the *wave*

A LIFE CHANGING JOURNEY INTO
THE HEART AND MIND OF THE COSMOS

JUDE CURRIVAN PhD

DEDICATION

For our Bill,
with love and gratitude

Copyright © 2005 O Books
O Books is an imprint of John Hunt Publishing Ltd., The Bothy,
Deershot Lodge, Park Lane, Ropley, Hants, SO24 0BE, UK
office@johnhunt-publishing.com
www.O-books.net

Distribution in:
UK
Orca Book Services
orders@orcabookservices.co.uk
Tel: 01202 665432 Fax: 01202 666219 Int. code (44)

USA and Canada
NBN
custserv@nbnbooks.com
Tel: 1 800 462 6420 Fax: 1 800 338 4550

Australia
Brumby Books
sales@brumbybooks.com
Tel: 61 3 9761 5535 Fax: 61 3 9761 7095

New Zealand
Peaceful Living
books@peaceful-living.co.nz
Tel: 64 7 57 18105 Fax: 64 7 57 18513

Singapore
STP
davidbuckland@tlp.com.sg
Tel: 65 6276 Fax: 65 6276 7119

South Africa
Alternative Books
altbook@global.co.za
Tel: 27 011 792 7730 Fax: 27 011 972 7787

Text: © 2005 Jude Currivan

Design: BookDesign™, London

ISBN 1 905047 33 9

A CIP catalogue record for this book is available from the
British Library.

Printed in the USA by Maple-Vail Manufacturing Group

the wave

A LIFE CHANGING JOURNEY INTO
THE HEART AND MIND OF THE COSMOS

JUDE CURRIVAN PhD

BOOKS

WINCHESTER UK
NEW YORK USA

CONTENTS

ACKNOWLEDGEMENTS

The foundations of this book go back nearly half a century to when I was four years old. It was then that I encountered my first experience of discarnate beings and it was then, that I knew there was more to the Cosmos than the physical world.

And since, I have had the privilege of learning from many teachers.

My teachers have ranged from respected university professors of physics and archaeology to an old woman sitting silently on a reed island in Peru; from the shamans, geomancers and wisdom keepers of many traditions to accountants - and include all my family and global network of friends.

They have included many discarnate beings; Nature spirits, Archangels, the aetheric guardians of sacred places, Ascended Masters and archetypal beings of Light

I thank them all, past and present and those whom I have not yet encountered.

My loving thanks go especially to my mother and brother. And to my darling husband whose loving presence and support is a gift beyond words.

I would not have been able to share the understanding offered in *The Wave* without the wonderful insight and support of my publisher John Hunt and my wise editor and dear friend Jeannie Kar, to whom I am ever grateful.

INTRODUCTION

My mother is a saint!

From the time she taught me to read, at the age of three I began to ask why and how the world is as it is. Despite my constant questions, she always tried to answer me as best she could, with loving patience and good humour. She encouraged me to keep on asking, and when my questions outstripped her ability to answer, she guided me to other sources of knowledge.

Like everyone else, the culture and environment into which I was born shaped my perception. I grew up in the north of England, the daughter of a coal miner who died when I was ten years old and my brother was seven.

In that environment, my cultural influences were materialistic and practical. However, the inspiration of my mother, my passion for understanding the world and my ongoing psychic experiences from the age of four shaped me in a different way from most people around me.

As I grew up, these various threads of understanding, perception and experience wove themselves together to form my Cosmology – my explanation of why and how the Cosmos is as it is and an understanding of my purpose and place within it.

Cosmology, derived from a Greek word *kosmos*, meaning order, is just that – a way of explaining the Cosmos. To qualify as a Cosmology any such explanation needs to be comprehensive, internally consistent and equate with the entirety of our experience and perception.

How we perceive and understand the Cosmos is affected by and affects everything in our lives. Individually and collectively, our Cosmology *is* our reality, for we can only real-ise what we can imagine.

Aspects of the world, which are physically unseen, but which the perception of our psyche renders real to us, are thus an intrinsic component in our Cosmology. And so perhaps, the old adage of 'seeing is believing' should rather be considered as 'believing is seeing'.

Seeing the world

Throughout human history, and probably back to the very inception of what it has meant to be human, we have sought to understand the Cosmos and our place within it.

Different cultures at different times have emphasized different aspects of our human experience in explaining the world and providing answers to the questions of who we are, where we come from and what, if any, is our purpose on Earth.

To indigenous shamans, the path to understanding is the way of direct experience and the innate feeling of being a thread in the vast web of life that is the Cosmos.

To the mystics of many traditions, intuitive and psychic revelations filled with the wonder of miracles, has been the vocational path to glimpsing its creative purpose.

Whilst to scientists and geomancers, both ancient and modern, the way of the mind has opened up a vast storehouse of cosmic knowledge.

It is this third way of perceiving which we have increasingly explored over the past three centuries.

And three hundred years ago, the way in which humanity collectively 'sees' the world was revolutionized when the philosopher Descartes freed the investigation of the physical world from the control of the Catholic Church with the introduction of the scientific method.

Science

Until then, almost all philosophers had combined observations of Nature with intuitive understanding and speculation. But with the birth of the scientific method, its pioneers began to experiment with the physical world around them and to test their theories of how it worked.

These were no ad hoc investigations. The power of this approach was that it had a defined method, which aspired to be objective and sought results able to be replicated.

Its basic premise was that those aspects of the world that could be measured could be progressively reduced to their fundamental building blocks, leading to an ever-deeper knowledge of the ultimate structure and nature of the universe.

Scientific discoveries progressively described a beautifully ordered world, which seemed to operate like a vast intricate machine.

But whilst many of the pioneers of science continued to see the guiding hand of a Creator underlying this exquisite order, the schism of science and spirit had already begun.

The material world?

By the end of the nineteenth century, the cosmology of a materialistic and mechanistic Cosmos was firmly established. Ever more people pushed the presence of a creator or higher consciousness ever further to the periphery of 'real' life, to be evoked only in times of extreme need.

But the birth of the twentieth century witnessed a second scientific revolution as scientists first glimpsed the quantum world and the cosmology of a relativistic universe. Moreover, experiments into the fundamental building blocks of matter, and observations, which peered out ever further into the vast reaches of Nature, replaced a world of separate materiality with one of profoundly interconnected energy fields.

Nonetheless, whilst this now century-old revolution overturned the previous mechanistic worldview, it did so without acknowledging the inclusion or influence of consciousness.

And so, for most of western society, including the overwhelming majority of scientists, the paradigm of a materialistic universe with by now little, if any, space for spirit or purpose continued and indeed appeared to deepen its hold within the collective psyche.

The concept of spirit was not the only casualty of what to most people was a progressive modern world which brought undreamed of material prosperity. The experiential and perennial wisdom of indigenous peoples and that of the ancient sages was also marginalized. But perhaps above all it was the voice of emotional and intuitive awareness, which was ever more consistently denigrated and deemed to be without merit in the modern world.

The energetic world

A further century of scientific research has realized phenomenal insights into the nature of the physical world. Discoveries of the behaviour of energy and matter at the microscopic scale of the quantum world have been harnessed to develop the computing and communications technologies, which underpin our global economy.

But now a further revolution is underway. And it revolves around our understanding of consciousness.

For despite over a century of intense research into the interface of mind and brain, scientists seeking to validate their assumption as to how the phenomenon of mind arises from the mechanics of brain activity have been totally unsuccessful in doing so.

Whilst many scientists are content to develop applications from the amazing insights reductionist science has revealed, a growing number are realizing that the prevailing paradigm of scientific materialism is only a partial perception of the Cosmos.

And they are also recognizing that the increasing scale of anomalies, irreconcilable theories and those which only account for a very small proportion of observed phenomena, require a radical new way of perceiving how the world works and why it does so.

The conscious world

We stand at a crossroads.

The current scientific paradigm of a fragmented and materialistic Cosmos is under siege. Whilst the success of its approach has carried us an enormous way into understanding the physical world, its innate limitations are now holding us back from a more profound realization of its true nature and purpose.

At this crossroads, it is ultimately our understanding of consciousness that will choose our path.

Viewing the universe as a random explosion of energy without innate purpose and considering consciousness only as a consequence of physical evolution, will lead us one way.

Perceiving the Cosmos as an inherently conscious and purposeful co-creation, will lead us another.

For the first time in our human history, the understanding and wisdom of many different cultures are freely available to us. We are beginning to discern the underlying principles, which are common to all traditions, and to reconcile these with the new wisdom arising from the pioneering findings of wholistic science.

Such a new approach to science seeks to understand the world as a whole and, in so doing, is beginning to realize that the Cosmos is indeed greater than the sum of its fragmented and materialistic parts.

Initially at the very edges of collective thought, individuals have been making discoveries and undergoing direct experiences, which have transformed their perception of the world and its 'realities'. Some have utilized scientific methods, only to discover anomalies, which cannot be contained within the mainstream paradigm. Others have been drawn to the rediscovery of ancient wisdom, for so long deemed heretical or decried as naïve. Still others, rebuffing the dogmas of organized religions, have been seeking their own path to inner divinity.

It is the exploration of these apparent paradoxes and anomalies, which is reconciling science and spirit into a universal model of consciousness. The new wisdom arising from this leading edge research is in many ways restating and augmenting the wisdom of the ancients. And as we pursue a deeper understanding of what life is, we are also rediscovering the gnosis, or inner knowingness, of our heart-felt experiences and the power of our intuition.

What we are beginning to discover, as we re-engage our hearts, minds and the purpose of our experiences is nothing less than a revelation of the profound interconnectedness and harmony of the Cosmos, its underlying principles and the primacy of consciousness.

A new wisdom

Here and now, we gather at a momentous time; when our understanding of the Cosmos and of what it means to be human is on the threshold of a quantum leap of awareness.

In our exploration of the world, we have traveled far. But in our journey, we have become fragmented. We have dis-membered our psyche, and separated mind from heart and soul.

Now, we are beginning to re-member. As individuals and collectively, we are glimpsing the underlying principles of harmony and unity, which pervade the Cosmos. And the global family of humanity is beginning to celebrate rather than fear the diversity of our different ways of 'seeing' and experiencing.

The emerging wisdom of wholistic science is reconciling with and expanding the perennial wisdom of the ancient sages. And in re-marrying heart and mind, a practical, empowering and creative spirituality is being birthed from their union.

The following pages of *The Wave*, share the unfolding steps of this journey into the heart and mind of the Cosmos and the homecoming to the wholeness of who we really are.

PART I

RECONCILING NEW AND ANCIENT WISDOM - HOW THE UNIVERSE IS AS IT IS.

Throughout *The Wave*, we will use the term Cosmos, with a capital C, to encompass not only the physical world – the universe – but the entirety of all physical, emotional, mental and spiritual realms.

As we begin our journey of exploration, in these first four chapters however, we will focus primarily on the universe of manifest form.

We will discover how the latest scientific insights are providing a radically new understanding of how the universe is as it is and see revealed the incredible harmony and order that underlies its apparent diversity.

And we will also see how the perception of the wholistic science that is now emerging is reconciling science with the perennial wisdom of all ages.

The materialistic and fragmented worldview of the universe to which many people – and most scientists - still adhere, is already a hundred years out of date.

So let us now begin our journey home.

The real voyage of discovery consists not in seeking new lands but seeing with new eyes.

Marcel Proust (1871 – 1922) French novelist

CHAPTER I

A THEORY OF EVERYTHING?

There is one central fact that can be distilled from our advances in understanding over the last century and on which pioneering science and the wisdom teachings of many traditions agree – throughout the universe, consciousness expresses itself as energy. All energies are manifested as waves – and it is from the vast and ever-changing interaction of these waves of energy that the entire universe, at all scales and levels of existence, including ourselves, is continuously created.

There is also an implication of this new understanding that affects every one of us.

As we gain a deeper awareness of the underlying principles of consciousness and energy, which pervade and guide these cosmic waves and their cycles of influence, we are empowered to perceive and experience the world as being profoundly harmonious. Harmony with which we are able to consciously resonate and embody.

But not only is wholistic science demonstrating the underlying interconnectedness and harmony of the physical world, it is beginning to offer glimpses beyond space and time and a deeper understanding of consciousness as the creator of the manifest universe.

Taking us from the fragmentation of a worldview, which denies our spiritual essence to a perception, which reconciles science with spirit, it offers us a deeper understanding of who we really are, and empowers us to live in harmony with the Cosmos and ourselves.

We will begin our journey of exploration by seeking to understand how waves form the tiniest building blocks of the material world and the structure of space and time itself. And to do that, we need to go back to the start of the twentieth century.

Matter is energy

The first sign of trouble in the perception of a mechanistic and materialistic Cosmos, which had developed since the time of Isaac Newton, appeared mundane. It came when physicists were unable to explain the radiation emitted by a hot oven.

Such radiation is in the form of electro-magnetic energy, extending from short wavelength, high frequency x-rays, through the rainbow of visible light to the progressively longer wavelengths and lower energies of heat waves, microwaves and radio waves.

According to the then prevailing theory, electro-magnetic energy forms a continuous spectrum. But when the total radiation of an enclosed oven at any given temperature was calculated according to the theory, a nonsensical answer resulted – that the energy would be infinite.

It was through seeking to explain this conundrum between theory and observation, that the entire edifice of nineteenth century physics was overthrown.

To understand the observed energies of hot body radiation, in 1901, the physicist Max Planck was able to show that the energy of electro-magnetic radiation is not continuous, as had been thought, but increases in discrete steps as its frequency increases and its wavelength shortens. In effect, there is a minimum packet or 'quantum' of energy associated with each wavelength or frequency of such radiation.

The key was his realisation that the radiation within an enclosed oven can only be expressed as whole numbers of complete waves of energy, and that the waves themselves are only able to embody a whole number of quanta. This constrains what otherwise would be the continuous and thus infinite expression of energy, to its finite and observed level.

Other apparent anomalies could also be explained by such quantization, leading Albert Einstein to describe electro-magnetic radiation such as light, as a stream of particles, which came to be called photons.

This in turn reopened an old debate, as two hundred years earlier Newton too had described light in this way, only for this to be apparently disproved by the following deceptively simple yet crucial experiment.

Waves *and* particles

The experiment comprises a solid screen into which two parallel slits have been cut. At a distance behind the screen and parallel to it, is positioned a photographic plate. When first one and then the other slit is covered and a beam of light is shone onto the screen, the light shining through the uncovered slit forms a pattern on the photographic plate which is an image of the slit.

However, when both slits are open, the light shone through them and onto the photographic plate creates what is known as an interference pattern, a pattern of alternating dark and light bands, which arise from the interpenetration of waves.

If Newton had been correct, and light is formed of particles, the effect of their being beamed through the double-slits would be to replicate the effect when only one slit is uncovered. But the interference pattern created by the double-slit was taken to prove that light is comprised of waves.

Clearly, Einstein's photons are not the corpuscular particles that Newton had envisaged, as the combined evidence of quantization and the interference pattern of the double-slit experiment; shows that light and other electro-magnetic radiation exhibit both wave-like *and* particle-like properties.

By the nineteen-twenties, physicists were still struggling to understand this apparent paradox, which was soon to become even more perplexing.

By now, Einstein had come up with his famous equation $E=mc\approx$, which equated energy and matter. And a young French scientist Louis de Broglie, realised the astounding inference that, as Planck had equated energy with wavelength and frequency and Einstein had equated energy with matter, so matter itself must have wavelength and frequency.

Shortly afterwards, remarkable proof of this came, when essentially the same double-slit experiment was carried out: but this time with a beam of electrons being substituted for the light. Sure enough, when the electron beam was shone through the double-slit, an interference pattern characteristic of waves was seen.

And so it was that at the subatomic scale of the quantum, waves were seen to behave as particles and particles as waves.

All matter, which we consider to be solid, is thus essentially wave-like and energetic. The reason we are not aware of this in our day-to-day experience is that the wavelengths of matter are extremely tiny and so are far below our threshold of awareness.

No more separation

However, as it turned out, the reality of wave-particle duality was only the beginning of the extraordinary discoveries arising from the exploration of the quantum world.

At these minute scales of existence, experimenters were becoming aware of the unsettling truth that observing a phenomenon actually changed it. Indeed, the very act of observation causes the wave-like properties of quanta to essentially collapse and transform into those associated with particles.

No longer could observer and observed be deemed to be separate – a key requirement of reductionist science.

This way-shower to our deeper understanding of perception and consciousness was, however, ignored when the consensus of physicists declared that such influence was limited to the scale of the quantum and played no part in the macro-scale world of human experience.

Intrinsic to the unavoidable influence of an observer was a further, equally profound implication. The precision of determining an object's position at the quantum scale was found, by Werner Heisenberg, to be inversely proportional to the precision of determining its velocity – the more you know about the one, the less you know about the other.

Enshrined in what came to be known as the Heisenberg uncertainty principle, this requires that, at the quantum scale, the position and velocity of quanta can only be determined in terms of probabilities described mathematically in terms of waves.

But this fundamental principle of uncertainty is not just a limitation of measurement; it describes an innate property of the physical world.

At increasingly tiny scales, as the position of a quantum becomes ever more constrained, fluctuations in its motion become ever greater. Such oscillations pervade Nature and throughout the vacuum of space. Whilst the overall energy of this vast ocean of space averages out to zero, the fluctuations at the tiniest scale of the quantum foam forms a vast maelstrom of what is referred to by physicists as zero point energy.

Time and space are relative

Whilst physicists such as Heisenberg were probing ever deeper into the subatomic world of quantum mechanics, Einstein and others were exploring the large-scale fabric of space and the meaning of time.

It began when, as a sixteen year-old, the young Einstein asked the apparently simple question of what happens if we chase a beam of light? A decade later, his answer revolutionised our understanding of space and time.

What he discovered is that space and time are not the absolute and passive backdrop to the universe, as postulated by Newton, but are relative to the position of an observer and are dynamic with regard to his or her movement.

In effect, we cannot differentiate movement at a steady speed from remaining stationery, unless we have something to perceive relatively, as a benchmark or a frame of reference, and against which to measure such motion.

We may have experienced this for ourselves when sitting in a train pulling gently out of a station. Without a noticeable acceleration to let us know that we are moving, it may appear that the train next to us is travelling backwards even when to an observer on the platform, it is the second train, which is stationery, and we are moving.

However, Einstein realised something even more profound. He deduced that observers in relative motion to each other will measure distance and time differently, and that these differences are not merely perceptions but are intrinsic to the space and time nature of the universe itself.

This revolutionary understanding dawned on Einstein, when in his inner vision, he chased a beam of light and realised that, unlike the pursuits of material objects, however fast he travelled, he could never catch up.

Experiments have consistently shown that, unlike other phenomena, which he had realised were always measured differently by an observer in relative motion, the speed of light to any observer, is always measured as being constant in a particular medium such as a vacuum - regardless of any benchmarks for comparison.

However fast an observer or material object chases a beam of light, it will always be measured to move away at a constant speed. Moreover, an observer rushing towards an oncoming beam of light, no matter what his speed, will still measure the oncoming light at the same constant velocity.

It required Einstein's genius to realise that this is because as the speed of an observer or material object increases, time itself slows down. And as the speed of travel increases, time progressively slows down, in perfect correspondence, such that the speed of light is always observed as a constant.

The speed of light

A huge body of experimental results supports this theoretical framework of relativity, which states that the speed of light in a vacuum, denoted by the letter 'c', is a limiting constraint of the universe. And whilst recent experiments have demonstrated faster than light travel is possible, all evidence continues to insist that any signal or information cannot travel through physical space and time faster than the enormous speed of light – measured in a vacuum as 186,282 miles per second.

As we shall explore later, this limiting speed of light and other characteristics of space and time have profound implications for how we experience consciousness in the physical world.

Einstein also realised that it was not only time which slowed as the speed of an object increased towards the limiting speed of light – when time effectively stands still – but that space too is affected.

As the relative speed between two observers increases, to each, not only does time slow down, but the length of the other also reduces along the direction of travel.

For example, if an observer were to measure a space ship before a flight, as a hundred feet in length, his later measurement of the ship when it is travelling at about 87 percent of the speed of light would show it being only fifty feet from front to back.

Yet, to each observer, his or her own length and duration of time appears to be as normal. This perception of normality is crucial because it means that the laws of physics themselves are identical to all observers undergoing constant-velocity motion – regardless of their vantage point in the universe.

Einstein's insights thus intimately connect space and time, to the extent that to describe one without the other is in effect meaningless. Rather than seeking to separately understand the nature of space and time, since Einstein, physicists have described and explored the interwoven fabric of the universe as spacetime.

However, it is in yet a further realisation of this giant of human thought by which most of us know of Einstein's genius. In what has been described as the most famous equation in the world, $E=mc\approx$, where the energy (E) of an object is equal to the product of its mass (m) and the speed of light (c) multiplied by itself, he showed that mass and energy are interchangeable and related by the speed of light.

Given the enormous value of the speed of light, the inclusion of the term $c\approx$ in the equation shows that the energy 'frozen' in even a small mass is huge.

This simple equation underlies the Sun's ability to convert hydrogen nuclear fuel to helium and thus radiate life-giving heat and warmth to the Earth over the last four and a half billion years and for many billions of years yet to come. Ironically, the same equation describes the awful destructive power unleashed by the hydrogen bomb – whose detonation remained a perpetual grief to the pacifist Einstein.

Spacetime

As if this still was not enough, Einstein then applied his insights into relative motion into an all-encompassing theory, of general relativity, which sought a still deeper understanding of spacetime and the nature of gravity.

Being struck by the experiential similarity between gravity and acceleration, led him to consider the proposition that accelerated motion is indistinguishable from the effects of gravity.

He realised that the very presence of a massive body actually distorts spacetime, and it is the effect of this distortion, which is experienced as gravity. In a simplified way, we may envisage this by placing a heavy ball on a flexible rubber membrane. The heavier the ball, the greater is the distortion – or warping – of the 'spacetime' membrane and by analogy, the greater the effect of gravity.

Einstein's mathematical model of the relativistic universe also required the entire fabric of spacetime itself to be dynamic, carrying with it, like a great tide, the cosmic flotsam and jetsam of untold billions of galaxies.

However, Einstein who was unhappy with this conclusion arising from his own theory and preferring a static and essentially eternal universe, inserted into his equations, a factor which offset this innate effect. When his original theoretical conclusions were subsequently verified; by Edwin Hubble's observations of distant galaxies, which showed that the universe is indeed expanding, Einstein removed this so-called cosmological constant and called it his greatest blunder.

In still later hindsight, as we shall soon see, his 'mistake' may have inadvertently opened the door to an even deeper perception of the Cosmos.

The concept of an expanding universe implies that it was once smaller than it appears to be today. And it was by following this trail of logic back to its beginning, which birthed the so-called big bang theory of the origin of the universe.

Over the intervening decades, refinement of the theory and ever more penetrating observation have supported its basic premise that sometime around 14 billion years ago, the physical universe was born in a cosmic maelstrom. And from this explosive expansion from its almost unimaginably minute beginnings, has been expanding ever since.

Having discovered how space and time are intimately interwoven and how the vast reaches of space are permeated by the unending turbulence of quantum energy oscillations, the big bang shows us that the fabric of spacetime itself is dynamic.

Thus, given that all energy can be expressed as waves, two further extraordinary insights arise.

The first is that, rather than considering the origin of the physical universe as an explosive bang, we may instead perceive it as a vast radiating wave of spacetime, an insight with which the Vedic seers of ancient India would have been familiar.

The second insight also relates to the nature of spacetime as being innately energetic. We will explore cycles of time on many levels of experience later. But now we are faced with the awareness that time itself *is* energy. The wavelengths and frequencies of such cycles thus not only represent the measurement of time but actually embody its intrinsic energetic and wavelike nature.

In the beginning

Several generations of cosmologists, have attempted within the theoretical framework of the big bang, to understand the array of fundamental particles and forces, which shape the universe, and have sought answers in its very earliest moments.

The fundamental particles, which came to form the matter with which we are familiar – protons, neutrons and electrons – were created during this early epoch.

And it was during this timescale that a fourth elementary particle, the neutrino, was also created. Having no charge and a tiny mass, whose value is yet to be experimentally confirmed, its minimal interaction with other matter causes it to remain an as yet enigmatic constituent of the universe.

Within only one hundred thousandth of the first second after the big bang, which marked the beginning of time itself, two forms of quarks, the elemental building blocks of nuclear matter, were clustering together in groups of three, to create the familiar protons and neutrons which comprise atomic nuclei.

These two forms of quarks, which are known as 'up' and 'down' by physicists, carry electrical charges of $+2/3$ and $-1/3$ respectively. The combination of two 'up' quarks and a single 'down' quark forms a positively charged proton, whereas the combination of one 'up' quark and two 'down' quarks creates a neutral neutron.

Before the first second of physical time had elapsed, the nuclei of the lightest elements, hydrogen, deuterium and helium had already begun to coalesce. And over the following three minutes, such nuclei continued to synthesise in a primeval fog of hot plasma – a world as yet without light.

Over the following one hundred thousand years, shock waves, akin to sound, rippled through the early universe, as it continued to expand and cool, creating eddies from which aeons later stars and galaxies would be seeded.

And during this early epoch, as the universe continued to expand and cool, the colossal flux of negatively charged electrons, were slowing down sufficiently to be captured by the positively charged atomic nuclei to form electrically neutral atoms.

As they did so, energy was released in the form of photons; the primeval fog cleared and there was light in the darkness.

This contemporary understanding of the origin of the universe is remarkably consistent with the metaphorical and symbolic perceptions of the ancient sages. From its beginnings as a spacetime wave, we now consider that the primeval ocean of energy was pervaded by sound, and subsequently materialised by the manifestation of light.

The Biblical words of Genesis, derived from the even earlier creation myths of Mesopotamia, in describing the primeval void as the *Deep*, also liken it to an ocean of energy. And by referring to the initial creation as the coming of light into the darkness of the void, they presage the science of nearly three millennia later. In the words of the apostle John, two millennia ago, *'in the beginning was the Word'*. And this symbolic reference is now also shown to reflect the physical reality of creation.

A cosmic symphony

In seeking to replicate the environment of the early universe, experimenters and theorists have identified a number of particles, some of which are unstable and only able to exist under these extreme conditions.

The stability of 'up' and 'down' quarks, electrons and neutrinos has enabled them to persist for some 14 billion years and will do so for many more billions yet to come. And it is this family of four particles, which comprise the fundamental 'notes' as it were of the matter of the universe.

However, at higher energies, two other families of four related particles are encountered. Each of these has exactly the same characteristics as the four fundamental particles, except that, in embodying greater energy, they are heavier in mass.

In essence, we may consider these three families of particles as forming the chords of a cosmic symphony. The fundamental notes are formed by the familiar particles, which comprise our everyday experience of matter. And the higher, more energetic notes, rather like overtones in music, form the matter we find in stellar and cosmic environments.

Following Einstein's insights into the nature of the forces of electro-magnetism and gravity, later investigation of the atomic nucleus revealed two further fundamental forces whose influence only prevails on these tiny scales.

The strong nuclear force, which effectively glues neutrons and protons together in the atomic nucleus, was, subsequently able to be correlated with electro-magnetism into the explanatory framework of quantum field theory. And in a similar way the weak nuclear force whose influence enables the disintegration of nuclei through radioactivity was also able to be reconciled with electro-magnetism.

These four fundamental energetic forces are each perceived to be mediated by so-called force-particles; electro-magnetism by the photon, the strong nuclear force by a particle called a gluon, the weak nuclear force by two related particles, termed the W and H bosons, and gravity by the aptly named graviton.

These discoveries relating to matter and forces have been progressively encompassed within a theoretical framework, referred to as the standard model of the universe.

But whilst the standard model is a triumph of theoretical and experimental physics, it does not explain why there are three families of fundamental particles, or why there are four particles in each family.

Although, as we have already seen, such fundamental particles also embody wave-like properties they are treated within the standard model as point-like with no internal structure. And as we shall shortly discuss, such an assumption leads to untenable conclusions when applied to the extreme conditions of the very earliest moments of the physical world.

The tip of the iceberg

There is powerful observational evidence and strong theoretical support, to indicate however that it is not the constituents of matter and energy, which are familiar to us and which we have to date observed and measured, which form the major constituents of the universe.

It is only in the last few years, that a fifth cosmic force has come to the attention of physicists. Yet, it has overturned much of their previous understanding and confidence in being able to progressively explain the entirety of the material world.

Hitherto unsuspected but pervading all of spacetime, it is in essence, a cosmic antigravity. Termed dark energy, whilst its ultra-weak influence is only felt at the colossal scale of galactic clusters, it controls the expansion and future destiny of the entire universe.

And when measurements of the light-emitting visible matter within galaxies showed it to be dramatically insufficient in enabling them to hold together, given their observed speeds of rotation, the presence of so-called dark matter was also revealed.

Astoundingly, it is now estimated that dark energy and dark matter, the nature of both as yet unfamiliar to us, constitute in total about 95 percent of the entirety of the universe. With dark matter estimated to comprise about 25 percent and dark energy about 70 percent, only a meagre five percent of the universe is made up of the fundamental particles and energies described by the standard model.

The essence of dark energy is as yet unknown, although shortly, and in Chapter 3, we will explore how its presence is crucial in understanding how the large-scale universe has evolved.

In seeking to understand the nature of dark matter, possible candidates such as black holes - collapsed massive stars, so dense that not even light can escape their gravitational pull – have been eliminated, given that theory requires the dark matter to be distributed throughout space.

And whilst the enigmatic neutrino, may yet be found to be a constituent of dark matter, its postulated mass and estimated abundance suggests that it would be insufficient to account for the great bulk of the shortfall. Other possibilities relate to super-heavy particles, theorised to have been created in the extreme energies of the early universe and which may have survived to the present; but these too, are yet to be found.

An inflationary universe

With telescopes that are ever more powerful and the evolution of detectors able to energetically map a wide spectrum of electro-magnetic radiation from short wavelength gamma rays to microwaves and radio waves, it has become apparent that the energy density of the universe in all directions as seen from the Earth, is extraordinarily smooth.

With irrefutable logic, theorists realised that to achieve this, the earliest epoch of the universe must have been highly ordered before being accelerated apart by the aftermath of the big bang.

There were technical reasons within the standard model, which could not accommodate the means whereby such order was communicated, but in 1979 physicist Alan Guth, offered a possible solution.

Guth calculated an outcome to Einstein's equations, which showed that a massively exponential burst of expansion could have been a trigger for the big bang itself,. Moreover, it would have allowed the time needed for the ordering of the universe to have been accomplished and thereafter for such homogeneity to expand in line with observations.

Before such inflation, the stuff of the universe was in much closer proximity than assumed by the unmodified standard model and was able to blend and achieve the smoothness required. Cosmologists have thus commonly accepted the insertion of this inflationary process into the big bang scenario.

Guth's premise is that the initial energy of the universe was carried by what is termed the inflation field, which the model begins by assuming was at an unstable state above its minimum energy level.

The potential energy, then released during its transformation to its minimum state, drove the initial inflationary burst and the resulting formation of matter and radiation.

And essentially, it is the ongoing expansionary force of the inflation field which has now been discerned as dark energy.

A consequence of the inflationary big bang model, is that as the universe continues to expand, its totality of matter and radiation loses energy to gravity which in turn loses energy to the inflation field.

By retracing the logic of this energy transfer, cosmologists conclude that, at the onset of the big bang, the inflation field itself did not require much energy since the very expansion it triggered would enormously increase the energy it carried and reconcile this with observations.

This enables the model to provide a mechanism for the large-scale universe we see today from a beginning, which was not only miniscule in spatial terms but in the energy it required to be born and evolve to its present complexity.

One further possibility is that rather than the transformation of the inflation field to its minimum energy state taking place in the briefest burst of time at the beginning of the universe, that its characteristics have enabled a much gentler and ongoing transition by which the wave of spacetime continues to expand.

And in this scenario, the universe may yet prove to be cyclic. We may shortly be able to determine whether the expansion will ultimately cease and then, like the peaking and falling away of a giant wave, for spacetime to contract once more - an echo of many ancient and mystical traditions for whom such cosmic cyclicity was fundamental.

A theory of everything

Over the last century, quantum theory has been able to describe the world at atomic and sub-atomic scales with incredible accuracy. Similarly, the theory of relativity has been equally successful in doing so at the huge scales of planets, galaxies and the universe itself.

However, astonishingly, these twin pillars of twentieth century physics are fundamentally incompatible with each other, as the force of gravity has been unable to be accommodated within the quantum framework of the standard model.

In most instances, this has not given most physicists much cause for concern. Focussing on how the universe functions rather than why it is the way it is, the study of the minute scales which are the remit of quantum theory are rarely perceived to encroach into the realms of the large-scale and massive bodies which are the concern of relativity.

But this is not the case in the circumstances pertaining during the very earliest moments after the big bang, when the colossal mass of the entire physical universe, is deemed to have been constrained within an almost unimaginably tiny space.

And as conditions at that time determined the form of the world today, understanding them and how they came about is crucial to our deeper understanding of the universe now.

When relativity and the quantum theory of the standard model are forcibly conjoined under these circumstances, they are only able to describe this earliest epoch of the universe in terms of masses, densities and temperatures which are infinite. – and as we saw in the breakdown of nineteenth century physics, this is a sure sign that the theoretical framework has in effect broken down in depicting these extreme conditions.

The perception of point-like fundamental particles as postulated by the standard model is key to this computation of infinite density, as without spatial extent, the model predicts no end to the closeness to which the particles can be packed.

Whilst other scientists became enamoured with the powerful insights, which each theory offered, Einstein was not one to close his mind to this catastrophic dilemma. But now, he was striding far beyond others into the unknown. And without the discoveries that would have supported his flights of intuitive genius, for the last thirty years of his life, he struggled without success to derive a unifying 'theory of everything', or TOE.

However, in recent years, and with the benefit of discoveries unavailable to Einstein, a radical new way of understanding the universe has begun to emerge. Like a phoenix rising from the flames of the initial cosmic fireball, it offers the possibility of unification and a description of the world from its very beginning.

Musical strings

Scientists are sometimes also musicians or poets. And sometimes this supports a revolutionary discovery being described in words of symbolic power. It seems however, that the discoverers of string theory had no such artistic aspirations.

Nonetheless, their theory may offer us the most profound insight into the nature of the universe, which science has yet offered us, and the tantalising possibility of reconciling science with perennial wisdom.

The philosophers of ancient Egypt, Chaldea and Greece perceived the Cosmos as essentially harmonic and described it in musical terms. Their understanding of natural harmony and archetypal patterns of vibration, which underlie the manifest world, is one we will explore in the next and following chapters.

But now, we will journey alongside the scientists who, beginning in the nineteen-seventies, took the first tentative steps in perceiving the universe, as did these ancient sages, as being ultimately harmonious.

They proposed that instead of point-like particles, the fundamental building blocks of the physical world are one-dimensional vibrating strings, whose oscillatory patterns and resonance form the notes of a cosmic symphony.

By 1984, Michael Green and John Schwarz, were able to show that string theory had the potential to describe all of matter and the four fundamental forces then known, with the ability to encompass gravity and thus reconcile it within a comprehensive framework of Nature.

The scale of such strings is almost unimaginably tiny. The theory postulates their existence at the level where, in the standard model, quantum fluctuations prevent the reconciliation of gravity. At less than 10^{-35} metres, known as the Planck length, such strings are many orders of magnitude smaller than our current technological ability to experimentally detect.

Over the intervening two decades, the theory has continued to develop and indeed has undergone a series of revolutionary leaps, where new insights have encompassed and superseded the prior, more partial understanding.

By1995, five competing versions of string theory had been formulated. And whilst all described vibrational patterns of one-dimensional oscillating strings of the same length, they varied as to whether such strings were in the form of closed loops or were open – with different characteristics of fundamental particles and forces arising from each formulation.

But in that year, and initiated by Edward Witten, the latest incarnation, which has become known as M theory was able to show that what appeared to be five possibilities were in fact different translations of the common music of strings.

Higher dimensions

A fundamental requirement of M theory is that the strings vibrate not in our familiar four-dimensional spacetime (three dimensions of space and one of time), but within eleven dimensions.

As had been the case for the earlier iterations of string theory, such additional spatial dimensions were, in M theory, initially deemed tiny and at the scale of the strings themselves. But intriguingly, the latest understanding is that the scale of such dimensions may be significantly larger than previously suspected.

And completely unexpectedly, as the theory continued to be developed and refined, a further fundamental constituent of the M-described Cosmos, emerged from the shadows.

These multi-dimensional objects, termed branes, may form the framework within which strings oscillate and to which they are energetically connected.

The mathematics of the theory, demonstrates that branes would be invisible to three-dimensional electro-magnetic forces, which are essentially trapped within their boundaries. Thus, our bodily human senses and the myriad of instruments used by science to observe and measure the physical universe would be impotent in probing for higher dimensions.

However, an insight by Theodor Kaluza nearly a century ago, showed that whilst electro-magnetism is manifested within physical spacetime, its underlying mathematical waveforms can be expressed in a higher dimensional reality. And whilst as yet unproven, it may be that Kaluza's insight offers us a key to unlocking the door to these higher realities.

Whilst these higher dimensions also appear impervious to the effects of the strong and weak nuclear forces, M theory supports the premise that the effects of gravity may be able to transcend the brane boundaries and thus may provide a further key to determining their presence.

And as physicists come to terms with, and continue to explore, the implications and realities of higher dimensions the question of whether spacetime is truly fundamental, is now being asked.

The holographic universe

In 1947, Dennis Gabor introduced the theory of coherent wave interference, which enabled the development of the hologram, where the splitting and re-convergence of light beams projects a three-dimensional image from a two-dimensional surface. Nearly half a century later, the principle of holography would find in the waveform nature of strings and M theory a natural and unifying complement.

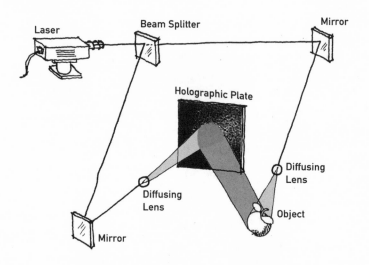

Fig 1.1

A hologram is created by the splitting of a single beam of laser light into two. One beam is then reflected off the object to be photographed and the other aimed to interfere with it with their interference pattern recorded on film. When light is then shone through the holographic film, a three-dimensional image of the recorded object is produced.

Parallel research into the disorder – and intriguingly, information - inherent within the super-dense interior of black holes has shown that its maximum value is proportional, not as might be expected to its volume, but to its surface area.

Correspondingly, if the maximum disorder/information in any given region of space is proportional to the region's surface area and not its volume, then perhaps the attributes that have the potential to give rise to that disorder, and embody that information, actually reside on the surface or boundary of the region and not within its volume.

This gives rise to the possibility, first expressed by Gerard 't Hooft and Leonard Susskind in the early 1990s, that the universe, is in fact the projection of processes taking place on a bounding surface – exactly the principle of the hologram and potentially able to be encompassed by and expressed within M theory.

In 1997, Juan Maldacena was able to add substantially to the realisation of this possibility. Mathematically, he demonstrated how the physics witnessed by an observer 'within' a hypothetical five-dimensional spacetime Cosmos, could be described in terms of the physics taking place on its four-dimensional boundary. And in doing so, he also included the additional 'curled up' dimensions required by M theory.

Whilst, for the surprising but valid reason that working with such a hypothetical five-dimensional case, is mathematically simpler than with the 'real' universe of four-dimensional spacetime, nonetheless, this deeper understanding of the holographic principle may offer a quantum leap forward in the exploration of the underlying realities from which the world of materiality is born.

Sacred science

We have arrived at the current limits of where science has led us in the understanding of the physical structure of the universe on its tiniest and largest scales, and to our most hopeful framework for a grand unification of its fundamental laws.

Whilst most scientists appear to be stuck in a mechanistic and materialistic worldview, which is about a hundred years out of date, the pioneering edge of physics is showing that the physical world is a vast matrix of energy.

And as we shall see in the next and later chapters, their concept of the manifest universe being essentially a projection of a cosmic hologram is one, which whilst using metaphorical and symbolic language, the ancient sages would have found familiar.

They would also have recognised, in M theory and the concept of strings, the presence of the universal harmonies they revered.

The holographic principle and M theory also open up exciting avenues of research into higher dimensional expressions of gravity and electro-magnetism and ultimately deeper insights into the Cosmos and the nature of consciousness itself, which we will explore in later chapters.

However, to begin to understand how such newly emergent wisdom, and much more we have yet to discuss, reconciles with ancient sacred science, we now once more, need to journey back in time.

Chapter 2

Perennial Wisdom

The technical triumphs of reductionist science have enabled us to see further into the universe and deeper into the nature of matter than ever before. However, in doing so, the prevalence of its approach – which reduces phenomena to their component elements without consideration of the whole - has literally prevented us from seeing the entirety of the forest by its focus on the detail of the trees.

The progress of such science and its incalculable influence on our collective worldview has been an amazing journey of discovery. But a growing number of scientists are beginning to consider that it has taken us to an extreme perspective from which we need to restore balance.

And as we shall see in the following chapters, a radical new wholistic approach to science is now emerging, which does seek to understand the whole and to discern answers to the questions of why the Cosmos is as it is, and not merely how it is.

Perhaps, one of the greatest disservices of reductionist science and the mind-set it has engendered has been its view that the history of humankind has been a linear progression from primitive superstition to an epitome of sophisticated understanding.

But now wholistic science is reconciling new and ancient wisdom as it rediscovers and values the insights of traditional teachings, which perceive the Cosmos as an interconnected whole.

Such perception has enabled wisdom bringers throughout all ages, to attune to and thus gain intuitive insights and higher awareness of universal truths. And whilst often described in symbolic language that reflects the cultural awareness of their place and time, these truths are perpetual and continue to be valuable way showers for our ongoing journey of discovery.

To appreciate their relevance for us now, we need to reconsider the perennial wisdom of the ancient sages and to understand how they saw the world. And as we retrace their footsteps, we may perceive the echoes of their insights whose principles resonate with the discoveries of pioneering science today.

Ancient wisdom

To the Vedic seers of ancient India, the entire universe formed a cyclic breath of Brahman, the ultimate consciousness of God. We now know that the universe did begin with an out-breath which cosmologists term the big bang.

And a possibility, which awaits confirmation, is that such an out-breath may indeed form part of a vast cosmic breath when, at some point in the far distant future, the expansion may peak, and the wave of the physical world then contract once more, as an in-breath to complete one cycle and begin another.

The Greek philosopher Plato famously likened the manifest world to a dark cave. Sitting within the cave, with his back to the entrance is a solitary being, the representative of humanity. As light streams through the entrance, it projects myriad moving shadows onto the cave wall, and it is these, Plato maintains, which the being perceives as the reality of existence, rather than recognising the beams of light which are their true source.

His insight of two and a half millennia ago, is redolent of the multi-dimensional characteristics of a Cosmos, restated by M theory, where what we perceive as 'reality' may be a huge and intricate holographic projection.

The Greek philosophers also ascribed to Hermes Trismegistus - the name they gave to the deity known to the ancient Egyptians as Thoth - a teaching, which again presages the holographic principle.

This was the hermetic dictum of 'as above, so below', which relates to the microcosmic world of diverse forms, as replicating the macrocosmic whole. Just as in the creation of a holographic object, where, if the entire image is subdivided into multiple parts, each part fully embodies the whole.

In the mystery schools of Plato and Pythagoras, the sages initiated their students into the profoundly harmonic nature of the universe and perceived numbers and geometry as the fundamental manifestations of the Creator.

In seeking to understand the world, they explored numbers, not at the mundane level of arithmetic, which for most of us is the case today, but on symbolic, mythic and Cosmological levels of awareness.

As they peered into the essence of reality and beneath the rich diversity of natural forms, they discovered archetypal patterns. And in the idealised forms of geometry, they saw revealed the harmonic coherence of fundamental relationships woven into the fabric of space and time.

These initiates of the Platonic and Pythagorean mystery schools were called *mathematekoi*, a word encompassing the understanding and awareness of everything in the Cosmos. Using pebbles as counters and the simplest of tools to create geometric forms, they were themselves the inheritors of the even more ancient wisdom of the Egyptians and Chaldeans.

They and later philosophers perceived the relationships within and between numbers and geometry as resonant wave-guides, archetypal pathways for energetic forms and structures to manifest.

Now the latest insights of M theory echo that ancient understanding with the postulation that the physical world is made up of the ultra-minute waveforms called strings, reverberating in different ways to produce the various fundamental 'notes' of energy and matter.

In the next and following chapters, we will see how the diversity of physical forms is generated from the fundamental notes created by such patterns of vibration.

The Greeks realised that it was from the simplicity of whole number relationships that such diversity arises. And by taking the first steps to understand the quantised nature of the world, they discovered the deep wisdom embedded in whole numbers.

For each integer between zero and ten, meanings were ascribed, whose themes are repeatedly found throughout the ancient world and whose perennial wisdom, revealing deeper realities beyond the world of appearances, continued to echo through metaphysical and esoteric teachings until the coming of reductionist science.

Let us now become initiates ourselves as we consider the essence of number and geometry, and perceive them not as inventions of humanity but as profound revelations of the holographic nature of the Cosmos.

The spirit of One

Virtually every spiritual tradition and ancient wisdom teaching has seen in the perfection of the circle and the number Zero, transcendental symbols of the Cosmos.

It is from the circle's centre-point of creation, that spirit is birthed into matter and the waves of energy rippling outwards embrace the entirety of physical experience. All is embodied within the One-ness represented by the O and indeed, when we speak the word 'One' itself within the very shape our mouths make, the concept of One encompassing all else is realised.

Only one measure is needed to denote a circle – its radius. And through all scales of existence, the unbroken, ever continuing line denoting its circumference relates to its radius through the ratio of pi, itself a transcendental number without end or repetition.

The geomancers of ancient Egypt, China and Mesopotamia also saw this idealised whole in the dome of the heavens above them and in looking around themselves witnessed Heaven meet Earth around the circle of the horizon. And cosmologists today observe the universe as such a homogenous expansion from the initial event of the big bang.

The sacred marriage of Two

Using only a simple hinged compass, the Greek *mathematekoi* drew twin circles, side by side, the centre of one passing through the circumference of the other. In their pairing, known to the Greeks as the *vesica piscis*, the womb-like space of overlap contains all the proportions to generate the shapes of Nature.

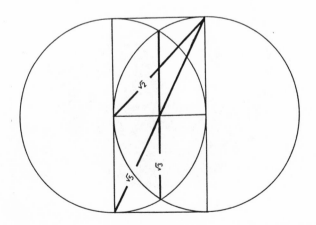

Fig 2.1 The sacred marriage of the vesica piscis.

In becoming Two, the fundamental separation of the world and its essential duality is realised. And yet, the two circles remain interlocked and the diverse generation of physical form requires the sacred marriage of their ongoing relationship. Thus, duality is shown to be merely an illusory separation.

It is from the interplay of such polarities and their manifold expression, that the world is generated.

This is seen in the iconic symbol of the Chinese Taoists – the mandala of yin and yang, which perfectly reflects the ancient perception that the expression of such polarities, are innately relational. Bounded by the cosmic circle and differentiated by the inner flow of a balancing wave, the light and dark of the expansive yang and the passive yin are depicted, and from within each, the seed of the other emerges.

Fig 2.2 The mandala of yin and yang, their cosmic polarities balanced by the wave of awareness that flows throughout all experience.

And the inner wave of the yin-yang symbol further reveals their relationship as a consequence of its periodicity - the rising aspect of the wave expressing the yang principle in all its diverse forms and its falling away, embodying the yin.

The ancients well understood the dynamic tension expressed by Two-ness. And it is only within the next number Three, that they considered that resolution and reconciliation is effected, experience is completed and unity restored.

The wholeness of Three

The triangle, its three sides culminating at three points or apices, is the simplest geometric form expressing such reconciliation. In its restoration of unity, as architects have long known, it appropriately represents the most stable of two-dimensional physical forms.

And it is within the confines of three spatial dimensions that the physical world is manifest.

This perception of tripartite wholeness reveals itself, not only in geometric form, but also throughout myth and the teachings of ancient cosmologies. In the Vedic pantheon, Brahma the Creator, Vishnu the Preserver and Shiva the Destroyer, represent the eternal cosmic cycles of birth, life and death. Such cycles, ever the same and yet ever changing, play themselves out in space and time. And within the same tradition, the three cosmic principles of experience or *gunas* continually express themselves in an ever-creative dance.

Even within the Chinese Taoist symbol of yin-yang, which emphasises the duality of experience, balance is achieved through the reconciling wave, which flows through the centre of the mandala.

Such fundamental wholeness is also embodied in the almost universal presence of trinities of male, female and child archetypes in ancient beliefs. To the Egyptians, the mythic Osiris, Isis and Horus, embodied these cosmic principles. And to the Greeks, from the relationship of Aphrodite the goddess of love and Ares, the god of war, the conception of their child Harmonia mediated and resolved their innate conflict.

Fig 2.3 The Caduceus has been a symbol of healing for millennia. In this depiction the central staff that grounds the energies is surmounted by the wings of spirit.

In the healing symbol, known as the Caduceus, found in various forms throughout the ancient world, two serpents intertwine around a third central staff. Representing the interplay and balance of energetic polarities, they heal into the wholeness of their resolution.

Throughout folklore too, three-ness expresses the mediation of polar opposites, or the completion of three-fold experiences. Initiatory journeys involve the instigation of the mission or quest, the inner-tuition of the learning process itself and the integration of the wisdom acquired through endurance and courage. We delineate our experiences into past, present and future, speak of stories as having a beginning, a middle and end and perceive ourselves as embodying heart, mind and will.

The physics of Three

Embedded within the laws, which regulate the physical world, these themes of mediation, resolution and completion of three within one are also expressed repeatedly.

In Einstein's equation E=mc$\approx$, energy and matter, which together embody the universe, are reconciled through the mediation of the speed of light.

The inherently stable structure of the atom is also based on the balancing masses, forces and charges of the proton, neutron and electron.

And it is three harmonic families of fundamental particles, which make up the universe and not two or four.

It is also three laws of physical motion, which as Newton discovered, completely describe movement in three-dimensional space and which are applicable throughout the physical world.

Ultimately, on all symbolic, energetic and experiential levels, we may perceive such three-in-oneness as being fully expressed within the contiguous nature of a wave in its rising, its peaking and its falling away. Whilst in its rising and falling the polarity expressions of yang and yin are overt, it is in the turning points of its peaking and re-forming that the cycle is able to complete and move on.

The elemental Four

As we have already seen, in Einstein's description of general relativity three-dimensional physical space is intimately connected with the concept of time to form the fabric of four-dimensional spacetime.

To the ancient geomancers who first measured space and time, their innate relationship was already apparent. Early metrology almost universally divided the circle of the horizon into four cardinal directions – north, south, east and west. And such directions divided the cycle of the year into four quarters, expressed by the winter and summer solstices and the spring and autumn equinoxes. Such cosmic symmetry is also reflected in the human body whose primary orientations on the Earth are forwards and backwards, and to the left and the right.

This ancient perception of the Four-ness of space and time, was embodied in the cross-cultural symbol of the equidistant cross within a circle representing the Earth, as it still does in astronomical and astrological literature.

Almost all ancient cultures identified the fundamental 'elements' of the physical Cosmos as being essentially four-fold in nature - Earth, Water, Air and Fire.

But as experimental scientists from the sixteenth century onwards began to separate and identify the chemical constituents of matter, which ultimately became the Periodic Table of 93, naturally occurring such elements, the ancient perception was seen as being naïve and obsolete.

Yet from their own alchemical processes of metal-working, glass production and use of minerals, the ancients were clearly aware that the four 'elements' they denoted as being essential were capable of diverse expression.

And by verifying that all chemical elements are only found to exist in four states or phases, solid, liquid, gas or plasma, the essential 'elemental' composition of Nature continues to support the ancient metaphysical perception.

To the ancients the vibrations of consciousness in their spiritual, mental, emotional and physical expressions also related to the essential elements – Earth with physical experience, Water with the flow of feelings and emotions, Air with the intellectuality of the mind and Fire with individuated spirit. The fifth element Aether was perceived as the all-pervasive presence of cosmic consciousness, ever flowing and vivifying the physical world.

It was only in the mid twentieth century and after the penetration of the atomic nucleus that science revealed that four fundamental physical forces pervade the universe. And these too may be seen as being essentially equivalent to the ancient understanding - the force of gravity as equating to the element of Earth, the weak nuclear force to Water, electro-magnetism to Air and the strong nuclear force, which provides the energy of the Sun's furnace, to Fire.

The geometric harmony of Five

With Five, in the exquisite harmonic geometry of the pentagram, we see embodied the human form as depicted by the influential Roman architect Vitruvius and Leonardo da Vinci. With head held high and arms and legs spread, the idealised dimensions of the human body as expressed in this canon of man, are replete with harmonic ratios.

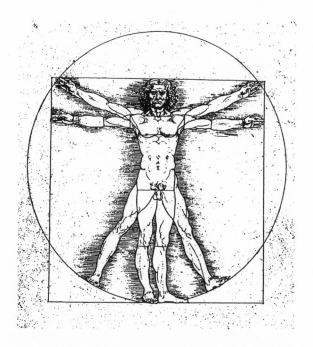

Fig 2.4 The canon of man drawn by Leonardo da Vinci, encompassed by and touching both the circle of spirit and the square of Earth.

Whilst the Greek philosopher Plato is credited with the discovery of the five idealised polygons named after him, it is evident that these were known since Neolithic times as is demonstrated by the group of five stone objects excavated in Scotland, which someone had deliberately and clearly shaped over five millennia ago. These now reside in the Ashmolean museum in Oxford, a mute reminder of perennial wisdom.

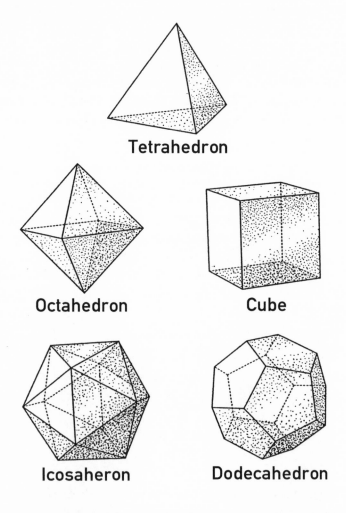

Fig 2.5 The archetypal forms of the five Platonic solids.

The five Platonic solids are the only forms, which incorporate geometric relationships whose angles, sides and faces are identical. And the *mathematokoi* considered them to be the universal building blocks of three-dimensional structure and of its interface with spirit.

As is appropriate to their cosmic nature, all five Platonic solids can geometrically nest within each other and with their vertices touching the surface of a single encompassing sphere.

When the centres of the faces of each of the five solids are joined, one of the other Platonic solids is traced out, to form its 'dual' or partner. And rotating them three-dimensionally and altering the viewpoint from which they are observed creates a wealth of transformations and reveals further harmonic relationships within and between these fundamental forms.

But when we consider three spatial dimensions, we do so measuring each dimension as being perpendicular to the other two. And as such, we perceive them as though they formed the parallel faces of a cube. Yet such a perception is merely a convention and not an inherent attribute of space. As we manipulate the Platonic solids, we may instead begin to consider dimensions as being expressed by the planes represented by the faces of these polygons.

Such a revision of our perception not only enables us to see how we are conditioned to think and thus experience in particular ways, but may also offer insights to the exploration of multi-dimensional physics which is required by both M theory and the holographic principle.

Multi-dimensional geometry

For example, M theory posits a total of ten spatial dimensions (and one of time) within which strings are free to oscillate. Three of these are the large-scale dimensions familiar to us, and the additional seven are minute and deemed to be the same scale as the strings themselves.

But one of the currently unanswered questions of M theory, is how, at the inception of the universe, did the ten minute spatial dimensions, transmute into the large-scale three dimensional world.

As we consider the Platonic solids, and the dual partnerships they form with each other, one relationship is particularly intriguing in this regard.

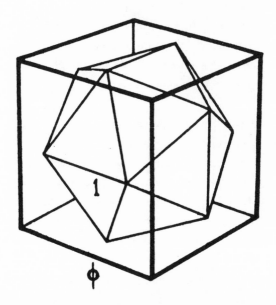

Fig 2.6 The twelve corners of the icosahedron are connected by an inner three-dimensional trinity of phi rectangles and are encompassed by an outer cube, embodying the same transcendental geometry.

The twenty faces of the icosahedron form ten dimensional planes and the six faces of the cube similarly form three-dimensional planes. Given that the dimensional ratios of M theory are ten and three and considering that, the cube is the dual of the icosahedron, could their inherent relationship, discovered by the ancients, hold a profound insight into the creation of space itself?

In the Platonic tradition, an essential element was also ascribed to each polygon. The six-faced cube was associated with Earth, the twenty-faced icosahedron with Water, the eight-faced octahedron with Air and the four-faced tetrahedron with Fire.

And the twelve-faced dodecahedron, the fifth and only Platonic solid with pentagramic faces, was associated by the Greeks with a fifth and spiritual element they called Aether.

The Aether

This enigmatic fifth element was accepted as an all-pervasive constituent of the Cosmos for over two millennia – its presence perceived as underlying and breathing spirit into all physical manifestation.

In the mid-nineteenth century, physicists studying the nature of electro-magnetic waves considered that a universal medium was required to enable their propagation. Mis-perceiving the insight of the ancients, they designated the term 'luminiferous aether' to describe it.

But a famous experiment by Albert Michelson and Edward Morley in 1887, which proved the constancy of the speed of light, also demonstrated that its motion requires no such medium.

And from that moment, despite the erroneous equivalence of the luminiferous aether with the ancient concept of Aether, scientists dismissed the entire idea.

A further century of exploration, however, has theorised a form of all-pervasive energy field, named after mathematician Peter Higgs, which essentially is a re-consideration of the ancient concept.

In the Aether's modern day incarnation - the Higgs Field - is an ocean of energy, a cold relic from the big bang responsible for many of the properties of the wave/particles of matter and energy and with a uniform and non-zero value throughout all of space. And it is the resistance by the Higgs Field to accelerated motion, which is theorised to give mass to quarks, electrons and neutrinos.

The energy of such a Higgs Field however, not only pervades space, but also contributes a uniform negative pressure which has the same properties as the recently discovered fifth cosmic force of dark energy. And like the Aether of the ancients, the energetic composition of the fifth force is as yet unknown to science.

The ancient Chinese perception, as incorporated in the tradition of feng shui, also counted five 'elements'. These however, are somewhat different in essence from their western counterparts in that they are considered more as dynamic influences rather than fundamental building blocks of form.

To the Chinese geomancers, the five 'elements' of Fire, Earth, Metal, Water, and Wood also equated with cosmic influences and were imbued with the astrological essence of each of the five visible planets.

Human experience on Earth was thus perceived to resonate with Heaven through the association of Fire with fiery and energetic Mars, Earth with grounded and practical Saturn, Metal with the interplay of relationships as embodied by Venus, Water with the inner reflectivity and outer flow of communication expressed by Mercury, and Wood with creative and expansive Jupiter.

And it is in the five-fold form of the pentagram or its three-dimensional equivalent, the pentagon, that the transcendental relationship known as the 'golden section' or phi is revealed, as we shall now see. The aesthetic beauty of the golden section is universally appreciated in art and is revealed in the ideal proportions of the human body. And throughout nature, phi is a revelatory treasure of the expression of cosmic evolution at all scales of existence.

Fundamental phi

The symbol of the five-pointed star lies deep within our human psyche. From the ceilings of Egyptian temples and tombs over four millennia old to the flags of the United States and sixty other countries and the logos of numerous companies, it bridges cultures and eras.

The Greek geometers understood that all the relationships between the interconnecting network of sides, which arise when a five-pointed star is constructed, and when its points are connected to form a surrounding pentagram, are in a constant and self-replicating ratio to each other, which they denoted by the Greek letter φ (phi).

Fig 2.7 The transcendental essence of φ (phi) is embodied in the geometry of the five-pointed star.

Phi may also be derived by dividing a line such that the ratio of its smaller to its larger portion is the same as the ratio between the larger portion and the whole.

Numerically, the value of phi is transcendent, like pi, an irrational number, which effectively continues, never ending and without repetition. Expressed to a mere three decimal points as 0.618, this truly cosmic relationship may uniquely, also be expressed as its inverse, as the number one divided by phi equals phi too – 1.618 – again transcendentally extending without end.

The thirteenth century mathematician Fibonnacci, revealed phi through a series of numbers named after him. Beginning with zero and one, each number of the series is the sum of the preceding two numbers: 0 + 1 = 1, 1 +1 = 2, 2 + 1 = 3, and so on and thus the three-in-one nature of unity finds yet another and profound expression.

The Fibonnacci series can be extended indefinitely: 0,1,1,2,3,5,8,13,21,34,55….. By then dividing each term by its predecessor, a series of ratios arises; 1/1, 2/1, 3/2, 5/3, 8/5, 13/8….. And by converting each ratio into decimal form and graphing these, a wave emerges which pulses above and below the value of phi. As the series continues, the pulses approach ever nearer to, but never reach, this unattainable ideal.

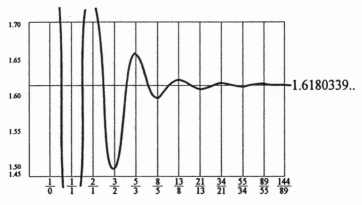

Fig 2.8 When the successive ratios derived from the numbers of the Fibonacci series are plotted on a graph, the waveform nature of φ (phi) is revealed.

And the universal power of the Fibonacci series may also be expressed as a spiral, with the ever more perfect expression of phi emerging as it unfolds from its centre point.

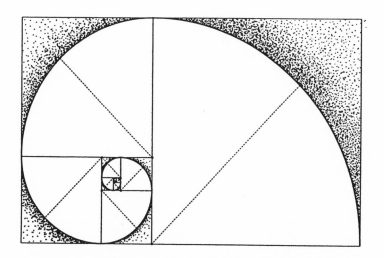

Fig 2.9 The golden spiral, born from the immanent 0 at the beginning of the Fibonacci series, is manifest throughout the whirlpools of Nature.

It is this self-replication of phi as seen in the evolution of these never-ending waves and spirals, which is revealed as the key to its ubiquity in natural forms. From the unfolding of leaves around a central stem, the seeds in the head of a sunflower, the growth of a Nautilus shell, the shape of a whirlpool to the arms of a spiral galaxy, phi pervades the universe.

The geometry of the pentagrammic star also embodies this innate self-regeneration. The central space bounded by the five sides of the star, is itself a pentagram. And by forming a smaller five-pointed star whose apices coincide with those of this inner pentagram, a still smaller pentagram is created at its centre.

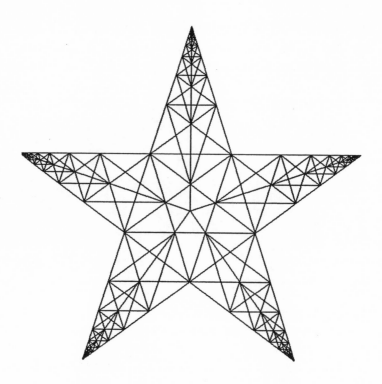

Fig 2.10 The holographic principle of the many within the one is revealed through the generative geometry of the five-pointed star.

And drawing a pentagram around the original five-pointed star, forms the template for the generation of ever-larger stars and pentagrams.

Such self-regeneration, repeating the same shape at different scales is archetypally embodied in fractal geometries, whose mathematical expression forms the underlying order of complex systems, and to which we will return in the next chapter.

And here again, within the self-replication of phi, we meet the holographic principle.

Throughout Nature, five-ness and its holographic and evolutionary harmonics are encompassed by a rich diversity of living examples – from seashells, plants and the human body, to the ebb and flow of the populations of animals and the structure of spiral galaxies.

The archetypal proportions of phi sometimes known as the golden mean or golden section also abound throughout sacred architecture since ancient times. In its manifest and symbolic expression of cosmic harmony, its dimensions are innately beautiful and intuitively nurture our senses. And in our sensual and spiritual delight of buildings; such as the Parthenon in Athens, the cathedral of Notre Dame in Paris and the Great Pyramid at Giza; as their creators intended, their embodiment of phi resounds throughout space and time.

The cosmic order of Six

In the number Six, the ancients recognised the ordered integration of structure and function.

And as we shall see in the next chapter, the innate order of the universe is expressed at the most fundamental level by the exquisite harmony and interplay of six cosmic numbers whose values, set from the very beginning, have enabled its purpose and evolution to be fully expressed.

Nature abounds with such hexagonal forms embodying maximum efficiency in the use of materials, labour and time and the least wastage. At a Cosmic level, it should therefore come as no surprise that the writers of Genesis considered that the world was created in six days.

Six circles fit perfectly when drawn around a central one. But when the circles are replaced by six-sided hexagrams, the packing array becomes even more efficient.

In nature, such tessellated arrays, incorporating strength and stability are found in the form of beehives, where their structure allows the maximum amount of honey to be stored in the most efficient way and a multitude of crystalline forms balancing positive and negative charges with the least expense of energy.

Fig 2.11 The ancient symbol of the six-pointed star embodies harmony and order. The size of the inner circle, which it encompasses, and the outer circle which surrounds it form a 2:1 relationship – an octave of frequencies.

Symbolically, the hexagram finds an alternative expression in the Star of David, in alchemical tradition known as the Seal of Solomon and in the Hindu tradition as the Mark of Vishnu, the archetypal preserver of the world.

In many ancient traditions, the number Twelve, whose properties emerge numerically and geometrically from those of the hexagram, was perceived to perfectly express the essence of completion and wholeness.

Whilst in two dimensions, six circles fit perfectly around a central one, in three dimensions, it is twelve spheres around one, which embodies such order and integration.

Transcendental Twelve

Supreme mythic and symbolic significance was also ascribed to the wholeness of twelve around one. Across the ancient world, this archetypal relationship was seen in the cycles of the heavens, where twelve solar months and thirteen lunations combined to complete the year and during which time, the Sun, the centre of life-giving heat and light, made its way through the twelve-fold zodiac of constellations.

In many traditions, the solar hero, exemplified by Jesus in the Christian teachings born at the winter solstice, at the turning of the year and the re-birth of the light, was invariably surrounded by twelve followers, disciples or attendants.

And in order to manifest such wholeness, societies, real and mythic, sought to embody this cosmic ideal,; as in the twelve tribes of Israel, the court structure of the ancient Chinese emperors, the Athenian culture of Solon and the Arthurian court of Camelot.

Ultimately, the completion of the inner journey to spiritual wholeness was at the esoteric heart of many of the symbolic associations with twelve around one, as described in the twelve labours of the Greek hero Hercules and the astrological numerology of the zodiac, where the essence of each sign offers a further insight into human personality.

It is within the twelve-faced dodecahedron, the fifth Platonic solid, that the symbolic and energetic harmonics of twelve-ness are combined with the self-regenerative evolution of five-ness and phi. Given these profound spiritual and transcendental associations, it is then no surprise that the Greeks related the all-pervasive Aether to this form.

The rainbow bridge

With the number Seven, we encounter the triadic nature of the cosmic male, female and child as experienced through the four-fold nature of our human experience embracing our individuated spirituality, mind, emotions and physical body. And our personality and human experience is intimately woven within the energetic resonance of cycles traditionally ascribed to the number Seven.

The geometric expression of Seven is also revealing as it neither fits perfectly within a circle nor forms a partnership with any other number. It is the essence of aloneness, of self as expressed through the individuated consciousness of our personality.

Yet to initiates its 'hidden' relationship with the number twelve as seen in the resonance of three plus four equalling seven and three multiplied by four equalling twelve are clues to a deeper metaphysical significance to which we shall return in Chapter 9.

The ancient Vedic teachings of India saw our personality-based consciousness energised into physical form through seven chakras (in Sanskrit, meaning spinning wheel or vortex). Similar to the *lata'if* of Sufi tradition, these subtle energy centres are deemed to be located up the primary axis of the body. Positioned just in front of the spine, they range from the root chakra at the pubic bone to the crown chakra at the top of the head.

Contemporary exponents of energy medicine now associate these subtle energy chakras with our physical endocrine system, which produces and regulates hormonal balances throughout the body and thus mediates our physical, emotional and mental well being.

This ancient seven-fold correlation found cosmic resonance through the astrological association of the seven visible luminaries of the Solar System. And the energetic essences ascribed to the Sun, Moon, Mercury, Venus, Mars, Jupiter and Saturn, were each considered to influence particular chakras and thus aspects of our personality.

For writers culturally as disparate as Biblical scribes, Greek philosophers, Chinese geomancers and Shakespeare, the ages of man's earthly journey too, are held to be seven in number.

In Seven, we thus find the periodic rhythm of personality based experience and two final correlations expressed in light and sound.

When Newton first shone the white light of the Sun through a glass prism and separated it into the colours of the rainbow, he recreated the seven-fold wonder of Nature, which has been a symbol of human hope since the earliest antiquity. We perceive the seven colours of the rainbow through the neural mechanism of our eyes, whose rod and cone shaped receptors, are sensitive to different wavelengths, which combine to form the seven resonant colours of visible light.

As in music, where it is also the innate harmonic relationship between wavelengths of sound, which creates the seven-fold range of notes culminating in what we refer to as the octave, the frequencies of visible light too spans the same relationship of wavelengths as expressed in the octave

But as is evident, when we sing the rising cadence of doh, ray, me, fa, soh, la, te ... by stopping at the end of this seventh note, we instinctively feel that there is something 'missing'. And it is only in the sounding of the 'missing' eighth note, the higher doh, which both completes the lower octave and becomes the first note in a further and higher octave, that we feel whole.

The cosmic harmony of Eight

The higher and eighth note, which completes the octave, represents a sound whose wavelength is exactly half – and thus whose frequency is twice the first note. This 2:1 ratio of wavelength and frequency is repeated with each higher octave and represents a fundamental property of energetic waves, called resonance.

Such resonance is fundamental to the harmony of the Cosmos and expresses itself in a myriad of diverse ways.

The numerical symbol for Eight - 8 - is a ninety degree rotation of the symbol for infinity, ∞. Each essentially epitomises a continuous energetic flow, where the completion of a cycle is the beginning of the next. And seen clearly in the infinity symbol, the flow is depicted as two juxtaposed and balanced waves.

The essence of the number Eight is thus the continual weaving together of the world of energy, expressed as waves, and the eight-legged spider is prominent in many ancient and indigenous traditions as the archetypal weaver of the resonant web of life.

And in modern times, scientists have re-interpreted this eight-fold tapestry as the Periodic Table of the 93 naturally occurring elements from hydrogen to uranium.

In the mid-nineteenth century, chemists began to group the elements together, according to similar physical properties and realised that these properties repeated in periodic cycles.

The two-dimensional table, which emerged, was made up of vertical columns of chemical families exhibiting similar properties, and horizontal rows, which reflected gradations in those properties. Each row was found to complete the expression of these properties in an eight-step cycle or octave, which was eventually discovered to relate to the completion of orbital shells of electrons at different energetic states around the atomic nuclei.

Thus the periodic recurrences of chemical characteristics, as we now appreciate, are essentially harmonic notes, each an octave apart.

Consciousness and the star-tetrahedron

Perennial wisdom also recognises resonant harmony in the combination of numerical attributes, such as those found in the tetrahedron, the Platonic solid associated with the element of Fire.

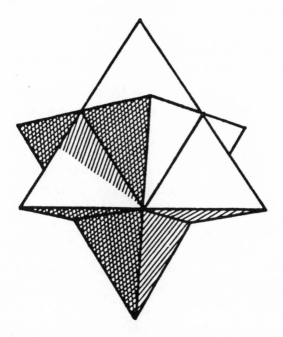

Fig 2.12 Within the star-tetrahedron is the coming together of Heaven and Earth.

The essence of this geometrical harmony is enhanced further in the form of the star-tetrahedron, where two tetrahedra are interspersed as shown in fig 2.12, forming a three-dimensional representation of the Star of David symbol.

The eight-fold resonance of the octave is reflected in this three-dimensional form by being 'anchored' by the eight corners of the star-tetrahedron, which also innately embodies three-ness through its triangular faces.

In Chapter 7, we will consider how consciousness may be embodied in physical form through the mediation of energetic biofields. And in the unfolding understanding of these supra-physical energetic templates, the metaphysical geometry of the star-tetrahedron is being perceived as key.

DNA and the I Ching

When the double-helix structure of DNA was decoded in 1953 by Francis Crick, James Watson, Maurice Wilkins and Rosalind Franklin, it was found to be made up of four types of genetic bases, now known by the letters, A, T, G and C. The bases form pairs, A always with T and G always with C. And in turn, permutations of three out of the four bases group together to form different amino acids, which link together to form the proteins from which all biological organisms build their physical bodies.

The total number of possible permutations of the four bases engenders the 64 so-called DNA codons of the genetic code.

And in 1973, philosopher Martin Schönberger discovered that astoundingly, these are exactly the same permutations of binary pairs, which are organised into the matrix of 64 hexagrams in the ancient Chinese I Ching, or Book of Changes.

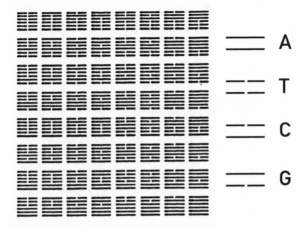

Fig 2.13 The sixty-four hexagrams or kua of the I Ching and their bi-gram counterparts in the four bases or codons of DNA.

The perennial wisdom encoded in the I Ching is universal in its attributes and has been used as a psycho-spiritual resource for millennia. It is based on a system of 64 six line hexagrams called *kua*, made up of different combinations of the binary systems of yin and yang, depicted as broken (- -) or unbroken (- -) lines respectively.

The structural code of DNA is binary and organised into the triadic structures of amino acids. And each *kua* of the I Ching, also encodes the binary attributes of yin and yang organised into a triadic form exactly analogous to the DNA code.

In the seventeenth century, the German mathematician Gottfried Wilhelm Leibnitz learned of the I Ching through Jesuit scholars and referred to its fundamental relationship to confirm his system of binary mathematics, whose on/off series of ones and zeros form the basis of today's digitalised computer science.

As each codon of DNA encodes information of the biological attributes of an organism, so each *kua* of the I Ching encodes an archetypal attribute of the human psyche. For both, their generic combination of binary separation and triadic resolution optimise the means by which information is stored, processed and retrieved.

The completion of Nine

To the ancients, Nine represented completion and the culmination of the nine-month gestation period of a human baby provides both a physical and symbolic metaphor

However, other aspects of completion relating to nine-ness are more often emphasised in the ancient texts, amongst the most prominent being the themes of judgement, redemption, acceptance and forgiveness – and ultimately reconciliation

Such themes relate to the human personality. And it is within ancient Sufi and mystic Christian doctrines that the nine-fold analysis of personality types and the guidance for their transmutation, known as the enneagram (from *enneas*, the Greek for nine and *gramma*, meaning written) is derived.

And the numerical nature of nine as the product of three and three reinforces the symbolic aspects of the trinity and in their raising to a higher power, the re-integration of their innate unity.

Greater than the sum of its parts

As Nine completes, so Ten is seen to stand at the threshold of a new and higher empowerment.

Ten incorporates the pantheon of numerical archetypes within itself and, as a whole, is greater than the sum of its parts.

The Pythagorean initiates referred to Ten as 'the higher unity wherein the One is unfolded', and Ten represents the power to generate numbers beyond itself. In adopting a ten-based numerical system, the raising of a number to the nth power of ten thus does not change its essential nature but literally, symbolically and energetically expands its power.

Just as the perfection of One is deemed immanent, Ten is its manifested expression. We designate ten out of ten as an expression of such perfection and through the ten fingers of the human body, the ancients perceived the power to create all the inventions and achievements which allowed man to achieve dominion.

Fig 2.14 The cosmological model of the Tetraktys.

Within the Pythagorean mystery school, the ten-point construct known as the Tetraktys, was used as the basis for Cosmological study. Consisting of four levels, it was set out as a triangle. Beginning with one, the next levels comprised two, three and four points respectively, exactly as in a modern game of ten-pin bowling.

This simple two-dimensional form, inscribes a wealth of wisdom.

Its levels embody all the elemental and geometric associations of four-ness as we have previously noted. Within its layout, the geometries of all five Platonic solids are captured and its numerical values of one to four encompass the fractional lengths of a vibrating string, which produce the natural notes of the musical scale.

The universal insights embodied within the ten-fold Tetraktys, found an alternative expression within the ten-fold divisions of the symbolic Tree of Life, known as Sephiroth, of the Jewish mystical tradition of Cabalah.

But whilst the Greek philosophers contented themselves with perceiving the geometric perfection of the universe encoded within the Tetraktys, the Cabalistic philosophers perceived the spiritual journey to enlightenment as being embodied within the essence of the Sephiroth.

Exquisite harmony

As we continue to explore the resonant harmony and the archetypal patterns of the Cosmos, we shall return to the thematic essence of number and form as intuitively perceived by the ancients.

We will also continue to encounter the holographic principles understood by the ancients and being rediscovered by leading-edge science as we progressively embrace the wholeness of the Cosmos and of our spiritually based human experience.

Throughout the ages of the human journey, there has always been access to higher awareness attuning through dreams and intuitive inspiration to the universal truths of the Cosmos. And Pythagoras, Newton, Einstein and many others, if not all, who have acknowledged such expanded perception as the primary source of their revolutionary insights, have been initiates to the deeper mysteries of perennial wisdom.

But now we will turn our attention to six numbers, which reveal the exquisite harmony of the universe from its beginning and which have shaped its history and destiny.

We will also discover how new theories are expanding the ancient perception of profound order underlying the apparent chaos of the world.

And we will begin to explore the deep mystery of time.

CHAPTER 3

EXQUISITE HARMONY

I have only been able to write this book, and you to read it, because, from the very beginning, the universe was set up in an extraordinarily special way.

As cosmologists have continued to uncover its mysteries, they have discovered six cosmic numbers whose values, profoundly embedded in Nature, are incredibly finely tuned. Were any of them to have values only marginally different from those measured we, and the entire physical world, would not now exist.

And as we explore each of them in turn, and understand why their values are so crucial to the evolution of complexity and life throughout the universe, we may see further evidence of an underlying harmony and purpose, which has been present from its inception.

The first cosmic number

Represented by the Greek letter ε (epsilon), the first cosmic number is a measure of the force which binds together the protons and neutrons within atomic nuclei.

This power of attraction represented by ε is known as the strong nuclear force and its value determines the efficiency of nuclear reactions. The value of ε is thus crucial to the entire alchemical process by which all 93 naturally occurring elements within the physical universe are ultimately synthesised, from the lightest, hydrogen, to the heaviest, uranium.

And it is in its dynamic relationship with the extreme temperatures and pressures within the interiors of stars, that enables the elements to be birthed in the proportions we observe throughout Nature and which ultimately gives rise to biological life.

We can see the importance of ε by returning to the first second after the big bang, when the binding power of the strong nuclear force had already begun to exert its power and the nuclei of the lightest elements - hydrogen, deuterium and helium - had begun to form.

Over the next one hundred thousand years, as the universe continued to expand and cool, eddies of primarily hydrogen gas, began to form as the seed points for future galaxies and the first generation of stars.

It would however, take a further billion years or so, before these first stars, the crucibles for the creation of heavier elements, began to coalesce out of the vast birthing fields of primeval gas clouds.

Under the influence of gravity, the gas forming these embryonic stars slowly spiralled inward, and began to heat up to the point where in the central and hottest part of the interior of the newly birthed stars the nuclear fusion of hydrogen to helium could be ignited.

Whilst this primary fusion reaction converts the great majority of the mass of the hydrogen fuel into heavier helium atoms, a tiny amount, 0.007 of its mass, is released as energy, mainly as heat.

And it is the specific efficiency of this energy release, which is expressed as the cosmic number designated by ε that is crucial for two reasons.

Firstly, it controls the speed by which hydrogen is converted to helium, and thus determines the lifetimes of stars. And secondly, it controls the subsequent synthesis of all heavier elements, required to enable the formation of planetary systems and the evolution of biological life.

It is the combination of both of these factors, which allows the time and conditions to ultimately enable the development of all complex physical forms.

The death of a star

Whilst a star continues to burn hydrogen, the value of ε allows the outward pressure of the heat generated to perfectly balance and thus to hold off the inexorable collapse of gravity. But as this primary fuel is exhausted, gravity prevails and the core of the star implodes. Now however, the higher temperature generated by the collapse, is sufficiently energetic for helium to fuel transmutations to still heavier elements.

Depending on a star's mass and thus available fuel, this alchemical process may generate progressively heavier nuclei, releasing energy at each stage and so enabling it to continue to hold off gravitational collapse.

However, a crisis is eventually reached when the stellar core has been transmuted into iron, as it is from this point onwards that, to create heavier nuclei, energy must be input rather than being released.

And it is this pivotal energy crisis, which now drives the final stages of a star's life.

For smaller stars, gravity now takes over for the final time and the star shrinks to a shrivelled husk of cold and dark matter. But for heavier stars, substantially above the mass of our own Sun, the final implosion sets off a gigantic explosion. And in the maelstrom of the dying star, the necessary energies are generated to enable the synthesis of the remaining elements up to the heaviest, uranium.

By about five billion years ago, several generations of stars had been born, lived and died in such cataclysmic explosions resulting in vast and chemically rich interstellar clouds.

It was within such a cloud that our own Sun and Solar System were birthed, seeded by the elemental gifts of these earlier suns, which enabled biological life on our planet to evolve.

We are literally star seeds.

All this has only been possible because the specific measure of ε is 0.007. Were its numerical value to be less than 0.006 or greater than 0.008, such elemental synthesis and thus all complex physical forms, including ourselves could not have evolved.

The bonding of neutrons and protons

The value of ε also offers an understanding of why atomic nuclei are comprised, not only of protons (whose positive electric charges in stable atoms are balanced by the negative charge of orbiting electrons) but include neutrons too.

Were nuclei only to be composed of protons, being of the same positive electric charge, they would repel each other, preventing nuclei comprising more than a single proton from forming. However, the inclusion of neutrons in the nuclear mix, contributes their mass to the cohesive effect of the strong nuclear force, without them exerting any additional electric repulsion – or upsetting the overall balance of charge between protons and electrons, whose interaction comprises another crucial relationship, as we shall see.

The fine-tuning of ε then ensures that the initial nuclear attraction between a single proton and neutron is sufficiently strong to bond the two particles together, and thus support the synthesis of heavier nuclei.

This is imperative for the initial build-up of hydrogen to helium, which must go through an interim stage – that of two hydrogen nuclei combining to form a nucleus of deuterium (heavy hydrogen). Were the value of ε to be only 0.006 instead of 0.007, the deuterium nucleus would be unstable and thus unable to provide this crucial bridge.

Equally, were the value of ε to be greater than 0.008 the binding force between protons would be so strong, that there would have been no hydrogen remaining in the early universe to provide stellar fuel and thus provide the long-term heat and light to sustain the evolution of biological life.

And as was shown by cosmologist Fred Hoyle, even a few percentage points change from the actual value of ε would have cataclysmic effects.

Creation of a carbon nucleus with six protons and six neutrons arises from the combination of three helium nuclei. In calculating details of this synthesis in stars, Hoyle realised that there is little chance of three such nuclei coming together at the same time.

And he determined that the process completes via an intermediate stage, where two helium nuclei energetically combine to form the nucleus of the element beryllium, before then combining with a further helium nucleus to form carbon.

The problem is that beryllium is unstable and would decay before the third helium nucleus comes along to complete the process. But as he discovered, the carbon nucleus uniquely embodies a crucial resonance, which enhances the beryllium-helium interaction and thus the transition to carbon.

Fig 3.1 The tetrahedral form of carbon from enables the least force to be applied to achieve the greatest strength – as shown by the geometric form of diamond. In 2004, astronomers discovered a diamond of crystallised carbon 2,500 miles across in the constellation of Centaurus. They called it Lucy.

Moreover, as Hoyle calculated, a change in only four percent in the actual value of ε would severely curtail the synthesis of carbon and thus the evolution of all carbon-based life, including us.

The spacetime universe

The processes from which the current complexity of the universe have unfolded, have taken an enormous amount of time. If the initial set-up conditions had not supported the actual duration of this cosmic timetable, complex biological life forms could not have evolved.

The ancient geomancers recognised the interplay between time and space and integrated them in their metrology of the Earth and its cycles. And today, cosmologists do so in the measurement of the spacetime universe.

We measure its vastness in light-years, which represent the distance a beam of light travels in a year, at a speed of 186,282 miles per second.

As we peer into the far reaches of space, we are only able to observe stars and galaxies by the light they emit. And given that no physical signal travels faster than light, the enormous distance it travels in a year also represents our observing a bright object as it emitted that light a year ago.

Therefore, the further out we look, the further back in time we journey. So by looking at a star we are actually looking backwards in time – we are looking into the past.

Observations by the latest generation of instruments, such as the Hubble space telescope, have enabled cosmologists to estimate the radius of the physical universe to be some 14 billion light-years in extent and thus to be about 14 billion years old.

It is this almost unimaginable scale and duration, which has allowed the necessary time to elapse for biological life to evolve.

And as we shall now see, it is the incredible fine-tuning of the second cosmic number expressed as the letter N, a measurement of the ratio between electrical and gravitational forces - which set at the moment of the big bang has enabled this to be the case.

The perfect balance of large and small

N measures the relationship between the electrical forces, which hold atoms and molecules together, and the vastly weaker force of gravity. Its enormous numerical value of 10^{36} (ten followed by thirty-six zeros) is critical in enabling gravity to be the large-scale organising force of the universe, whilst allowing stable and complex structures to develop.

For any two objects, the strength of the gravitational attraction between them is proportional to their masses multiplied together, and falls away in proportional to the square of their distance apart.

At the level of our everyday experience, gravity is a predominant force and thus the gravitational attraction of the enormous mass of the Earth holds us securely on its surface.

On still larger scales, it is gravity, which is the organising force pervading the universe, holding planets in their orbits around stars and stars within galaxies.

The reason why gravity is able to predominate on larger scales is that the vast majority of the positive and negative electric charges within atoms and between molecules, balance themselves out. When the balance of such forces is disturbed, for example by the energetic release of electrons to form electric currents, the imbalance only accounts for a minute proportion of the existing charges, whereas, the force of gravity applies to all matter, at all times.

But on the tiny scale of atoms, whose masses are minute, the effect of gravity become utterly insignificant in comparison to the forces of electric charge. It is these forces and not gravity, which hold negatively charged electrons in their orbits around the positively charged atomic nucleus and which bind atoms together to form molecules.

Were the value of N to be only marginally less, or greater, the universe could not have supported the evolution of complexity. Either it would have run its course too rapidly or the imbalance between the small-scale electrical forces and the large-scale forces of gravity would have dramatically limited the options for diversity.

But the exquisite tuning of the actual value of N has one more intriguing aspect.

As we explore what it means to be human, the number N ensures that we are poised midway – a billion times bigger than a molecule and a billion times smaller than a star – held in the balance of these forces which have shaped us.

The significance of three

As we now consider the third of these six cosmic numbers which are crucially embodied in the physical world from its beginning, a theme is beginning to emerge.

Whilst small variations in the values of both ε and N would have enabled some type of universe to form, if either ε or N were to vary by more than a few percentage points, such a world would have been still-born and unable to support the evolution of complexity and life.

The next number, represented by the letter D for dimension, may seem simple and mundane in comparison to the influence of both ε and N to life on earth, yet its value too is crucial for our existence and perception.

D represents the number – three - of extended spatial dimensions in the universe. We use this term when we talk about 3-D when describing the combined length, breadth and depth of an object and of the physical world as a whole.

As physical dimensions can only be structured as whole numbers, were D to have a value of two or four, physical life as we know it would again be unthinkable.

However, as we have already seen and will continue to explore, some cosmologists believe that what we experience as three-dimensional space (and four-dimensional spacetime), may actually be a holographic projection emanating from a two-dimensional boundary termed a brane.

If this is the case, the number of spatial dimensions and thus the value of D may represent the simplest form engendered by such a holographic universe

Ripples in the universe

The very earliest epoch of the universe existed in an incredibly ordered state. And the next cosmic number, represented by Q, is a measure of this intrinsic smoothness of spacetime, an innate feature of the universe from its inception.

As we have already seen however in Chapter 1, slight ripples akin to sound waves pervaded the early universe, creating eddies which would form the seed-points for primeval structure.

It is the amplitude, or height of these ripples, which is represented by Q. And a discovery in 1965 by physicists Arno Penzias and Robert Wilson led to its measurement.

In that year they identified the residual energy signature of the big bang in the form of background microwave radiation, which they found pervades all of space. Following their discovery, satellite mapping has progressively measured its strength in all directions.

Its numerical value is tiny and amazingly consistent throughout the universe. At 10^{-5} (one in one hundred thousandth) it would be equivalent to a wave only three inches high on the surface of the deepest ocean on Earth.

The precise tuning to this value ensured that the primeval eddies which rippled through the early universe, were sufficiently powerful to create areas of greater density which under the influence of gravity, enabled the formation of stars, galaxies and even vaster clusters of galaxies, whilst sustaining a remarkably smooth and thus stable universe in which, over the aeons needed, stars and whole planetary systems were able to evolve.

As for all six cosmic numbers, the finely balanced value of Q is crucial to our existence. Were it to be slightly less, any initial spacetime eddies would have been insufficient to allow stars and galaxies to form and the universe would have endured only as a sterile expanse of formless matter.

Alternatively, were its value to be marginally greater, the turbulence caused by the primeval eddies - whose effects were amplified as spacetime expanded in the aftermath of the big bang - would have prevented the stable conditions required for stellar and galactic formation.

Our future destiny

The future destiny of the entire universe depends on the values of the two remaining cosmic numbers, which relate to its continuing rate of expansion, beginning with the big bang, and its inherent density.

From the observed rate of expansion, a critical density – where ultimately the forces of gravity and expansion would be theoretically balanced – has been able to be calculated.

The ratio of the actual density of the universe to this critical value, is known by the Greek letter Ω (omega) and is the next cosmic number. If Ω is greater than unity, gravity will prevail. And at some point in the far distant future, perhaps many tens of billions of years or more away, the universal expansion will end and the entirety of spacetime will rebound into a slow starting but increasingly rapid gravitational collapse.

If Ω exactly equals unity, and thus the expansionary force and gravity are perfectly balanced, whilst the expansion will eventually stop, the universe will then remain static.

And if Ω is greater than unity, then the force of expansion will overcome gravity and the universe will go on expanding indefinitely.

But what is it that makes up the actual density, which determines the value of Ω ?

As Einstein showed us, energy and matter are equivalent and thus the density, measured by Ω comprises all the matter and all the energy in the universe.

Until a few years ago, scientists believed that the universe was entirely composed of the observable matter of stars and galaxies spread throughout space.

But as we have seen in Chapter 1, familiar matter and energy now appears to constitute only some five percent of the overall matter/energy 'stuff' which comprises the universe. The remaining 95 percent is made up of dark matter and dark energy whose natures are as yet unknown.

As astronomer Martin Rees has described, cosmologists now realise that the observable stars and galaxies of the universe are *just white foam on the wave crests, not the massive waves themselves*.

In Chapter 1, we have seen that calculations of the gravitational influence of dark matter have shown it to account for more than five times that exerted by 'ordinary' matter. Without yet knowing its constituents, this still allows cosmologists to incorporate its effects into the calculation of the actual density of the universe, and thus increase the value of Ω from about 0.05 to at least 0.3 – in other words, thirty percent of the critical value.

But what about the other 70 percent?

The beginning of the universe

As we further consider the value of this crucial ratio, we need to go back once more to the earliest moments of the universe.

Despite the uncertainty in its current value, in the beginning, the value of Ω must have been very close indeed to the unity value of the critical density. The reason for this is that as the universe expanded, any difference between the forces of gravity and the forces of expansion would have been dramatically exaggerated and the universe today would be very different to what is actually observed.

In effect, the big bang was initiated with an incredible degree of fine-tuning, by an expansionary force which was almost exactly sufficient to balance and ultimately offset the decelerating force of gravity.

At one second after the big bang, to arrive at the present day universe, cosmologists calculate that this initial value of Ω could not have differed from unity by more than one part in a million billion (one in 10^{15})!

A fundamental law of physics, known as the first law of thermodynamics requires that the total energy/matter in a closed system is conserved. It may take many forms, and change from one to another – but in its entirety, its value always remains the same.

Thus, despite the duration of the last 14 billion years and the incredible evolutionary journey of the universe, this fundamental law requires Ω to retain its initial value.

So, what constitutes the missing component of Ω ?

The cosmic force of expansion

The third constituent of the universe, which contributes to the necessary value of Ω, now appears to be the cosmic force of expansion, the recently discovered dark energy, whose strength also defines the sixth and final cosmic number, denoted by the Greek letter Λ (lambda).

Over eighty years ago Einstein inserted a cosmological constant in the equations of relativity. And although for the wrong reasons – he was seeking to engender a universe he thought should be static – Einstein's 'mistake' is now seen as presaging the discovery of dark energy.

Whilst its strength differs from the factor inserted by Einstein, dark energy provides the same negative pressure effect he envisaged, of offsetting gravity. And indeed, the latest calculations of its influence suggest that it does comprise about 70 percent of the overall mass/energy density of the universe and thus increases the value of Ω to very close to unity.

The force of dark energy is so weak that its influence is only apparent at the largest scales of the universe – greater than the group size of galactic super clusters or about 200 million light-years. As such, we may consider its characteristics to be a property of the universe as a whole.

Whilst as we have seen, its current nature is unknown, it may thus represent the inflation field through which the expanding wave of spacetime continues to embody its innate order and homogeneity and its ultimate destiny.

Perfect precision

The ancient philosophers perceived the integration of cosmic order and structure to be embodied in the number Six. And in these six cosmic numbers we see the astounding manifestation of the underlying principles of the Cosmos.

Were any one of the six - set at the very beginning of space and time - to vary only marginally from their measured values, the universe as we are able to experience it, would never have arisen.

That all six numbers are tuned to such perfect precision both individually and in concordance requires us to ask fundamental questions.

Are they merely the almost unimaginably fortuitous outcome of a random combination of factors producing a uniquely sustainable universe by chance?

Or does their combination, represent a single example of a vast array of random possibilities, which in other spacetimes forms a congregation of universes – a multiverse - all engendering different conditions and unfolding, if at all, in a myriad of ways?

Whilst the multiverse scenario is a theoretical possibility and the concept is supported by a number of cosmologists, its underlying assumption too, is that our own universe is a random occurrence

However, given the numerical values and fine-tuning of the six cosmic numbers, the multiverse scenario requires the creation of billions of trillions of universes, the vast majority stillborn or sterile, for the probability of ours to exist as a chance outcome!

Another theoretical suggestion, which again presupposes that the Cosmos is inherently purposeless and random, is that of parallel universes. In this hypothesis, every choice taken on every scale throughout the universe creates 'parallels' where the choices not taken in our universe are taken in other universes.

If this suggestion is taken to its logical conclusion, there would literally be an infinity of other parallel universes.

As a means of avoiding a discussion of the possibility of our universe as purposeful and consciousness as primary to its creation, both scenarios of the multiverse and parallel universes, posit alternatives that are extreme in their requirements for either billions of trillions or indeed an infinite number of other random universes.

And as we have already seen, when physicists encounter infinity, it is a sure sign that they are on the wrong track.

A further alternative, and the one perceived by all perennial wisdom teachings is that the initial set-up conditions of the universe were purposeful and created by consciousness to explore the evolution of the complexity and diversity of physical life.

And as we seek to expand our understanding of consciousness and the interface between mind and matter, the evidence of harmony, order, meaning and purpose, which pervades the universe, will be our continual way shower.

The nature of time

As we have seen, the spatial constituents of the earliest epoch of the universe were in an amazingly ordered and uniform state.

We will return in later chapters to consider the fundamental question of why this was so, but for now, we will begin our exploration of another mystery intrinsic to the universe – the nature of time and the direction of its 'arrow'.

What is time? What is it that we experience as time and what does that mean for our perceptions of reality? And whilst we seek to measure its apparent flow, is it a fundamental aspect of the physical world or a consequence of our minds enabling the ordering of our experience?

Of fundamental importance to our quest is that whilst Einstein showed that relative movement *within* spacetime results in different experiences of time, the symmetrical expansion of spacetime as a whole enables us to consider that a clock on Earth measures the same elapsed time from the beginning of the universe as one on a distant galaxy.

And it is this intrinsic symmetry of the entirety of spacetime that enables us to state that the universe as a whole is some 14 billion years old.

As we have just seen, observers at rest to each other are carried along by the expansion of spacetime and occupy the same freeze-frame perception of the 'now' of the present moment.

But, as we saw in Chapter 1, the action of moving relatively to something or someone *within* spacetime, causes time itself to slow down and thus different 'nows' are experienced by different observers.

As however in the symmetry of the universe, no vantage point in space or time is more valid than another, reality encompasses all such 'nows' - all events in spacetime without distinction between past, present and future. – and thus the only reality is space and time in their combined entirety.

There is no flow of time. Events just are – they all exist – occupying their particular point in spacetime. The flowing sensation comes from the conscious awareness of changes in our perception.

And it is in only in our mental freeze-frame that a sequence of events seems to evolve as a continuous story.

Rather like a DVD, every moment of 'now' is a still frame which when all run together creates the sense of the whole continuous picture and enables a coherent experience to unfold.

However, as with a story captured on DVD – and for the universe as a whole – the perception of change does embody a direction in time.

Unlike the symmetry of the spatial dimensions of the physical universe, this arrow of time, requires an underlying asymmetry for its unfolding and again we may find an answer as to how this arose, in the extreme order prevailing at the beginning of the universe.

To do that, we need to explore the concept of entropy.

Order and disorder

Entropy is the measure of the disorder inherent in a physical system. The second of the four laws of physics, which relate to the inter-relationships of different forms of energy, or thermodynamics, it states that the entropy of any such system is statistically liable to increase.

Essentially, this is because there are generally far more ways in which a system can be disordered than ordered. And the more complex the system is, the greater the disparity in the number of such states and thus the increasing likelihood of a trend to higher entropy.

For example, consider a pack of twenty-six cards, each displaying a letter of the alphabet from A to Z. Whilst there is only one way of arranging the cards to obtain the ordering from A to B to C and soon to Z, there are an enormous number of ways of shuffling the cards to obtain the disorder of them being out of alphabetic sequence. The likelihood of the cards being disordered – and therefore in a state of high entropy – is vastly greater than their being in a state of order, or low entropy.

However, there is one crucial aspect of the second law of thermodynamics, which we will need to continually bear in mind. It is that order *can* nonetheless evolve within an overall trend to disorder, as long as in the formation of such order there is overall a more than compensating generation of disorder.

For example, in our pack of letter cards, order can arise, such as in the formation of words. However, such order requires energy to be introduced – in this instance, by human intention.

Entropy and the arrow of time

The equations describing entropy are symmetrical with regard to time. In other words, from any given moment the second law of thermodynamics indicates that entropy of a system can theoretically increase not only towards the future, but also towards the past.

But whilst such a trend to overall disorder is universally confirmed with regard to the future, when applied to the past, it is forcefully contradicted. All our experience and observation of the physical world tells us this. Milk that is spilled does not become un-spilled and at my last birthday I was, at least in age if not in spirit, a year older and not younger.

Following this line of reasoning, as we journey back to the big bang, we realise the universe itself must have begun in a state of very low entropy for it to have been increasing ever since – for the last 14 billion years.

We find that the current order of the universe is a relic of its cosmological beginning. And, as we have seen, the set-up conditions were perfect for starting it off in such a state of extremely low entropy.

The mechanism for the achievement of such initial order is gravity.

It was the enormously high density of the evenly distributed primordial gas, which exerted gravitational attraction and enabled progressively larger clumps of matter to form around the tiny ripples through which, as we have seen, the early universe was suffused.

The extraordinary order prevailing at the birth of the universe has thus enabled entropy to increase ever since, and in so doing, empower the arrow of time to take flight.

Consciousness

However, entropy is not only a measure of disorder it is also a measure of the possible states a particular system may experience. As each state embodies information, the level of entropy represents the maximum level of information able to be encoded within a system. The universe is thus again, set up perfectly to enable the maximum level of information – consciousness – to be expressed as it unfolds in spacetime.

The realisation by cosmologists that the universe of spacetime is an entirety which like a DVD is complete from its beginning, but whose story unfolds in awareness through the mediation of consciousness, is revolutionary to our perception of who we really are.

And as we expand our awareness, we liberate ourselves from the constraints of physical perception and are able to begin our exploration of the wider Cosmos which transcends spacetime.

In Chapter 6, we shall return to the discussion of the meaning of time and our perception of it. But now, as we begin to consider the evolution of complexity, we will find that it is the arrow of time, which lies at its heart and which is key to the physics of history.

Harmonic relations

As we saw in Chapter 2, the ancient geometers sought archetypal patterns and harmony, which they discerned to be the underlying templates for the diversity they saw in Nature.

However, with the limited analytical tools at their disposal, they were unable to probe deeply into those phenomena of nature, which are complex or exhibit chaotic behaviour.

And this remained the case for over two millennia until the advent of computers enabled the calculation of enormous volumes of data and facilitated the comprehension and description of increasingly complex systems.

In the early 1960s, the mathematician Benoit Mandelbrot began a decade-long study of phenomena, which exhibited fluctuations and irregularities, seeking underlying patterns in such diverse examples as the fluctuations in stock market prices and the naturally occurring shapes of coastlines and mountain ranges.

When he scrutinised a vast range of data, he saw in these systems – whether occurring in space or time – a revelation of self-similar patterns repeating at ever larger and smaller scales.

As we have already seen, such self-similarity and scale invariance are innate within classical geometry. But what Mandelbrot now discovered was that these forms of harmonic relationships underlie the diversity of chaotic and complex phenomena too.

He termed the building blocks of such patterning, fractals and the description of such fractal-based systems, chaos theory - perhaps an ironic name as the theory actually describes the underlying order inherent in such chaotic behaviour.

For such systems, what happens in the future is extraordinarily sensitive to tiny influences.

This aspect of the theory has become widely known as the butterfly effect from what is probably its best-known metaphor; where within the Earth's weather system, it has been estimated that a miniscule factor such as the beating of a butterfly's wings in one part of the atmosphere can eventually result in a major weather effect elsewhere.

And chaos theory offers dramatic insights into phenomena such as earthquakes and as we shall see, paves the way for yet a deeper understanding of Nature's apparent complexity and its underlying simplicity.

The power law

Before chaos theory, most researchers had sought to understand and predict the occurrence of earthquakes using statistical methods in attempts to determine their frequency and scale.

A basic outcome of such methods is known as a Bell curve, whose familiar shape indeed resembles a bell. If a group of similar objects are measured, for example the heights of a hundred adult men, the results will follow such a curve, with the greatest number clustering close to the average and a rapid falling off in the incidence of heights that are significantly different to the average.

On this basis, if there was such a thing as typical earthquakes, they too should cluster around an average value, with quakes significantly beyond the Bell curve being extremely rare.

However, this is not the case.

What seismologists have found instead is that over an enormously wide scale the frequency of earthquakes varies in a direct and linear way with the energy they release. The statistics for all earthquakes, over a huge range of energy release, show that a quake, which releases twice the amount of energy, is four times as less likely to occur.

Where, as in the case of earthquakes, the continuing doubling of the frequency of one factor (e.g. the energy released) elicits a constant response in the frequency of another factor (e.g. the rate of occurrence), the harmonic nature of the phenomenon and the resonance underlying its entire manifestation, is revealed.

Such a relationship is known as a power law. The inherent simplicity of such laws underlies the complexity of the phenomena they describe. Any system, which obeys such a power law, is scale-invariant, self-similar and based on a fractal pattern, and as such, the term typical just does not apply.

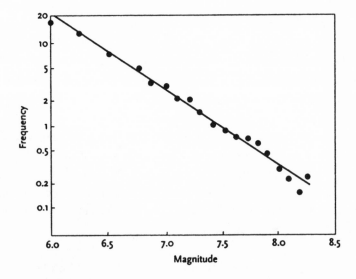

Fig 3.2 The Gutenberg-Richter power law of earthquakes shows that when their magnitude doubles, their frequency is reduced by a factor of four – this 2:1 relationship represents the harmonic of the octave.

For earthquakes, this means that the same factors, which cause a small quake, can also trigger a cataclysmic event. And the unavoidable consequence of such power law adherence is that whilst general characteristics are discernible, the accurate prediction of a specific quake is impossible.

Critical states

Whilst chaos theory can explain unpredictability, it is by itself, insufficient to explain major shifts or upheavals. And for this we need to develop a deeper understanding of systems which are not in equilibrium – and especially those that are poised on the critical knife-edge between order and chaos.

Such non-linear systems, where a tiny event can trigger either a small dislocation or a catastrophic upheaval, are inherently unstable and described as being in a critical state.

Their characteristics are found across a huge range of phenomena and their mathematical signature has been discerned in events apparently as diverse as the contagion of epidemics, the collapse of ecosystems, stock-market crashes and the spread of forest fires.

Increasingly, it is being recognised that inter-connecting networks of many types have a tendency to naturally organise themselves in such states. In computer generated simulations the self-organisation of criticality appears to show up in systems which are slowly driven away from equilibrium, and in which the actions of any individual element are dominated by its interactions with others.

Of fundamental importance to the behaviour of all such systems is that they are open to energy supplied from outside. And it is the way in which such energy is supplied which is key to such self-organisation.

In a series of ground-breaking experiments, physicist Per Bak played with sand piles and discovered the key.

Bak and his colleagues Chao Tang and Kurt Wiesenfeld sought to understand the difference between a pile of sand sitting passively in equilibrium and the same pile of sand to which grains are added.

What they found was that gradually adding grains increases the height of the pile, until at some point the addition of one more grain causes the pile to collapse. At this critical point, the collapse can be minor, with a few grains falling down the slope of the pile, or a catastrophic avalanche.

As grains continue to be added, other collapses, minor and major, ensue. A stage however comes, when as more grains are added, on average the same number of grains topples off the pile and thus the amount of sand in the pile remains the same – the system is in a state of self-organised criticality.

Further experimentation both by computer simulation and by building real piles of sand and other materials has shown that the character of the continual battle between order and disorder in such systems, and the perpetually shifting interactions which it engenders, is the same. And this is the case despite the diversity they exhibit and regardless of almost every last detail of the objects and elements making up such systems.

How they behave seems to be solely due to the basic relational issue of how easy it is for an ordering or disordering influence at one point in the system to bring order or disorder to another point nearby.

In addition, it appears that only the physical dimensions of the elements of the system in question and their basic geometric shape, matter in effecting this influence and thus the behaviour of the system – but nothing else.

This is amazing. For what this universality tells us is that substance, or phenomena, embodying the same two criteria will fall into the same critical state of organisation, regardless of how utterly dissimilar they may otherwise appear to be.

Thus if the characteristics of the critical state of one example in a universal class of phenomena is understood, then *all* other members of that class are understood too.

And because the critical state only appears to depend on the two fundamental factors of size and shape, to model its behaviour, a simulation can effectively exclude all other details, which make up the overt complexity of a 'real' system.

History matters

One inherent aspect of many critical systems and the influence of their innate order-disorder factors is that they are time dependent.

Occurring most naturally in processes of growth and evolution, what happens in their past, shapes the present and what happens in the present shapes the future.

Whilst this appears to be self-evident, the fundamental laws of the micro-world and the underlying principles pertaining to systems in equilibrium are independent of the direction of time. So, the search to explain the characteristics of complex systems had until relatively recently, also focussed on a quest to discern trends, cycles and periodic behaviour.

As we have seen, the spread of influence is crucial to the behaviour of a critical system. But not only does influence take time to effect, in many instances it is not a simple, one-way process.

Where an influence generated by one element in a system on another, results in a reverse influence, the system is said to exhibit feedback. Such feedback can be positive or negative, depending on whether the reverse influence is greater or lesser than the original.

An example would be the well-known principles of diminishing and increasing returns encountered when for instance an innovative new product is developed and sold. Initially, sales are boosted and profits or returns increase. But once the market for it is satisfied, sales decline – and returns diminish. Only by further innovation do sales and thus returns increase once more.

Where the impact of the influence is reversible, in essence the system is independent of time. But when the processes of feedback are irreversible, the system is not time independent. What happens in the future depends on the accumulation of what has happened in the past – and the history of the system matters.

Such feedback processes are an intrinsic component of self-organising critical systems, which as we have noted, are prevalent in contexts involving growth and evolution.

Whilst their study is still in its infancy, bringing these new tools to bear is dramatically extending our understanding and is beginning to resolve deep mysteries relating to the Earth and its history, to which we will return in Chapter 7.

And the insights they offer into the evolutionary and revolutionary aspects of collective influence and behaviour are also being considered as being applicable to human interactions and the functioning of social and economic systems.

Such universal classes of systems and their common behaviour are a further revelation of the simplicity of the underlying principles from which the diversity of the universe is manifest. A simplicity which as we can now see not only informs the relationships embodied in the classical geometry of the ancients, but the fractal geometry of the emergent new wisdom.

Underlying order

The processing power of computers has enabled a myriad of complex phenomena to be distilled into the essence of their underlying patterns and harmony.

This technological prowess and our latest understanding is progressively enabling us to perceive these dynamic patterns of a creative Cosmos, which the ancients could only intuit and weave into myth and symbol.

To the Egyptian priests, whose civilisation lasted for over three millennia, the manifest world arose from the sundering of cosmic Unity. Whilst peace and harmony represent order and thus an implicit return to Source, they saw the forces of chaos in all their aspects, as embodying the diversity of separation.

But whereas in the continual battle between the cosmic principles of order and chaos, personified by the deities Horus and Set, the Egyptians recognised the creativity inherent in their conflict, by spiritually imbuing the cosmic power of Horus within the physical body of the pharaoh, they ensured that order prevailed throughout the land.

As the cosmic order, which underlies chaos, is now being revealed, the tools are also becoming available to express its diversity as simple patterns of waves.

And now as we rediscover the manifold waves of energy through which consciousness expresses itself and remember the ancient reverence for sound and light, we shall discern new insights into the cosmic symphony that is the world.

CHAPTER 4

WAVES OF CREATION

The mystical origins of many spiritual traditions depict an initial void from which higher consciousness created the diverse manifestation of the physical world.

The ancient Egyptians called this ocean of potentiality *Nun*. To the Vedic sages of India, it was *Nirguna Brahma*. And the Sumerians and later Biblical writers described it as *the Deep*.

This ancient wisdom perceived the physical world as being breathed into existence by the aether of an immanent Creator causing the myriad waves of the universe to foam on the surface of this endless ocean of possibility.

And for all, the sounding of the Word and the coming of the Light are embodied as energetic wave-guides for the innate essence of divine harmony and creative purpose.

As we have seen, the big bang origin of the universe is remarkably congruent with these ancient intuitive insights.

Physics has now equated matter with energy. The perceived separation of material objects has been replaced by energy fields, which incorporate harmonic patterns of waves. And isolated mechanistic events have been replaced by the perpetual interaction of dynamic processes.

Now, as we discover how the harmony of the world is expressed through the waves of sound and light, we will see how they bring to dynamic life, the potentiality of the energy fields, which pervade the universe.

Wave patterns

Waves come in many different forms.

The simplest is the familiar sine wave, so-called because of its sinuous or serpent-like undulations, which move from peak to trough to peak again in a continuing flow of energy.

Where such waves are free to move, they will do so until their energy eventually dissipates. But where they are generated for example, in a closed space or by stroking the strings of a musical instrument whose ends are fixed, the waves are not free to travel and instead set up standing patterns of vibration.

Spirals and vortices are other examples of waves, emblematic of Nature's dynamic cycles and which all adhere to a handful of underlying harmonic and archetypal forms as we shall now see.

Even the phenomenon of the seasonal cycle – from spring to summer, autumn and winter, is in actuality a spiral. The path of our Earth, orbiting around the Sun, traces a helix as the Sun itself moves around the galactic centre, carrying us through space at 600,000 miles per hour.

So, the macrocosmic helix of the Earth's galactic journey mirrors that of the microcosmic helix within us, that of our DNA.

In the spirals, which emanate and grow from a central originating point, we see the evolutionary urge revealed throughout Nature. The

Fibonacci series, from whose mathematical relationships the golden ratio is born, may be expressed as a spiral, with the calm eye at its centre representing the initiating 0 of the series, the One-ness from which everything else grows.

And as this golden spiral unfolds, the ever more precise ratios of phi embodied within its turning, enable its dynamic balance. Such Fibonacci spirals are seen throughout Nature from pinecones to seashells, rams horns to spiral galaxies; for they are the genesis of life.

A further fundamental pattern that spirals express in Nature, is that of a vortex sheet where eddies of alternative polarities branch out from a central axis. Such a phenomenon may be seen when a stationery object interrupts a moving stream of air or water, for example when the oar of a boat is rested on the surface of a fast flowing river. And conversely they also arise as the wake of a moving object - such as an aeroplane when it disturbs still air, or a boat as it sails across still water.

The V formation of flying geese also takes advantage of such a vortex sheet to minimise the energy required to undertake their long migratory journeys. Only the lead bird needs to work at flapping its wings. The others benefit from the undulating spiral wake of the vortex sheet trailing behind; and simply relax and allow its waves to move them up and down. When the lead bird becomes tired, it moves to the back of the formation and another bird takes its place.

The growth of plants too, exhibits the alternating rhythm of a three-dimensional vortex sheet as they unfurl around a central stem. As patterns of dynamic energy, they embody in their spirals, the golden ratios of phi, optimising by this means, their access to sunlight and rainfall.

Cosmic doughnuts

Another fundamental form of spiral is known as a torus or vortex ring.

Such spirals are the embodiment of regular cyclic patterns where two periodic motions interact with each other in such a way as to become locked together into a repeating rhythm in a regular and predictable way.

Fig 4.1 The ever-creative spiral embodied within the torus.

The torus continually curves back on itself around a spherical or doughnut shaped ring; In Nature such forms are dynamic, yet stable. Found within the structure of DNA, a number of researchers have speculated that certain of the vibratory patterns of quantum strings may also take such a form.

Mathematical waves

In the eighteenth century, the Frenchman Jean Fourier developed a mathematical framework for converting all such patterns – and indeed, *any* pattern – into a mathematical language of simple waves, and further showed how these could be reconverted back to the original pattern.

Such Fourier transforms may in fact be a key to the innermost workings of the universe. And indeed, they were the powerful tools which two centuries later were used by Dennis Gabor to derive the theory which led to the development of the hologram.

The key to holograms

The vast matrices of waves, which comprise the universe, are in continual interaction. And just as their apparent diversity is based on fundamental patterns, so the complexities of their interactions also arise from the interplay within a small number of fundamental relationships.

It is in these relationships between waves that harmony is born.

The energy carried by a wave is expressed in terms, which relate to its length or conversely its frequency of vibration. The shorter the wavelength, or the higher the frequency, the greater is the energy of the wave. Thus for example high frequency X-rays embody more energy than low frequency radio waves.

Science describes the manifold interaction of waves as interference; And it is the form that the interference takes which determines its harmonious or disharmonious outcome.

The combined energy of waves whose peaks and troughs coincide – when they are said to be in phase - is additive and their interference is said to be positive. But where waves interfere such that the peak of one coincides with the trough of the other, their energies cancel out and their interference is described as negative.

One particular example of positive interference is when waves of identical frequency and co-incident phase are combined. Known as coherence, this is the underlying principle by which the intently focused beam of a laser is produced.

Interference and coherence are key to the phenomenon of the hologram. Fourier's equations were used by Gabor to convert a picture of an object into a blur of wave patterns on a piece of holographic film and to devise a way of converting the image back to the original object.

The hologram is produced when a single beam of the coherent light of a laser is split into two. One beam is bounced off the object to be photographed and the second beam aligned to interfere with the reflected light of the first. The resulting wave pattern is recorded on film. A three-dimensional image of the object is then created when light is shone through the film.

One of the most intriguing and significant aspects of the holographic principle, which is innate to the Fourier language of waveforms, is that the entirety of the whole object is recreated in every part of the fractal geometry of its three-dimensional image.

This manifestation of the One in the many, is an underlying principle of perennial wisdom and as we explore further, we will discover its presence throughout the universe.

Sound and light

The principles we have just described apply generally to waves and we will return to them again in later chapters. But now, let us move on to begin the exploration of our human experience of sound and light.

The universal principle of the conservation of energy states that energy may change its form, but in its entirety is neither created nor destroyed. And Nature is replete with such changes in form, or the transduction, of energies.

The waveforms of sound and light are particularly adept at this alchemical transformation, which gives rise to a multitude of technologies including the telephone, hi-fi, television and computers.

For example, when you pick up the telephone to make a call, the sound energy of your voice is transduced into the electro-magnetic signal which goes through the telephone lines to the telephone handset of the person you are calling, where it is transduced back to the sound energy of your voice.

And our perception of the physical world is, only able to be accomplished, through the transduction of the many different forms of environmental energies into the electrical signals, which form the language of our body and our brain.

Sound originates in all vibrating bodies, whether they are musical instruments, the voices of children or trees rustling in the breeze. When surrounded by an elastic medium, such as air, the pulsating waves of sound travel by alternatively squeezing and expanding it.

The normal range of human hearing covers about ten octaves of sound frequencies, from roughly 20 cycles per second (cps), to approximately 20,000 cps. At acoustic ranges above (ultra-sound) and below these ranges (infra-sound), our bodies still react vibrationally to acoustic phenomena even though we may not physically hear the sound.

The spiral of sound

Like other vertebrates, the human embryo spirals into life. By 24 weeks, the ears of the foetus are completely functional, with the baby fully responsive to the sounds of the outer world.

Chinese acupuncturists, recognising the holographic principle that the part models the whole, map the entire body onto the ear and thus in treating any malady, will first treat the corresponding part of the ear.

Both the outer and inner ear are spirals. The inner ear or cochlea (Greek for snail shell) is encased within a hard shell and filled with liquid. Around its central axis threads a Fibonacci spiral of sensitive hairs, which decrease in thickness as the spiral winds tighter. Sound vibrations entering the vortex of the outer ear are guided to impinge on the base of the cochlea and then travel in waves up and around the inner liquid.

The waves making up each sound then break, depending on their wavelength, at a different point along the spiral triggering the sensitive hairs at that location. The hairs then transduce the energy of the sound waves into electrical signals, which are transmitted to the brain for interpretation.

The physical properties of sound waves are similar across an enormous range of frequencies. The generic term *light* however refers to the entirety of the electro-magnetic spectrum whose waves express a variety of apparently diverse aspects extending from the ELF, (extra low frequencies) of long range waves, pulsing at a few cycles per second, to high frequency cosmic rays with frequencies of 10^{24} cps – a frequency range of over 70 octaves.

Within this huge range of waves, spanning the frequencies, which represent a mere octave, is the rainbow of light which is visible to the human eye.

When Newton shone white light through a prism and thus separated it into its constituent wavelengths, he revealed the seven familiar colours of the rainbow. We see visible light thus because these colours are the only combinations possible which the human eye can detect with the rods and cones of our retinas.

The rods are only sensitive to white or black, but our eyes incorporate three kinds of cones, which are sensitive to the red, green and blue range of wavelengths. It is through the combination of their input, passed to our brains in the form of electric signals, that we perceive that which we call colours.

Music

The basis of the musical scale used in the west today, derives from that taught by Pythagoras, the Greek philosopher who was the first to teach its principles outside the temples of Egypt, Chaldea and India.

Its notes are based on fundamental ratios of simple whole numbers, and the creation of the complete scale begins with a string, or wire, of any length fixed at both ends to a stable base and pulled taut, as in a guitar or violin.

When the string is stroked, it will vibrate at its fundamental note, which is dependent on its length.

And when a finger or a bridge is positioned at the halfway point on its length, a higher note will be produced when either half-length is stroked, which is twice the frequency of the fundamental note – the interval known as the octave.

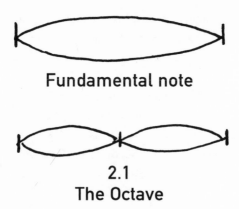

Fundamental note

2.1
The Octave

Fig 4.2 Nature's fundamental harmonic - the octave

Dividing the string at two-thirds of its length thus creates two notes an octave apart. By then continuing to divide each two-thirds section into an ever-smaller sequence of two-thirds ratios, a range of higher notes is produced, each in a harmonious relationship with the ones before and after. And on the thirteenth step, the cycle is completed when the original note is sounded once more – although slightly flat.

The full cycle ranges over seven octaves. So to now gather the twelve notes (and the thirteenth which completes one octave and begins the next) within the span of a single octave, only requires the length of the shorter strings to be doubled as every doubling lowers the note by an octave but maintains the note.

This chromatic scale of the ancients is harmonically resonant with the physiology of the golden spiral of our inner ear and with our body as a whole. It is represented by the white and black notes of the modern piano, but with one crucial difference.

Between the actual thirteenth note, devised by the ancient musicians and the ideal doubling, is a small difference in frequency – 1.34

percent – which was known to them and is termed the comma of Pythagoras.

With the introductions of orchestras in the seventeenth century, the difficulty of tuning across instruments resulted in the adoption of the even tempered scale used today, where the difference represented by the comma of Pythagoras is evenly distributed across the twelve notes ensuring that the thirteenth is an exact octave – or doubling – above the first.

Whilst pragmatic, this modern adjustment has moved away from the musical harmony with which our bodies are naturally resonant. But the rediscovery of the ancient rhythms and the therapeutic nature of music are now resurgent in our consciousness, as we seek the re-establishment of well-being, harmony and wholeness.

The hidden meaning of the musical scale

Within the completeness of the chromatic scale, the ancient musicians identified two smaller scales, which form the basis for the prevailing musical traditions of East and West.

The seven-note diatonic scale, which completes the octave with the eighth note, is familiar to us through the white notes on the piano keyboard.

The modern names by which we know the notes were introduced a millennium ago by Guido d'Aruzzo and the first letters of their Latin description reveals their Cosmological structure inherited from an earlier age. Traditionally sung from higher to lower, they were perceived as descending from Heaven to Earth.

Beginning with the higher DOH taken from *Do*minus which means absolute, the scale then descends through SI, taken from *Si*der, denoting all the stars in the firmament to LA from *La*ctea the name for the Milky Way galaxy, then to SOL the Latin name for the Sun, FA or *Fa*teas, the ancient name of the Fates or planets, MI from *Mi*crocsmia denoting the Earth, RE from *Re*gina Coeli, the Moon, known as the Queen of the Heavens and finally the lower DOH - *Do*minus, representing spirit revealed in man.

And the five-note, or pentatonic musical scale of the Chinese and Polynesian peoples also embodies five of the twelve notes of the complete chromatic scale and here again the musical system finds cosmological resonance with the five elements of the manifest and the un-manifest world.

Harmonics and resonance

There are two other characteristics of waveform interference, which pervade the universe and which are both readily experienced in sound.

The first, characteristic of most everyday sounds is a rich mix of frequencies, which give a sound its depth and timbre.

The second is due to the creation of higher overtones or harmonics of the fundamental note or notes being sounded; the quality of the overall sound then depends on their relative strength or weakness.

The creation of harmonics is a consequence of the principle of resonance, when an object vibrating at a certain frequency will cause another object whose innate frequency is the same or in harmonic ratio to the first, to vibrate in sympathy.

An easy way to demonstrate this is by sounding a tuning fork near a stringed musical instrument such as a guitar; when without being touched, the guitar strings will resonate with the tuning fork, vibrating at the same note.

And when a small piece of paper is placed over the guitar string that represents an octave higher than the frequency of the tuning fork, when the tuning fork is sounded, not only its fundamental note, but the higher octave will harmonically resonate and the paper will jump off the string.

For energy to resonate, regardless of its form, the interpenetrating wavelengths must be in harmonic relationship, when the frequency of one note is in a whole number ratio with its resonating note or notes.

Such harmonic ratios are inherently geometric, as in the case of sound where musical resonance is formed by notes an octave apart, where the frequency ratio is two to one. The harmonic ratio known as the perfect fifth occurs where the ratio is three to two and that known as the major sixth when the ratio is five to three.

Cymatics

The same ratios that are found in tonal harmonics are found throughout Nature. Researcher Hans Kayser discovered that whole number ratios of musical harmonies, such as the octave, the third (5:4), the fourth (4:3) and the fifth (3:2) correspond to an underlying numerical framework existing in chemistry, atomic physics, crystallography, botany and astronomy.

Two centuries ago, the German physicist Ernst Chladni found that when he evenly covered a flat metal plate with a thin layer of sand, that he was able to render the vibrations, formed by the playing of stringed instruments, as visible patterns in the sand.

Latterly, Swiss doctor Hans Jenny took up and expanded on Chladni's ideas, using a variety of media in addition to sand, to demonstrate the primacy of vibration in effecting the patterns found throughout Nature.

Jenny's simple method was to connect a metal plate covered with a variety of substances, such as sand, fluids and powders free to move, to an electronic oscillator controlled by a frequency generator capable of producing a broad range of vibrations. By then varying the wavelengths of the vibrations produced through the oscillator on the metal plate, he was able to show the effects of different frequencies on different substances.

And with the power of what he called cymatics, from the Greek word for wave – *kyma* - he saw revealed, as so many others before him, the fundamental three-in-one vibrational nature of physical manifestation.

Jenny described the triadic nature of phenomena as being made up of an underlying field of periodic vibration, which generates and sustains the pattern of form – its configuration – and the forces of dynamic processes. All three are aspects of the entirety of a phenomenon and no aspect can be removed without the whole ceasing to exist.

It is perhaps fitting that the cymatic pattern made by the sound of OM, through whose vibratory power the Vedas, the scriptures of ancient India, deem the entire universe is created and sustained, is a triad formed of a central point surrounded by two concentric circles.

And in the ancient science of sacred architecture, the most fundamental geometric harmonics revealed through cymatics, were incorporated in the dimensions and shapes of buildings, created as microcosms of the cosmic symphony, to ease and heal the body and free the spirit.

Perennial wisdom

The deeper we peer into the fabric of the physical world, the simpler and more harmonious the principles on which it is founded appear to be and the more we discover, reconciles with perennial wisdom.

Isaac Newton, when asked how he could see so far into the Cosmos, replied that he could do so only because he stood on the shoulders of giants. By this he acknowledged and honoured those pioneers who had journeyed the path of discovery before him.

Perhaps we too, at this momentous time in our history, when we seem to know so much, yet are beginning to realise that we know so little, need to honour and be open to the wisdom of those who have trod the path before us.

In these last four chapters, we have explored our understanding of how the universe is as it is. We shall now begin to seek answers to the question of why it is as it is and consider our unfolding understanding of the nature of consciousness.

At the heart of perennial wisdom is the perception of the wholeness of the universe ultimately expressed in and through man. The ancients and all spiritual traditions discerned creative purpose as pervading the world and ourselves as essentially spiritual in nature and undergoing a human experience.

So let us now see how wholistic science is being reconciled with this understanding of spirit.

PART II

RECONCILING SCIENCE AND SPIRIT - WHY THE UNIVERSE IS AS IT IS.

In these next four chapters, we will explore the nature of consciousness and how it transcends space and time.

We will see how the unfolding discoveries of wholistic science across many fields of enquiry and on all scales of existence are seeking answers to the question of why the universe is as it is.

In doing so, we will continue to amass the evidence for the underlying order and purpose which pervades the physical world and begin to consider the metaphysical realms of the Cosmos.

And we will discover how further insights into the universality of the holographic principle may offer us a key to reconciling wholistic science with spirit.

If you dream it, you can do it.

Walt Disney (1901 – 1966) American communicator

CHAPTER 5

THE CONSCIOUS UNIVERSE

The prevailing perception in western societies, and one portrayed by most scientists, is that the Cosmos is materialistic, random and mechanistic.

According to this worldview, we are each isolated from each other and separate from the world as a whole. We are also merely the serendipitous result of physical evolution, the fittest survivors in an unconscious and therefore unforgiving universe.

Yet, the pioneers of physics at the beginning of the twentieth century, in their discoveries of the quantum world, were already aware, at that scale at least, that the materialistic model was unsustainable.

They themselves, amazed at what they discovered, realised that at the tiniest scale of existence, matter was not as it had been previously understood. Instead, it behaved sometimes as a wave and only as a particle when it was observed. Perhaps their most astounding discovery was that in all cases, such wave/particle – or quantum - entities had no individual presence but only existed in relationship with everything else.

They also realised that the quantum field, which pervades the universe, is essentially non-corporeal. And that which we perceive as materiality, is fundamentally the manifest foam, the waves on the surface, of a non-manifest ocean

A number of the early quantum physicists, becoming aware that their discoveries were taking them into the realms of metaphysics, began to study ancient spiritual teachings in an attempt to clarify their understanding of this strange quantum world.

Yet, for most scientists, the implications were too revolutionary to accept and regardless of the evidence, they chose to regard quantum behaviour as being limited to the minute scale of the quantum world. And the wider implications of their discoveries were marginalised as they focused on their practical applications to develop technologies, which have transformed our material existence.

The radical challenge to the pre-existing worldview of these scientists, was apparent in the sign which the renowned physicist, Niels Bohr, hung up on his door - *'Philosophers keep out. Work in progress'* - which contrasted with the mystical yin-yang symbol he incorporated into his coat of arms.

As we have seen, the current generation of leading-edge scientists, are progressively perceiving the underlying waveform harmony and order of the universe at all scales of existence, an order which, according to the perennial wisdom of all ages, was and continues to be created purposefully.

The nature of consciousness

But a deeper understanding of the nature of consciousness and what it is that may purposefully create the world continues to evade the reach of science.

Or does it?

The Latin root of the term consciousness, *conscius*, means 'knowledge with experience'. At its most basic level, this refers to the experience of self and the world via the physiological processes of the body and the brain. But as we shall see, perennial wisdom and new scientific evidence is revealing a vastly greater perception.

Consciousness is notoriously difficult to define and scientific research has undertaken its study from opposite directions. The majority of researchers pre-assume consciousness and mind as solely the outcome of physical evolution and arising from the operations of the human brain.

Others, however, are prepared to consider the possibility of metaphysical realms and are exploring the supra-physical primacy of consciousness. In this model, the evolutionary development of perception effectively enables consciousness to express itself in ever more complex ways through the mediation of the mind and the physical processes of the brain and body.

As we have seen, the leading edge of physics, often considered to be the parent of all other scientifically based disciplines, continues to revolutionise our understanding of spacetime and the underlying fabric of the universe.

Yet, its 'children', the biological and so-called life sciences have continued, in the main, to adhere to a mechanistic worldview. And so the mainstream approach of neuroscience into the investigation of the human mind has been to assume that it is an emergent phenomenon of a materialistic brain.

Conversely, many physicists and cosmologists, busy with their own investigations, have been willing to leave the pursuit of mind and consciousness to the neuroscientists and psychologists, thinking it is unnecessary to their own line of research, and perhaps without fully appreciating the outdated understanding inherent in much of their colleagues approach.

And outside the disciplines of mathematics and systems analysis, few scientists are yet conversant with the power of complexity theory and the holographic principle to provide an explanatory framework, which as we will see is potentially able to incorporate a deeper understanding of the nature of consciousness.

But other scientists are progressively seeking to understand the human mind beyond the confines and perceived causality of the brain and in so doing, have pioneered the way for a revolution in science.

They have, in fact, paved the way for its reconciliation with spirit.

The role of science

The role of science is generally seen by many scientists as the asking and answering of questions relating to *how* the universe is as it is. The seeking of answers to the question of *why* the universe is as it is, most scientists have seen as the remit of philosophers.

But we are all human beings, and whatever our role in life, we are all seeking answers to the meaning and purpose of life on both personal and collective levels.

Whereas the idealised view of the scientist is as a rational and objective witness of the reality of the world, all scientists are human beings too and bring to their work, to a greater or lesser degree, their personal and communal cultural perceptions, beliefs and prejudices.

So on one level, whilst scientists may seek and indeed purport to be objective, as human beings they inevitably also bring their underlying personal beliefs to their work, and which whilst subtle and perhaps even subconscious, must affect their research in some way.

Paradigms

In 1962, Thomas Kuhn, a historian of science, wrote what has become a seminal work. In his book, *The Structure of Scientific Revolution,* Kuhn introduced the concept of paradigms – consensual ideas about the world which have been shown to work - and to which scientists, like all human communities, adhere.

In describing how scientific revolutions, which require a shift of the prevailing paradigm, come about, Kuhn found that they did so only when maladjustment or discomfort with the tenets of the pre-existing paradigm becomes unbearable.

In every revolution he studied, from that which was brought about by Copernicus in his assertion that the Earth orbited the Sun and not vice versa, to those relating to the discoveries of quantum behaviour and relativity, he found that scientists as a whole remained emotionally committed to the prevailing worldview.

Only when the level of inconsistencies and anomalies relating to the accepted paradigm, became intolerably great did the majority of scientists change their viewpoint.

As historian Michael Polyani in the early 1960s also discovered, such evidence is disregarded, even if it cannot be accounted for, in the hope that it will turn out to be false or irrelevant. Indeed, some scientists remain so incapable of accepting a new paradigm that it has been ruefully asserted that *'the progress of science is measured by funerals'.*

It is such dogmatic assertions of the prevailing worldview and the disregard of evidence that is sometimes termed scientism. And it is scientism rather than the ideal of science, which has attempted, at the threshold of each revolutionary leap forward, to bar the path to greater awareness.

Such scientism is sadly understandable given the peer group pressure within the environs of science itself and the perceived status of scientists in the wider community.

And with regard to the nature of consciousness and mind, not only the social and economic, but a deeper emotional investment too appears to be especially entrenched.

Science itself, at the time of its inception in the seventeenth century, was only free to follow its path of seeking to understand the physical world by its assumed liberation from questions of spirit and the then dogmatism of religion.

But the understanding of consciousness is not only revelatory in terms of the understanding of why the universe is as it is – but is essential to what it means to be human.

And now, the path taken by science and thus by us all, has come to a crossroads. We are now at the point where the nature of consciousness and our deeper understanding of it can no longer be avoided and the understanding of which will choose and guide our way forward.

The ideal of science is to be open-minded and willing to both see and follow the evidence wherever it leads. It is this frontier science, which sparks revolutions. And it is this science, which is seeking a wholistic understanding of the Cosmos.

Spirituality and religion are not the same

Just as science and scientism are not the same, neither are spirituality and religion.

Spirituality is based upon direct experience of non-ordinary states of mind and dimensions of supra-physical realities. Such experiences, which have been reported throughout history and across the world, do not require a special place or an intermediary to mediate contact with the numinous.

The revelatory awareness inherent in such experiences pervades perennial wisdom. And the teachings, which underlie the mystical origins of all the world religions, equally are based on their founder's experience of the spiritual nature of the Cosmos.

However, when such spiritual perceptions become organised as religions, the human tendencies towards the illusory comfort of certainty and control, which are offered by institutionalised religions, have often diminished the direct communion with the spiritual source of revelation. And as a result, the earlier spiritual perception has been transmuted to hierarchical and often dogmatic institutions.

Any spiritual revelation and the teaching which emanates from it - however universal in its underlying principles - still perceives those principles through the lens of culture, time and place. And because religious texts are generally constrained to their originating teachings, it is difficult if not impossible within their institutional framework to allow for the evolution and expansion of human awareness.

Yet, when the underlying teachings of all religions are examined, despite their different emphases and languages, they all express the spiritual nature of human experience. It is the immediacy and directness of such spiritual experiences throughout history, and amongst all peoples that continues to urge us forward in our search for the meaning and purpose underlying the Cosmos.

The universal mind

The distillation of such perennial wisdom perceives the Cosmos as a conscious inter-connected whole, and consciousness as all-pervasive.

The universal mind of the Cosmos expresses itself as energy. And through the archetypal patterns and harmony arising from the intention of the underlying order, energy manifests the physical world.

The initiatory teachings of many traditions, such as the Vedic path of ancient India, whilst revering higher consciousness, did not seek to worship the awareness itself, but sought to embody it within themselves as the fullest flowering of human potential.

The writings of the Vedic teachings – which go back at least five thousand years and probably much further – describe the individuated human soul as being a droplet of the infinite ocean of consciousness or as a spark of the immanent flame of *Brahman.*

Within such metaphors, which recur in the hermetic teachings of ancient Egypt and as we have seen in the Pythagorean and Platonic teachings of ancient Greece, we may see the workings of the holographic principle - the whole as embodied within the many.

The reconciliation of wholistic science with spirit empowers human freedom and the exploration and realisation of our potential as spiritual beings undergoing a physical experience.

A deeper understanding of who we really are, is now unfolding. And by being willing to be open to the deeper realities, which underlie the perception of materiality, we are able to raise our awareness of ourselves as co-creative participants in the meaningful evolution of the Cosmos.

The primacy of consciousness

A Cosmology which is based on the primacy of consciousness, and which has as its underlying principle the understanding that consciousness purposefully creates the physical universe is not incompatible with the findings of science.

But any new theoretical paradigm, which emerges from our deeper understanding of consciousness, must accommodate the anomalies and inconsistencies, which have revealed the inadequacy of that which has gone before.

Just as Einstein incorporated the universal principles discovered by Newton and showed them to be a partial understanding of a larger whole, so any paradigm, which incorporates consciousness as causal, must encompass the laws of physics as we know them and expand their applicability.

It is the further revelations relating to the holographic principle, waveform mathematics and the archetypal patterns of fractal geometry, which may offer us a key to consciousness and the beginnings of a framework for further exploration.

Nonlocality

But now we need to consider one of the most intriguing and ultimately paradigm shattering aspects of quantum behaviour.

In 1935, Einstein co-authored a paper with Nathan Rosen and Boris Podolsky, pointing out that an implication of the then emerging quantum field view of the universe, was that quantum events could be linked instantaneously across any spatial distance.

Their paper was actually intended as a rebuttal of quantum theory as they considered that such nonlocality would invalidate Einstein's own theory of relativity, which had determined that no influence or signal of any kind could traverse spacetime faster than the speed of light.

It took nearly half a century however, before a theoretical means of testing what had become known as the EPR (Einstein, Podolsky,

Rosen) paradox, was devised by physicist John Bell in 1964. And it took nearly two further decades before physicist Alain Aspect was able to experimentally and conclusively verify what Bell had suggested.

Aspect's experiment, based on Bell's insight, involved two detectors set 13 metres apart, which were able to measure the axis of spin of photons. And midway between the detectors, was positioned a container of energetically excited calcium atoms.

As was well understood, when calcium atoms revert to their normal unexcited state, they emit 'twin' photons, whose axes of spin are exactly correlated.

The essence of the experiment was to show that when the detectors were randomly and independently varied, and the spin of one of the twin photons was recorded by one detector, that the spin of its partner, immediately and spontaneously, flipped from its original state, to retain the perfect correlation between them.

In 1997, the experiment was further refined with detectors 11 km apart. Such a distance is approximately 10^{18} times (ten followed by eighteen noughts!) the scale of the atomic nucleus. A separation this enormous in comparison to the effective scale of localised forces, demonstrated that quantum nonlocality – spontaneous action at a distance - has no spatial limit.

Such quantum nonlocality, sometimes termed 'entanglement', means that, at least at the quantum level, two such entangled particles are instantaneously connected and are effectively a single entity – whether they are close to each other or separated by the entire universe.

But this incredible realisation has a further stunning implication.

Nonlocality in time

As we saw in Chapter 1, the theory of relativity integrates space and time into a combined four-dimensional entity called spacetime. And this means that the consequence of nonlocality in space – is nonlocality throughout time too.

The astounding reality of this has also now been proven in a series of experiments in which the detection of nonlocal behaviour has been shown to extend through time.

These involve a process of splitting beams of light and then converting the photons of the two beams into 'entangled' pairs. Each partner of the entangled photon pairs is then directed on a different route to a detector – thus ensuring that the photons travelling at the constant speed of light arrive at different times.

The subsequent interference patterns produced at the detector shows that the photons are entangled not only spatially, but also in time.

There are two other crucial aspects of such entanglement. The first is that future measurements of entangled photons whilst revealing the reality of temporal nonlocality, do not change the past – although they do however influence the level of information available to describe the past event.

The second aspect of quantum entanglement is that the effects arising from it are spontaneous and do not rely on any signal or influence of one partner on the other travelling *within* spacetime at a speed exceeding that of light.

This is enormously exciting, because essentially what it means is that at the immanent level of the quantum field, every event is correlated and thus 'known' simultaneously. Yet within physical spacetime, as we have seen, influence is mediated by the speed of light and thus causality and the arrow of time are preserved.

This provides a further and profound insight of how perhaps transcendental and all-pervasive consciousness may, through the structure of the universe, explore the unfolding of evolutionary experience.

But whilst science has been discovering the realities of quantum nonlocality, researchers investigating anomalies related to consciousness, have revealed that the power of the human mind also acts at a distance.

The mind/matter interface

To begin to appreciate the mind/matter interface we now need to review the pioneering experiments, which over the last three decades have been seeking to understand how the human mind may be influential at nonlocal levels beyond the brain. And to do that, it is helpful to first consider the following analogy.

The mapping of brain activity by neuroscience has shown that changes in brain function are clearly connected with changes in awareness. But this says little about the intrinsic nature of consciousness and its origins.

To help in elucidating this differentiation, the psychiatrist Stanislav Grof uses the analogy of the relationship between a TV set and the TV programme it transmits.

Whilst this analogy is much simpler than the incredible complexity it seeks to reflect in relationship to consciousness and the brain, and despite the entire television system being human-made, it nonetheless offers us a powerful and revealing insight.

Grof explains that, as we know, the output of a TV programme is dependent on the operation of the TV set. Malfunctions of specific components will typically result in the distortion of the picture or of the loss of sound. Like a neurologist who uses changes in consciousness as a diagnostic tool, a TV engineer can infer from the nature of the malfunction, which part of the set is faulty. And when identified and rectified, the set will be repaired and the programme broadcast again in its entirety.

We are aware that the TV set is merely the receiver of an electro-magnetic signal, which originates from elsewhere, and which is also the ultimate transmitter of the programme. We also know that the TV set itself does not generate or contribute anything to the content and form of the programme. And we would laugh at anyone who sought to understand the content of the programme or why it appears at a particular time by investigating the components of the set.

The fact that there is such a close correlation between the set and the quality of the programme does not mean that the entire secret of the programme itself lies within the set.

Yet this is what western materialistic science has drawn from comparable data about the brain and its relationship to consciousness.

Memory and the brain

Despite a century of intensive research, such an approach however, has been unable to produce any convincing evidence that consciousness is merely a product of the neurophysiological processes in the brain.

But in the early 1940s when psychologist Karl Pribram began to puzzle over memories, a way forward was revealed.

The prevailing view at that time was based on the research carried out two decades earlier by Wilder Penfeld, who had discovered when electrically stimulating the temporal lobes of the brains of epileptic patients, that they spontaneously retrieved memories in vivid detail.

Penfeld concluded that sequential experiences were recorded and stored at specific locations in the brain as units, or engrams, of memory. And so the search for the mechanics of engrams and the locations in the brain in which they were deemed to reside, became the focus of mainstream research into the nature of mind and the assumption that it arose from the mechanical workings of the brain.

But in 1946, Pribram went to work with the neuropsychologist Karl Lashley, whose own three-decade long research into memory had come to very different conclusions.

For Lashley had been unable to discover any evidence for engrams or for localised memory storage, and on the contrary he had found instead that memory appeared to be distributed throughout the brain as a whole.

To determine this, Lashley had first trained rats to undertake a series of tasks. Having then surgically removed various portions of their brains, he retested their abilities to undertake the tasks. Despite their motor skills being affected, he found that their memories were unimpaired even when he excised massive proportions of their brains.

This was also Lashley's finding for human patients who for medical reasons had had portions of their brains removed, but who never suffered the loss of specific memories. Other than the brains of epileptic patients, for reasons as yet unknown, Penfeld's findings have never been replicated.

The holographic brain

In the mid 1960s Pribram read an article, which would offer him the key to unlocking the puzzle.

The article, in the magazine *Scientific American* was a description of the first construction of a hologram and Pribram immediately realised that the 'whole in the many' aspects of the holographic principle might be able to shed light on the distributed nature of memory retention.

And it appears that it is not only memory, which might be processed holographically by the brain.

Intensive research had shown that there is no one-to-one correspondence between a visual image, which the eye sees and the way that image is represented in the brain. And further, like memory, that visual processing is also remarkably resistant to surgical excision.

Both memory and visual processing are amenable to holographic processing. The characteristic of the 'whole in every part' of holograms could explain how surgical removal of major parts of the brain would still enable memory and visual processing to continue. And secondly there would be no one-to-one correspondence for either.

But what wave-like phenomenon could the brain employ to carry out such holographic processing?

Pribram knew that electrical communications that take place between the brain's nerve cells or neurons do not occur alone. Neurons possess branches like tiny trees and when an electrical message reaches the end of one of these branches, it radiates outwards as does a ripple in a pond.

Because neurons are packed together so densely, these expanding ripples of electricity are constantly crisscrossing each other – an almost endless and myriad array of interference patterns and it is these, Pribram concluded, which may give the brain its holographic properties – mediated by the electro-magnetic waveforms of brain cell connectivity.

Holographic memory

Following Pribram's first article on the possible holographic nature of the brain in 1966, other researchers began to realise how the model is able to explain other neurophysiological features.

The human brain has a vast capability for the storage of information and brain researchers have struggled to come up with a mechanism, which explains its incredible capacity and its associated speed of processing data.

Holograms also possess an amazing ability to store information. By changing the angle at which two lasers strike a piece of photographic film, it is possible to record many different images on the same surface. And any image thus recorded, can be retrieved, simply by illuminating the film with a laser beam inclined at the same angle as the two original beams.

Another property of holographic recording provides a further analogy for the associative tendencies of memory. It occurs when the light of a single laser beam is bounced off two objects simultaneously and then is allowed to collide and the resulting interference pattern is captured on film. Then whenever the first object is illuminated with laser light, and the light that reflects off it is passed through the film, a three-dimensional image of the second object will appear, and vice versa.

So if our brain functions holographically, a similar process may be responsible for the way in which seeing certain objects evokes specific and related memories from our past.

Furthermore, a technique known as interference holography may also explain how we recognise both familiar and unfamiliar features of an image such as recognising the face of someone we have not seen for many years, despite the facial changes that have occurred in the meantime.

With interference holography, an object is viewed through a piece of holographic film containing its image. Any feature of the object, which has changed since the image was originally recorded, will reflect light differently. Viewing the new image will instantly reveal where it has changed and where it has remained the same.

Nevertheless, it is important to appreciate that the holographic principle does not require the entire brain to be the mediator of all mental processes. And indeed the brain seems to operate on both integrated and functionally specific levels.

And the increasing use of magnetic resonance imaging (MRI) techniques is beginning to reveal how these processes may complement and support each other.

The holographic recording techniques described above rely on the use of lasers, whose coherent light forms the wave interference patterns for information storage and retrieval. And as we continue to explore the nature of consciousness, we shall discover that such electro-magnetic energies are a vital and possibly universal conduit of its physical mediation.

The mind beyond the brain

The prevalent materialistic worldview considers that 'mind' arises from the properties of the brain. But this requires its influence to be constrained within the skull and what the five recognised bodily senses of sight, hearing smell, taste and touch, are able to perceive.

Thus, any evidence, which shows that the mind can operate beyond this field of influence – and thus on a nonlocal basis - is unable to be encompassed within this paradigm.

It is this evidence we will now consider.

The reality of psi effects

In 1995 the US Congress requested the American Institutes for Research (AIR) to review government-sponsored studies commissioned by the CIA. But these were no run of the mill studies. This was scientific research, which sought to test and measure parapsychological or psi effects of the human mind.

The extensive distances over which such effects have been measured, and the shielding which has been utilised to exclude electromagnetic influence, has proven that psi phenomena are not intrinsically electro-magnetic in nature. However, as we shall see, they may be physically mediated and localised through electromagnetic fields.

The AIR stated that the statistical results obtained by the experiments, were far beyond what is expected by chance. Having reviewed the experimental protocols, they refuted any possibility that the results could be due to any methodological flaws and also confirmed that they had been replicated at a number of laboratories around the world.

The Institute concluded that the reality of the phenomena was proven. In their view, future research should focus on how these phenomena work, and there was little benefit in continuing to undertake experimentation merely to offer further proof of their existence.

Psi experiments

But before we do go on to consider how such psi effects may arise, let us take a look at the sort of experiments, which developed from the 1970s onwards and which by the mid 1990s, led the AIR to their conclusions.

Psi effects have been experienced and reported throughout history and around the world. But with the schism between materialistic science and spirit, research into their nature has been emphatically marginalized. Only over the last three decades have some courageous investigators, often paying a high price in terms of the opprobrium of mainstream science, searched for ways to test the evidence.

Most researchers in the field of what is generally termed para-psychology do not claim to know what 'psi' is. Instead, they have, to date, tended to focus on measuring its effects. And as for all scientific endeavours, their experimental protocols have become progressively more rigorous, in their case often aided by the legitimate questionings of informed sceptics.

As is applicable to the study of all life sciences, they recognised that every form of human behaviour and performance varies from time to time. And to determine the confidence levels relating to a particular psi effect required statistical methods whereby, with sufficient repetition, a highly reliable estimate of the efficacy of a particular phenomenon could be determined.

Some sceptics continue to insist on the ability to reproduce a specific psi effect on demand as a major requirement for its acceptance. Yet this is exactly why, throughout the fields of medicine, psychology and sociology, such statistical methods have become an acknowledged means by which the behaviour of such complex systems is analysed. And to deny such a widely accepted means of scientific enquiry to the study of consciousness would be surely perverse.

The studies of psi phenomena have generally been classified into those involving passive awareness and those incorporating active influence. Nonlocal perception, such as the remote viewing of distant locations where a person can tune into an event happening in another place, or even another time, is deemed to be passive.

Nonlocal phenomena such as telepathic communication where one person can mentally communicate with and send thoughts and emotions to another person, and the ability to affect the outcome of ostensibly random events, in contrast denote an active mental influence.

Let us now review the evidence.

The ganzfeld method

In the mid 1970s, para-psychologist Charles Honorton and psychologists William Braud and Adrian Parker independently developed ways to facilitate states of consciousness, which were receptive to psi -effects.

Such states have been well known throughout metaphysical traditions for millennia. And one of the first texts from the ancient Vedic tradition of India, Patanjali's *Yoga Sutras* dating back three and a half thousand years, describes the attainment of psychic abilities through the yogic practice of deep meditation.

Involving an alert and receptive mind, combined with reduced sensory 'noise', these states of consciousness may be induced in sensory-isolation chambers.

Honorton, Braud and Parker developed a sensory deprivation technique, called the *ganzfeld*, a German word meaning 'whole field', to induce these psi receptive states in the laboratory.

The *ganzfeld* experimental method has three stages – firstly the preparation of two participants as the sender and receiver of telepathic influence, secondly the sending of the telepathic information and thirdly the evaluation of the outcome.

Researchers and sceptics had collaborated to agree guidelines for how such experiments should be conducted and evaluated, and the success of the technique has since generated dozens of independent replications. The rigour of the methodology has also enabled a constructive dialogue to be undertaken on the nature of the measured effects.

The protocol is simple and has been refined over many years, although the basic methodology remains the same - to ensure the physical and sensory separation of experimenter, sender and receiver and enable an unambiguous means of measuring the results.

A *ganzfeld* session begins with the receiver being comfortably seated in an isolated room, with earphones playing undifferentiated 'white noise' and translucent spheres placed over the eyes to provide an unchanging and low-level sensory medium. The sender is then placed in a second isolated room.

Nowadays a computer will randomly select a single video image from a random chosen pool of four, for telepathic transference. During the sending process, the sender then focuses on transmitting details of the computer-chosen image to the receiver.

During the sending process, the experimenter is aware of the four images of the pool, but unaware of which the computer has randomly chosen to be telepathically transmitted by the sender and therefore unable to add to their mental input.

Afterwards, the receiver ranks the four images in terms of their correlation with the image they telepathically received. The session is deemed a 'hit' if the receiver chooses the image intentionally transmitted by the sender, but a 'miss' if they select any other image.

In 1985, Honorton and sceptical psychologist Ray Hyman independently undertook meta-analyses of all *ganzfeld* studies up to that date, a total of twenty-eight experiments. That had provided quantitative data. When the hit rates for all the experiments were combined, both Honorton and Hyman found that the odds against chance were ten billion to one.

Critique of the methods used in the experiments included in these early meta-analyses, led to improvements in protocols which resulted in the computerisation of the process as described above. And for a further six years this *autoganzfeld* programme resulted in hit rates similar to those reported in the earlier meta-analyses.

By 1996, a total of 2549 *ganzfeld* sessions from a number of university and independent research laboratories in the United States and Europe were amassed into a meta-analysis by researcher Dean Radin, resulting in an overall hit rate against chance of over a million billion to one.

Random number generators

A further series of experiments designed to test for psi, utilised electronic random number generators (RNG) - a type of electronic coin-flipper - as the physical target for subjects to attempt to influence the outcome.

The technique relies on either electronic noise or radioactive decay times of radioactive elements to produce a random base line. As both sources act randomly, the use of either provides electronic spikes on an unpredictable basis. And when this is correlated with a timing mechanism and is computerised, a random series of ones and zeroes is generated.

Participants then focus their intention on influencing the outcome of these random events to produce results, which differ from chance. Often, they will be given feedback relating to their performance in the form of a digital display or an audio signal, and from these and many other experiments it appears that such feedback is a significant feature in facilitating psi effects.

In 1987, psychologists Roger Nelson and Dean Radin conducted a meta-analysis of 832 RNG studies carried out by 68 different researchers between 1957 and 1987 - which produced overall results against chance of better than a trillion to one. And continuing such experimentation at the Princeton Engineering Anomalies Research (PEAR) laboratory until 1996, results were produced from almost a thousand further studies, which closely replicated those of the earlier meta-analysis.

Under the leadership of engineer Robert Jahn, the PEAR results have also shown a number of interesting correlations.

For instance, when couples work together to attempt to influence RNG events, those of the same sex actually have a slightly negative impact, whilst those of the opposite sex have a significantly greater influence than either one of them does as an individual.

The greatest influence however, is effected by 'bonded' couples, who were shown to have over six times their influential impact as individuals. And these findings support the multi-disciplinary evidence that as couples bond, their holistic resonance and energetic coherence increases - from mutual body language, subconscious and conscious emotional responses to their telepathic connection.

Distant healing

Both *ganzfeld* and RNG experiments have been used to test for the psi effects of mental influence on a nonlocal basis. Another series of studies has sought to investigate the phenomenon of distant healing, which has been linked with the spontaneous remission, alleviation of pain and accelerated recovery of many patients around the world.

Unlike the clear-cut outcomes of the hit/miss psi experiments just described, the factors associated with distant healing are varied and the reasons able to be ascribed to someone's recovery may be many.

And so whilst a number of distant healing studies have demonstrated evidence for its positive effects, their methods have been criticised for their inability to exclude other factors, which may have been affecting the outcome.

However, during seventeen years of study, psychologist William Braud and anthropologist Marilyn Schlitz have conducted experiments with many hundreds of volunteers, to determine how people may be able to consciously influence the nervous system of remote participants and affect their blood pressure, muscle response and skin conductivity.

In one series of fifteen studies, which were subsequently replicated by four other investigators, the researchers continuously measured the electrodermal conductivity of the participants' skin - a measure of the unconscious fluctuations of emotion used for example in lie-detector testing.

In the studies, the sender was instructed on a random basis, usually by a computer, to attempt to arouse or to calm the distant receiver solely by thinking about them. At other times and again on a random basis, the sender was instructed to direct their attention elsewhere, to provide control periods against which to measure the active influence.

The meta-analysis of all nineteen studies showed that appropriate responses by the distant receivers to the intentions of the senders evidenced a combined effect of 1.4 million to one against chance.

Remote viewing

Unlike the experiments designed to test for the effects of nonlocal mental influence, remote viewing is an attempt to passively perceive information of a location or event at a distance.

The earliest known results of such experiments; were published by researchers Frederic Myers and Edmund Gurney in 1882. And a century later, their methods and results were closely replicated by researchers working for the US government.

In the early 1970s, the Central Intelligence Agency of the US government initiated a programme of study at the Stanford Research Institute (SRI) to determine the efficacy of remote viewing and its possible use for the gathering of intelligence.

In one well-documented case in the late 1970s, a remote viewer was able to accurately describe the location and interior details of a high security underground facility, having only been provided with its map reference of latitude and longitude.

For over twenty years the programme continued in various iterations under the leadership of physicists, Harold Puthoff, Russell Targ and Edwin May, leading to the conclusion that remote viewing is a real and nonlocal phenomenon, unconstrained by either distance or the presence of any electro-magnetic shielding around its potential target.

The American Institutes for Research who then reviewed the programme's results, having concluded that remote viewing is a real phenomenon, commented on the performance of the remote viewers.

They noted that a small number of remote viewers significantly outperformed the remainder. Only about one percent of volunteers who tested for remote viewing displayed consistent aptitude and neither training nor practice improved the performance of the others.

So whilst it seems that our ability to both transmit and receive nonlocal information is innate, rather like naturally having prodigious musical or mathematical gifts, it appears that the ability to consciously discern such information on a consistent basis is relatively rare.

Collective consciousness

The experiments we have reviewed to date consider the nonlocal perception and influence of individual human consciousness. But what about our collective consciousness?

Psychologists Roger Nelson and Dean Radin amongst others have undertaken experiments over the last fifteen years, which show that at peak moments of group attention, both at conscious and unconscious levels we are able to change the random outcome of events.

And emerging from the research carried on at the PEAR laboratory at Princeton University is a collaborative and ongoing study involving some seventy-five researchers around the world, called the Global Consciousness Project (GCP).

Set up in 1998, its purpose is to determine the evidence and study the influence of collective human consciousness through the large-scale sharing of reactions to major news events.

For this, the researchers use electronic devices called Eggs, designed to produce random data that is able to be affected – as in RNG tests – by the influence of human consciousness.

The project is ongoing and results to date indicate a strong correlation in regard to some events and virtually none in others. Overall however, the accrual of data so far indicates a probability of less than one in a million that the correlation with global events is by chance.

The current generation of Eggs however, are only able to measure the generic intensity of influence and not the intention or emotional attributes it embodies.

And if, as it appears, the level of influence is increased by coherent intensity, then an event which elicits varied or variable reactions or which occurs over an extended period of time would reduce the level of coherence and thus the corresponding level of influence.

But for those events, which invoke a generically coherent and intense response at a specific time or over a time period of relatively short duration, the influence should be significant. And this is seen in the Egg response both to the events of 11th September 2001 and the funeral of Pope John Paul II on 8th April 2005.

In contrast, as measured by the Eggs, the global response to the tsunami of 26th December 2004 was muted. But given that the appalling extent of the disaster only became apparent over the course of a number of days, this extended duration of awareness and reaction may be the cause of the Eggs' low level measurement.

Co-creating realities

All the experiments we have considered in this chapter demonstrate our ability not only to consciously perceive on nonlocal spatial levels but also to influence apparently random events.

Their cumulative results are undeniably far beyond chance and are demonstrating what metaphysical traditions have always maintained – that we individually and collectively co-create our realities.

In scientific terms, the resonance of our attention and intention causes the quantum field of free-wave possibilities to harmonise into the coherent standing waves of realised materiality.

And as we shall see, the higher our vibrational awareness, the more focused our attention and the more coherent our intention, the greater our empowerment to consciously co-create sustained health and well-being.

Expanding consciousness

Now let us continue our journey into the heart of what it means to be human, by considering how the nonlocality of our perception not only extends through space but also through time. And we will also see how transpersonal experiences involving altered states of awareness, are offering evidence for the expansion of the psyche not only throughout spacetime but into other realms of reality and for its continuation beyond the death of the body.

Chapter 6

Beyond space and time

The nonlocal effects of the psi phenomena that we have been reviewing in the previous chapter, beg the question, where do 'I' begin and end?

During our waking hours we are generally aware of the self-consciousness we call the ego. It is this self, which seems separate from others, which has a defined personality, a human history and a cultural heritage and affiliation.

Our conscious mind is continually interpreting our body's sensory communication and interaction with its external environment. And it is primarily by such perception that the psyche derives its sense of material individuation and ongoing sense of ego-self.

However, all such sensory information is filtered and interpreted through the lens of cultural conditioning and defined by the individual personality. And dependent on one's personality and cultural perception, it is the conscious mind, which thus pre-judges the possibility of nonlocal consciousness and psi effects – and thus delineates what we consider to be 'real'.

Reducing the volume of sensory input is one way of enabling the conscious mind to quieten and release the constraints imposed by the ego-self. The *ganzfeld* method of sensory deprivation, which, as we have seen, facilitates telepathic reception and other states of heightened awareness, is a modern technique, which continues the mystical traditions of millennia.

In all cases, the intention is to enable the mind to expand and explore nonlocal consciousness and other levels of awareness – and to 'let go' of its attachment and identification within the narrow confines of the ego.

Empathy

One such level of perception, as we shall now see, has been demonstrated by a number of researchers who have shown that, in addition to the conscious empathy we feel towards each other, such empathetic experiences are also manifested on a nonlocal basis in the functioning of our unconscious nervous system.

By having the participants in his experiments undergo electric shocks in one room, psychologist Charles Tart discovered in the 1960s that their pain were experienced on nonlocal levels by other participants in a separate room. But it was only through the receiving participants 'unconscious' physiological reactions that their awareness of the others' pain was registered. At a conscious level, they had no perception of the others' condition.

In the 1970s, physicists Russell Targ and Harold Puthoff also found the same empathetic connection when, by flashing a light in the eyes of a test participant in one room, a response was recorded in the EEG (electroencephalogram) readings - which record brain wave patterns - of a second participant in another, isolated room.

And with regard to the power of prayer and healing, researchers Elisabeth Targ, Fred Sicher and others have consistently reported that the most effective healing occurs when the healers focus their intention on the person being healed and then step back from their own egoistic involvement in the outcome, essentially allowing some higher level consciousness to energetically flow through them.

These experiments and many others all appear to demonstrate that it is generally through our unconscious mind or in altered states of consciousness that we experience greater resonance and coherence with an expanded field of awareness.

The individuation of our physical experience is perceived at the level of our ego-self. And it is this level of awareness that embodies the behavioural and attitudinal pre-dispositions of our personality and the influences of our cultural conditioning.

But as we then expand our perception beyond this perceived separation, through subconscious and supra-conscious states of awareness we experience the greater integration and wholeness of both our individual and collective consciousness.

Let us then continue to explore and expand our sense of who we may really be.

But before we do so, we need to return to our consideration of the nature of time, which we began in Chapter 3.

Nonlocality in time

As we continue to extend our understanding of other states of nonlocal perception, we will need to transcend the confines of our linear perception of time and begin to attune to the nature of spacetime as understood by cosmologists.

Intrinsic to Einstein's theory of relativity, as we have seen, is the realization that space and time cannot be considered separately but as the combined entity of spacetime. Just as space exists in its entirety, so logically must spacetime and thus time itself. So, as Einstein pointed out, the perception of the flow of time by our conscious mind is, in essence, a mental construction.

Einstein and others have shown that time travel to the future is available to us because the faster we travel relative to the speed of light, the slower time passes and thus we can intersect the 'future' at some point.

And on a miniscule scale the reality of this has already been demonstrated by astronauts, with Russian cosmonaut Valery Polyakov's extended mission on the Mir space station enabling him to hold the current record by travelling into the future by one one-fiftieth of a second.

However, the issue of travel into the past is much more problematic, although no-one has yet shown that the laws of physics absolutely forbid it. In theory there may be ways to do so. But none of the theoretical solutions for building a time travelling machine allows for it to journey further back in the past than the time it was actually constructed.

For example, if such a machine were to be built in the year 2012 and remained unused (as if!) for the next decade, it could then travel back to any moment during that ten-year period but no further back than the date of its construction.

And whist still uncertain, it seems very likely that the consequences of such a journey, even if it ever becomes technically feasible, would require the time traveller to re-intersect the historic spacetime line and correspond to its already enacted history.

This 'arrow' of time, which pertains throughout the universe, is as we have seen in Chapter 3, a consequence of the very high level of order pertaining at its inception. Thus, in accordance with this 'arrow', experiences *within* spacetime are generally subject to the principles of causality. And the signalling of any influence is limited to being transferred no faster than the speed of light.

These intrinsic conditions of causality not only enable the universe to unfold and evolve but allow the level of human consciousness associated with the ego-self to experience the implications of making choices through the process of cause and effect and thereby accrue learning.

But at nonlocal levels of perception, which transcend spacetime, and which include higher levels of individuated and collective consciousness and that of the entire Cosmos, it appears that the awareness of such experience is immediately available beyond the spatial or temporal limitations generally imposed by our conscious mind.

Experiences of such nonlocality in time, where people are aware of the future as if it was happening right now, show up during the investigation of the phenomenon of precognition. And it is to such experiences of perceiving the future, which have been reported throughout history as prophesies, premonitions and presentiments which we shall now turn.

Precognition

There is a myriad of historical anecdotes relating to precognition and almost every culture in the world has developed ways of divining the future, from the consultation of oracles, to the throwing of dice. As with the other aspects of research into consciousness, the investigation of such experiences has progressively opened itself up to the rigours of the scientific method.

One way of scientifically testing for such precognitive perception is to undertake what are called 'forced choice' experiments.

Such experiments are exemplified by a participant being asked to guess which one from a pool of selected targets will be randomly chosen by the experimenter, or nowadays by computer, at a later time – which might be moments or up to a year ahead.

The targets themselves could be, for example, cards with symbols drawn on them, coloured images or the outcome of a throw of a die. Later, at the agreed time, one target is randomly selected and if it corresponds with the one guessed earlier, the experiment records a hit.

In 1989, psychologists Charles Honorton and Diane Ferrari undertook a meta-analysis of all forced choice studies published in the English language literature up to that point. The database consisted of a total of over three hundred studies carried out by sixty-two different researchers and involved nearly two million tests by more than fifty thousand participants.

The statistical results of the meta-analysis showed that the evidence for precognition was a staggering 10^{25} (ten million, billion, billion) to one against chance. And even when the researchers excluded the extreme top and bottom 10 percent of the experimental results to obviate any possible bias, the combined analysis still showed the evidence for precognition as being a billion to one against chance.

Future contact

Another way to investigate the phenomenon of precognition is to explore whether the mind is in contact with its future state. And one way to do this is to see whether future perceptions interfere with present performance and specifically with tasks relating to reaction times to visual stimuli.

In the early 1980s psychologist Holger Klintman asked participants to undertake an exercise in recognition. He first showed them patches of colour, asking them to speak aloud as quickly as possible the colour they saw. And then he quickly showed them the name of a colour - which might or might not agree with the colour they had just been shown and which they had named - and asked them then to speak aloud the name he had shown.

What he found was astonishing.

The reaction times of the participants between seeing the original patch of colour and speaking its name, were faster when the image and the final colour name showed to them matched - and slower when they mis-matched.

After considering every other option he could think of, Klintman eventually came to the conclusion that somehow, the participants' precognitive sensing of the future stimulus travelled back in time.

When the participants saw for example a red swatch, they expected to see the name red following it. When it did, the precognitive signal between the colour and the name was coherent and their response was accordingly faster. But when shown a red swatch followed by the name 'blue', the future stimulus was a mismatch and suffered cognitive interference thus causing the reaction time to slow down.

Klintman then devised a series of double-blind experiments to test this idea, and after the completion of five such studies using alternative methods, he concluded that the effects were real, and computed the odds against chance as being half a million to one.

Significantly, he noted that, as for many other psi effects, participants were completely unaware on a conscious level that their performance was being affected by their own future perceptions. And Klintman's findings again suggest that the conscious mind of the ego-self generally filters out nonlocal psi perceptions from its ordinary awareness.

Presentiment

Another manifestation of the phenomenon of precognition is presentiment, where it appears that the body itself is registering some vague sense of future circumstances usually of a threatening or shocking nature.

There are many anecdotes relating to people who have had such experiences, for example, choosing not to fly on aeroplanes, which have subsequently crashed or travel on ships which have then sunk. Such feelings may generate conscious thoughts or be below the threshold of such awareness and acknowledged only at a physiological level - often as an uneasy or 'gut' feeling in the solar plexus.

It is such unconscious presentiment, that parapsychologist Dean Radin investigated at the University of Nevada in the mid 1990s.

In a series of experiments Radin studied the psychological reflex known as the 'orienting response'. This is well known from many studies of the fight or flight situation, and which is also present during less stressful experiences when confronting an unexpected or new stimulus.

For these experiments, Radin generated visual images selected from a large database. By randomly interspersing emotionally provocative subjects with calm scenes, the experiment elicited responses in participants, which were measured as unconsciously generated electrodermal activity before, during and after seeing the image.

Such activity measures the electrical conductivity of the skin and its recording during an experiment is an effective means of detecting unconscious changes in emotion.

As would be expected, during and after seeing the images, the participants recorded different levels of electrodermal arousal. However, what is far more interesting is that *before* seeing the images, the level of such arousal was higher for those images with a graphic emotional content and lower for the ones with calm depictions.

In other words, their *future* presentiment of the content of the randomly chosen images – of which the participants had no conscious awareness - was affecting the participants' unconscious nervous system in the present. And thus showing that the mind *can* travel forward in time and can create within us a reaction to that future event.

And since 1996, Radin's results have been replicated by Dick Bierman at the University of Amsterdam and researchers at the University of Iowa, which have corroborated the surely irrefutable evidence for such effects.

Do we really have free will?

But what do such psi effects mean for our understanding of free will?

An additional experiment carried out by neuroscientist Benjamin Libet in the late 1980s helps to shed further light on this question.

Libet conducted an experiment in which he asked his subjects to flex a finger at the exact moment of their deciding to do so and monitored their brainwave patterns throughout, to determine what effects their decision would have.

On average, the volunteers took about one fifth of a second to flex their finger after their monitored brain patterns showed that they had decided to do so – the expected time lag required for the brain to activate the body's neuromuscular system.

But what was completely unexpected was that their brains also displayed neural activity about a third of a second *before* they had consciously decided to move their finger.

Libet interpreted this as evidence that our sense of free will in deciding what we do, may be unconsciously determined before we are consciously aware of the decision. If mental intention, which is intrinsic to our perception of free will, arises elsewhere than in our conscious ego-mind, then is all our behaviour determined by processes beyond our conscious control?

However, given the evidence for presentiment, an alternative explanation may be that the one third of a second anticipation of a decision observed by Libet is the signal of a higher level of intention travelling back in time.

Whilst this may appear paradoxical – as we have seen, we need to revolutionise our perception of time – and what past, present and future mean within the spacetime of the physical world.

Future-present

One of the most persuasive aspects of our physical experience is the perception of time. But as we have already seen, we need to radically reconsider the nature of its apparent flow if we are to accept the findings of science and free ourselves from the illusory limitations of materiality.

But if you find such a reappraisal challenging – please don't worry and be assured that you are not alone!

In Chapter 1 we discussed the nature of the quantum world and how the behaviour of quanta, are able only to be expressed through probabilities. And we referred to the ongoing discussion amongst scientists as to how such probabilities become defined outcomes as the result of observation.

As we have seen in the last chapter, acts of attention and intention, at all levels of awareness, conscious and unconscious - sub and supra-conscious, individual and collective – are able to perceive and influence on nonlocal levels which transcend spacetime.

The focus or coherence of such intention may then be the means by which the probabilistic waveforms of the quantum field are manifested and 'particularised' in the standing waveforms of specific outcomes.

And in this model of resonance, the nodes of such standing waves are effectively the fundamental 'particles' of the energy/matter matrix of that which is manifest.

Such attention and intention may then be considered as transcending spacetime but whose outcomes are defined within spacetime as the present reality.

When we perceive the 'future' during precognition, are we then becoming aware of the more subtle energetic vibrations of the initiating intention?

If this is indeed the case, we would not actually be perceiving its outcome in a 'future' spacetime but would be tuning into the template of our individual and collective intentionality.

And as such, the 'future' perception would become progressively crystallised as the wave of the initiating intention flows towards the present.

Such a model not only agrees with the perception of spacetime, as defined by the theory of relativity, but also correlates with experimental findings of precognition, which generally affirms that the further ahead in time, the more uncertain and vague the perception.

In this model it is important to appreciate that it is not only at the level of our conscious mind, but on other levels of our expanded awareness, which transcend the perception of our ego-self - that are engendering attention and intention.

And this has important implications for our understanding of free will.

The scientific consequences of a materialistic paradigm essentially preclude free will, and the inevitability of destiny is an enduring theme that can be seen from ancient myths to the plays of William Shakespeare.

Yet, the perception of the conscious mind – the ego-self – is that we *do* have free will to make choices.

In the integrative model of consciousness, which we are considering in *The Wave*, choices may be made at many different levels of perception, enabling - on a conscious level - both a sense of destiny and a degree of free will to be embodied.

So now, let us go on to explore other experiences of expanded awareness and begin to consider their implications for the deeper understanding of our individuated and Cosmic consciousness.

Non-ordinary states of consciousness

At Princeton's PEAR laboratory, Robert Jahn and psychologist Brenda Dunne have shown that thought transference of images from one person to another is statistically more significant when archetypal images or those with spiritual or religious connotations are used. And metaphysical traditions are replete with such iconic or archetypal imagery and their associations with expanded awareness.

The materialistic worldview prevalent in western psychiatry has long derided such experiences as based on outdated superstition or has treated them as evidence of psychosis. And sceptics have deemed the vast compendium of such experiences throughout history, and globally across all cultures, as being too subjective to be scientifically verified.

Nevertheless, in the last few decades, significant strides have been achieved in the scientific investigation of such states or levels of consciousness and the first steps towards reconciliation with the spiritual nature of the Cosmos are being taken.

In the early 1960s Abraham Maslow, one of the co-founders of transpersonal psychology, conducted extensive research with many hundreds of people who had had spontaneous mystical or 'peak' experiences as he termed them. Instead of finding evidence of pathological or psychotic behaviour, which the materialistic paradigm of psychoanalysis has generally maintained, he concluded that they were conducive to self-realisation and high levels of development and functioning.

The use of such case studies is, in addition to the meta-analyses discussed in the last chapter, common in the research of all life sciences. And these qualitative experiences, when reported in detail and analysed in sufficient numbers, enable the phenomena they describe, to be amenable to scientific verification.

Such experiences of non-ordinary and transpersonal states of consciousness and the information retrieved from them are also challenging the narrow view of the potential of the human psyche and the limits of our perception.

And they are showing that such experiences and the expanded sense of perception and spiritual dimensionality they reveal, is not only intrinsic to human nature but is necessary for our mental, emotional and physical well-being.

Transpersonal awareness

The terms transpersonal and holotropic have been used to describe levels of awareness, which transcend the ego-self and vastly expand the sense of our personal identity and the perception of the wholeness of Cosmic consciousness - or what is often termed All That Is.

In such mystical states, one can undergo an immense range of nonlocal experiences. Episodes from the lives of immediate or remote ancestors, and memories of other lives are common occurrences. And profound identification with other people, groups of people, animals, plants, and even inorganic objects and processes, supra-physical and archetypal beings, devic, angelic and elemental beings, and extra-terrestrial beings abound.

Whilst such experiences have been recorded throughout history, Carl Jung in the early twentieth century was probably the first psychiatrist to give credence to the pantheon of mythical and archetypal beings and symbolic expression that characterise such levels of perception.

The ancestral, racial and collective memories, which his numerous clients reported to him during their experiences, led him to perceive a nonlocal psycho-spiritual connection between all members of the human race, which he called the collective unconscious. And Jung considered this to hold the entirety of humanity's cultural and historical heritage.

Jung also recognised the experiential languages of archetypal myth and symbol pervading such states. And according to him, the energetic influences of such archetypes are an essential part of our psyche and manifest throughout events of the world at large.

Such archetypes fall into two general categories. The first includes non-corporeal beings embodying primordial universal roles and functions, which represent intrinsic constituents of the collective unconscious. These, such as the Great Mother, are essentially cosmic principles and encompass the interplay of fundamental forces, motivations and attributes.

The archetypes of the second category represent various deities and demons related to specific cultures, geographical areas and historical periods. For example instead of a generalised universal image of the Great Mother as identified by Jung, we may experience her as one of her culture-specific forms such as the Virgin Mary or the Egyptian goddess Isis.

Indeed the spiritual pantheons of the great civilisations of the ancient world, such as Egypt, incorporated a profound understanding of the universality of cosmic principles and their manifest diversity, often being portrayed as deities.

And all these cosmic principles and archetypes may manifest in such expanded states of consciousness and in a holographic fashion, incorporate many cross-cultural instances of what they represent in the one representation.

In recent times, the experiences of these transpersonal states of awareness have been extensively recorded by anthropologists and transpersonal psychologists such as pioneers Abraham Maslow and Stanislav Grof.

Those experiencing such mystical states have included the founders of all the world's spiritual doctrines and religions. But as Grof points out, such experiences are bridges to the ultimate unity, and should not be confused with it. And mistaking such archetypal images for the source of creation has historically led to idolatry, dogma and exclusion.

By being open to the transcendental nature of such states and recognising that the beings encountered are aspects of an all-pervasive consciousness which transcends both their and our apparent individuation and is ultimately One - the universality of spirit and the wholeness of all life, may be perceived and embraced.

Near death experiences

Other - and sometimes extreme - ways to break through the barriers erected by the conscious mind of the ego-self have been taken during the initiatory rites of many traditions.

Ranging widely from drumming, ecstatic dance and the use of psychedelic plants such as the peyote cactus, to measures such as deliberately exposing the body to extreme temperatures, foregoing sustenance or imposing pain, such initiations have enabled aspirants over many millennia to achieve revelatory states of awareness.

Such states have also been experienced involuntarily by many other people as a result of accidents and illnesses and, at their most intense have catapulted them into what have become known as near-death experiences or NDEs.

Beginning with the pioneering work of psychiatrists Elisabeth Kübler-Ross, Raymond Moody and George Ritchie in the 1970s, the phenomenon of NDEs has been progressively investigated by a growing number of researchers, primarily other psychiatrists and medical doctors.

And for over twenty-five years, the International Association for Near Death Studies (IANDS) has amassed a substantial number of case studies from around the world and acts as a networking resource for health care professionals, researchers, as well as for those who have experienced NDEs and their families.

In 1982 the Gallup Organisation and near-death research studies established that as of that date, an estimated 13 million adults in the US alone had undergone one or more NDEs.

As is the case for every human experience, no two NDEs are exactly the same. However, when the reports are consolidated, there are aspects which continually recur.

These include the feeling that the 'self' has left the physical body, in many cases, providing information obtained during the experience, which closely correlates with eye-witness reports. Other recurring themes are the moving through a dark tunnel and encountering a bright light and feelings of powerful emotions, usually of joy and bliss but occasionally of deep distress.

Often family members who have already died, others close to the person undergoing the NDE, or archetypal or iconic beings are encountered. And a life review, where one witnesses one's previous actions with honesty but without judgement is a regular experience, as is an expanded awareness and the gaining of a profound sense of understanding how and why the Cosmos is as it is.

Whilst the decision to return to the physical body may be voluntary or involuntary, if it is the former it is often associated with a sense of unfinished business, and is usually to complete a service of some sort to loved ones.

Overwhelmingly, those who have undergone such an experience perceive the NDE as genuine. They often report it as being more 'real' than waking life and are able to clearly remember and lucidly describe their experience. And NDEs are reported as being profoundly different in their essence from either dream states or hallucinations.

In almost all cases, the NDE is transformative for the person experiencing it. And for the great majority of such people, it significantly reduces or completely removes any fear of death, as they subsequently consider that this involves the demise only of the physical body.

Medical evidence

An increasing number of medical doctors are undertaking research into NDEs, including a team at the University of Southampton in England who published the results of an initial study in 2001.

They spent a year studying people resuscitated in the city's General Hospital after suffering a heart attack. All the patients were for varying amounts of time clinically dead, with no pulse, no respiration and no brain activity.

Six percent of the patients experienced lucid and detailed NDEs. They all reported the features common to such experiences including feelings of peace and joy, increased awareness, seeing a bright light, meeting a mystical being or deceased relatives and arriving at a point of no return – from which they chose to come back to complete their physical life journey.

The Southampton doctors considered the possibility of a number of physiological causes for the NDEs before discounting them as being untenable.

All possible explanations that the NDEs could be hallucinations brought on by drug treatment, a lack of oxygen or changes in carbon dioxide levels were refuted. None of the NDE patients at Southampton had low levels of oxygen or received any unusual combination of drugs during their resuscitation and their experience was lucid, structured, easily recalled and clear.

In addition, during cardiac arrest, brainstem activity is rapidly lost, the brain is unable to sustain lucid processes or allow the formation of lasting memories such as those which are induced by the NDE.

By recognising that their results suggest that consciousness and the mind, may continue to exist after the brain has ceased to function and the body is clinically dead, the doctors at Southampton - along with a growing consensus of others around the world - are acknowledging both the reality of such experiences and that they are unable to be accounted for within a purely materialistic paradigm.

Near death awareness

Near-death experiences are often associated with near-death awareness (NDA) and again, working with terminally ill patients has enabled medical doctors to begin to correlate peoples' experiences as they approach death.

Whilst similar to NDEs, the experiences of NDAs occur without the sudden shift in physical conditions that usually precedes an NDE such as a heart attack, or serious accident.

The experiences of NDA during terminal illnesses, across all cultures, appear to support and prepare the person for physical death by reducing the potential fear of the cessation of the psyche.

Almost all such experiences are reassuring and involve the meeting of family members who have already passed over. However, unlike NDEs, the experience of NDA can occur when the person is fully conscious and may involve a dialogue with the beings encountered and the ability to interrupt that dialogue – unlike hallucinatory states – to speak with people physically present.

But beyond the experiences of NDEs and near-death awareness what other evidence is emerging for the continuation of the individual psyche after the demise of the physical body?

After death communication

There are three further areas of consciousness research which are the focus of investigation into the continuation of the psyche after the death of the physical body: the scientific evidence for Earth-bound spirits or ghosts, the concept of reincarnation and so-called 'after death communication', or ADC.

Such research continues to be controversial and appears to be still at the level of other areas of parapsychology a generation ago. The general quality of investigation is currently inadequate to provide unambiguous evidence and, as in other fields of consciousness research, co-operative efforts need to be made to emulate their improvements in methods and reporting.

But its significance cannot be overstated.

Whilst all spiritual traditions propose the continuation in some form or another of the psyche after the demise of the physical body, different religious teachings offer differing views as to whether the personal attributes of our ego-self continue in any way.

In this regard the evidence for after death communications or ADCs and also for ghosts or Earth bound spirits is crucial as both represent the continuation of personality based attributes.

The anecdotal evidence for ADCs is relatively common, especially between close family members and often occurs between the time of physical death and the consequential funeral. But for many, these intensely personal experiences are only shared, if at all, with other family members or friends, often for fear of ridicule.

And whilst an emerging number of books are publicising the subject and have developed a prima facie case, much more well-designed research needs to be undertaken to enable the sort of meta-analyses and correlation of case studies to provide irrefutable evidence of a 'real' phenomenon.

Earth bound spirits

The same is true of the numerous reports of ghosts or Earth bound spirits.

Here, it is very often reported that a traumatic demise or an intense emotional bond with a particular location is the cause of the ego-self aspect of an individual remaining Earth bound. It appears that in many instances, the psyche is unaware that it has 'passed over' and is often amenable to being 'released'.

Such release, to the psychically sensitive healers who engage with such presences, almost invariably involves the sort of transitionary encounters reported in near-death experiences.

The third area of research pertains to the concept of reincarnation, which is commonly associated with a belief that the spirit then returns to Earth to complete some learning process or to engage in the Cosmic conservation of energy known as *karma*.

Reincarnation

Scientific research into reincarnation has focused on verifying other-life memories, using the same criteria as for validating memories in someone's present life. As many details as possible are retrieved and then a search ensues to independently corroborate them.

Given that even in a current lifetime, such validation may often be challenging to obtain, to do so for other lifetimes, which may be centuries ago in our linear perception of time, becomes almost insuperable.

But yet again, there is a growing database of case studies where such evidence continues to accrue.

Perhaps the most persuasive evidence to date is provided by medical doctor and psychiatrist Ian Stevenson, who has amassed three thousand case studies of spontaneous other-life memories of young children.

Stevenson chose to focus on cases involving young children to minimise the danger of 'false' memories, which occur when a subliminal memory of something read, seen or experienced in some way and at some time in the current incarnation is mistaken for the memory of a past life.

Many of the children's memories refer to lives, which ended only a few years prior to their re-birth into their current life. And this has enabled Stevenson to obtain validating details of the earlier life and to correlate them with the children's reports.

The case studies also reveal a high incidence where the earlier death was violent. And Stevenson encountered a number of cases where for example, the knife or gunshot wounds, which were the cause of death in the previous incarnations, were able to be specifically matched, through autopsy reports, with birthmarks in the current lives.

However, given that many of Stevenson's cases involve the child's memories being of a pre-deceased family member, friend or neighbour, critics have argued that the children's reports may have been shaped by family and peers until they come to identify with the deceased

But such criticism is rebutted by Stevenson on the basis of a number of case studies where the child and its family have no acquaintance with the person the child remembers being, but yet the child's memories include verifiable details of its previous life.

The evidence for reincarnation does not, by itself, necessarily provide evidence for continuation of the ego-self aspect of the psyche beyond the death of the physical body. Nevertheless, at the very least, the research of Stevenson and other researchers is intriguing. And the enormous significance of such potential insights into consciousness surely requires that we retain open minds and follow where the evidence leads.

Gaia

There is no explanation within the tenets of a materialistic paradigm for nonlocal psi effects and the expanded awareness that is evident in holotropic experiences. And equally, there is no mechanism or reason that has yet been offered by that paradigm for the development of nonlocal mind and such higher level awareness to arise from a purely physical evolutionary process.

But by considering the primacy of consciousness as the source and purposeful creator of the physical world and ourselves as spiritual beings undergoing a physical experience, such awareness is both logical and inherent.

This perception inevitably raises questions regarding our relationship at the global scale with the Earth herself.

As we shall see in the next chapter, scientist James Lovelock has termed his hypothesis of the Earth as a single self-sustaining organism, Gaia, after the Greek goddess of the Earth. Whilst he did not go so far as to imbue Gaia with innate consciousness, we shall see in later chapters that other researchers are beginning to do so and thus reconcile their findings with the spiritual and metaphysical understanding of perennial wisdom.

So now, let us go on to tell the story of Gaia.

CHAPTER 7

GAIA

Astronomers estimate that by about four and a half billion years ago, the Earth had coalesced from the cloud of gas and dust, which had birthed our Solar System. But it would take a further half a billion years for her to cool sufficiently to enable an unstable but solid crust to form on the surface. And almost immediately we see in the fossil evidence of these oldest rocks that biological life was beginning to gain a foothold on the young planet.

As we go back to this beginning, we see revealed once again, the incredible harmony and simple order from which the abundance of life on our planet has evolved and which continues to underlie its diversity.

But the Earth herself is not a passive backdrop, an environmental stage on which the drama of life has unfolded. Instead, as perennial wisdom has always maintained and deep ecology is progressively discovering, the planetary body and atmosphere of the Earth and the entirety of her biosphere make up a single collective being.

In 1965, scientist James Lovelock used the name of the ancient Greek goddess of the Earth, Gaia, to embody this newly emerging understanding.

Let us begin to share her story.

The beginning of life on Earth

In 1953, scientists Stanley Miller and Harold Urey replicated what was believed at that time to be the early environmental conditions of the Earth. By mixing water vapour, hydrogen, methane and ammonia and passing electrical discharges through this elemental 'soup', they demonstrated how organic compounds and amino acids, the building blocks of biological life, could form.

Whilst ideas about the environment of the early Earth subsequently changed, in the late 1990s, a team of NASA scientists led by astrobiologist Louis Allamandola was also able to show how such organic compounds could form from basic elements and molecules - not within the Earth's ecosphere, but in the depths of interstellar space.

The team re-created the vacuum and very low temperatures of space in a laboratory, introducing a gaseous mix of water vapour, hydrogen, nitrogen, oxygen and carbon monoxide with a few grains of sand. And by irradiating the mix with ultra-violet light, they discovered that complex organic chemicals readily formed around the sand grains – including some which had been unknown up to that time.

The chemical residues that formed, spontaneously organised themselves into vesicles, - very small sacs of organic material. When these were analysed they were found to be similar to the fossilised organisms discovered within a meteorite, which had fallen in 1969 over Murchison, Australia.

The rod-like organic vesicles have very significant features in that one end is hydrophilic and the other end hydrophobic – so they both love and hate water. This enables them to be self-organising in the presence of water and thus establishes a simple sorting process.

In fact, the vesicle behaves like a lipid, a fatty or oily molecule that is a major component of living cells, serving a number of important functions. The most significant of these is the creation of a boundary or membrane, which isolates and protects whatever is inside from the harsh and potentially destructive environment outside.

The isolation of a collection of potentially life-making chemicals by such membranes, enabling them to carry on processes without external disruption, is a crucial step if life is to get started.

Astrochemists Sandip and Sonali Chakrabarti have also recently developed a mathematical model of how chemicals may evolve in a large cloud of interstellar gas and dust, several light years across and collapsing under its own gravity – essentially a model of the early Solar System.

The set-up conditions for their model, involves the presence of twelve elements including hydrogen, carbon and nitrogen. And the computer simulations they ran resulted in the formation of Anadine, one of the four bases for the genetic template encoded in DNA.

In addition, other recent discoveries by astronomers have also revealed huge swathes of gaseous interstellar clouds rich with water vapour and a multitude of organic compounds, many of which are unknown on Earth.

Panspermia

Such discoveries are providing powerful support for an idea put forward over thirty years ago by astronomers Fred Hoyle and Chandra Wickramasinghe, but whose roots go back to the Greek philosopher Anaxogoras over two and a half millennia ago.

Despite their eminence as scientists, Hoyle's and Wickramasinghe's hypothesis of panspermia – which means 'seeds everything' – was derided. But their argument that the building blocks for life on Earth may have arrived via the heavy bombardment of comets and other astronomical debris, to which the early Earth was subjected, is now rapidly becoming an accepted theory.

The prevalence of such organic constituents throughout the cloud of gas and dust from which the Solar System formed are also very likely to have also resulted in their presence within the embryonic Earth. And as the spinning of the planet inexorably drew its lighter rocks upward to form its surface crust, such organic vesicles, the precursors of life, would accumulate here too.

However, despite being able to show how such building blocks could easily assemble, Miller and Urey and every other researcher who has followed, have as yet been unable to replicate the leap of organising these building blocks into the simplest form of life – whose origins continue to remain a mystery.

The genetic code of DNA

Since the breaking of the genetic code in the 1950s, scientists have favoured the concept of genetic determinism, the notion that genes control biology. And they have considered the genetic coding incorporated in DNA to be the blueprint controlling the biological processes and structures of life.

This approach views genes as self-emergent, able to turn themselves on and off and thereby control the structure and functions of organisms. Accordingly, such a belief in genetic determinacy implies that the more complex an organism, the more genes it would possess.

Prior to the outcome of the Human Genome Project in 2001, which sought to map the sequence of the human genetic code, scientists had estimated that human complexity would require a genome in excess of 100,000 genes.

They considered that each one was associated with each of the seventy to ninety thousand proteins within the human body and a further 30,000 so-called regulatory genes, encoding information such as that relating to the physical patterns which specify anatomy and behavioural characteristics.

However, when the project reported its results, it revealed that there are only about twenty-five to thirty thousand genes in the human genome. Two-thirds of those expected, in line with the premise of genetic determinism do not exist. There are not even enough genes to code just for the proteins of the human body.

Indeed there is not that much difference between the numbers of genes in human physiology and that of primitive organisms. For example, the Caenorhabditis worm is only one millimetre in length and has fewer than one thousand cells in its entire body. But this primitive organism shares many of the characteristics of human biology and its genome comprises more than 18,000 genes. The human body which is made up of some 50 trillion cells, in comparison has only a further 15,000 genes compared to its simple predecessor.

An additional issue of the utmost significance concerns the fact that around ninety-five percent of the DNA within the genome seems to have no functional applicability whatsoever. Derogatively termed 'junk' DNA it may in actuality be involved in other processes, which are not directly associated with the coding of biological characteristics and which remain, as yet, unknown.

It thus appears that the prevalent view of the concept of genetic determinism is at least significantly incomplete and even fundamentally flawed. The unexpected results of the genome project require us to reconsider the question of from where and how does biological complexity arise.

Whilst mainstream emphasis has been on the 'power' of genes, other biologists have pursued research that reveals a radically different understanding concerning the expression of life. They have focused on how the organism's relationship with the environment and more specifically, its perception of the environment, directly controls behaviour and gene activity.

The mem-'brain'

One of the scientists, who are pioneering this radical new view, is cell biologist Bruce Lipton. The great majority of the genetic material within a cell is concentrated in its nucleus. And Lipton has pointed out that if genes do represent the control centre or 'brain' of the cell, then taking out a cell's nucleus should result in the cessation of all cell functions and the death of the cell.

However, such enucleated cells are able to survive for several months without genes and yet are capable of effecting complex responses to stimuli from the environment and from within the cell itself.

Instead, Lipton considers that it is the cell's membrane, its outer boundary and the first organelle – or rudimentary organ - that appeared in evolution, and the only organelle common to all living organisms, which represents the cell's 'brain'.

In its capacity as a semi-permeable barrier, the membrane enables the cell to both protect itself from the outer environment and maintain control over its internal conditions. However, it is not a passive boundary and actively mediates information between its outer surroundings and the cell interior via the proteins incorporated within it.

The process of adaptation by the cell is then effectively controlled by the membrane which recognises environmental signals through the activity of 'receptor' proteins which perceive both physical signals, for example in the form of electrically charged chemical ions, and energetic signals such as those carried by electro-magnetic vibrations.

Lipton has described the membrane boundary, which envelops every biological cell as comprising the structural basis of a life-based information processing system. The receptor proteins are attuned to distinguish harmonically resonant signals from the ambient background. And the cell's ability to do this resembles the mathematical use of Fourier transforms to decipher an underlying waveform pattern of information from overlying noise.

Cells selectively read or attune to only those signals that are relevant to their existence. And such signals cause the receptor proteins to bond with complementary effector proteins, which in turn control the cell's behaviour by activating internal processes via a group of proteins located within the cell itself.

Both receptor and effector proteins reside within the cell membrane and together provide the cell with its perception. They also appear to control the turning on and off of gene programmes and have been linked with genetic alterations that rewrite the DNA code in response to stress.

The evolution of perception

The capacity of a cell to handle information is determined by the number of receptor/effector protein complexes residing within the membrane. Due to its thinness, there is only room for a mono-layer of such proteins and thus the cell's ability to handle information is proportional to the surface area of the membrane.

In this model, it is the dynamic relationship with the environment through the process of perception, which controls behaviour, gene activity and even the rewriting of the genetic codes. Cells 'learn' and evolve by creating new perception proteins in response to novel environmental experiences.

In the case of a simple, single-celled bacterium, whilst most of its membrane receptor/effector proteins are needed to enable its survival, each bacterium is also capable of learning about six different environmental signals. And bacteria create an average of about six different plasmids ('new' memory genes in tiny circles of DNA) each derived from a unique learning experience.

The bacterium's limitation on the number of plasmids it possesses is not due to an inability to make DNA – for it can make thousands of copies of any of the individual plasmids it possesses. In Lipton's view, the limitation is related to the fact that each 'new' protein perception complex requires a unit of membrane surface area to express its functions. The inability to expand its membrane limits the bacterium's ability to acquire new perceptions.

But as perception increases, so does an organism's ability to survive. The limits inherent within an individual bacterium led to bacteria forming loosely knit communities and the development of mechanisms to copy and share the perceptions encoded in their plasmids.

Evolution then took further steps in the expansion of perception by the creation of extra-cellular matrices - membranes which enveloped entire bacterial communities. Such so-called biofilms enabled life on Earth to leave the oceans and make its first foray onto the land. And such primitive life forms continue to pervade Nature today in the form of surface films coating a wide variety of things from teeth to water pipes.

It was the exploitation of environmental niches by groups of bacteria specialising in different activities that may well have led to more advanced cells which incorporated a nucleus. And in turn, this development led to the evolution of multi-cellular life and the next great leap in the tidal wave of evolution.

By expanding the overall area of cell membranes, and thus perception, in a potentially exponential way, multi-cellular organisms provide the greatest opportunity for biological life to continue to evolve.

An example of this may be seen with regard to the evolution of the brains of vertebrate creatures – those with a backbone.

The first vertebrate brains were small and smooth spheres. But progressively, brains became larger and more of their surface became enfolded, enabling the area of their surrounding membrane, and thus perception, to be maximised.

And we can see this epitomised in the human brain, where such folding is only second throughout all biological life on Earth to that of porpoises and dolphins.

Lipton and others have pointed out that the optimal way to organise a two-dimensional membrane surface into a three-dimensional space is to employ fractal geometry. So here too we see the holographic principle at work in the evolution of biological perception.

In Chapter 1, we saw how cosmologists are suggesting that the boundary of spacetime itself may take the form of branes – the universal equivalent of the membrane of the cell.

Their hypothesis that the universe in its entirety may be a holographic projection arising from such branes may then correlate with the fractal microcosms of biological life.

And as we continue to explore the nonlocal nature of consciousness and its higher vibrational levels, in the workings of the holographic principle, we are now beginning to glimpse how the primacy of intention and purpose may be manifest through such projection.

Networks of influence

We have looked at the fractal evolution of biological life from the inside. Now let us briefly summarise how the fractal patterns of underlying order are able to account for its evolution from a perspective, which considers its dynamic co-evolution with the outer environment of Gaia.

As we shall see, networks of influence arising from the simple harmony and order of underlying patterns create complex and self-organising systems, which pervade Nature.

The importance of such networks and how they may help to account for the emergence of biological life has been the study of theoretical biologist Stuart Kauffmann.

Some substances act as catalysts triggering the formation of other substances, and which may create a complete cycle of catalysis, which returns to the initiating catalyst.

Such catalytic interactions for instance, underlie many chemical processes where one or more catalysts accelerate or inhibit the chemical reactions but without themselves undergoing any permanent change.

When this happens, a self-sustaining loop of interactions is then formed which feeds on, and grows from, the raw materials available, aided by the energetic through-flow of light or heat.

What Kauffmann has been able to show is that given a sufficient number of connections between the individual chemical compounds, or nodes, comprising the looping network of catalysis, the system undergoes an abrupt change – rather like the transition of liquid water to ice.

As he has argued, in a network with insufficient connections, there is no sign of life. But for a network with only a few more connections, it appears that life not only becomes possible but inevitable.

Seeking to understand how such networks might arise in the interaction of genetic material, Kauffmann recognised that genes exist in one of two states of activation – 'on' or 'off' – and thus are able to influence other genes with which they interact.

Looking for stable patterns, he theoretically modelled the nodal connections arising from the interaction of genes. With only one connection per gene, the model system showed that nothing much happened. With more than two connections, the system became unstable and 'chaotic'.

However, with exactly two other connections, the system behaves in a way that is both complicated and yet stable. As we have seen in earlier chapters, the fundamental stability inherent in such a trinity relationship is found throughout Nature and it is this intuitive knowledge that pervades the teachings of perennial wisdom and the wholeness perceived by such three-in-one phenomena.

Orderly attractors

To understand how genes may interact as templates for the replication of physical characteristics, we will need to understand a further aspect of fractal geometry.

Over the past thirty years, scientists have used the abstract mathematical concept, which they term phase space, to model the behaviour of the variable factors making up a complex system in the physical world.

In a wide range of cases, they have set up relatively simple nonlinear equations with complex outcomes and have solved them numerically by having computers trace out their solutions in phase space.

Such solutions in phase space take the shape of what are known as attractors. This refers to the zero point at the centre of the system's coordinates at which it would be in equilibrium or balance and to which its path is metaphorically 'attracted'.

To the great surprise of scientists, there are only three types of attractors. Simple systems, such as a pendulum, which is set to swing and which eventually comes to rest at a single point, in phase space takes the form of what is termed a point attractor.

The second type called a periodic attractor describes systems; that oscillate periodically. And it is the third, so-called strange attractor to which the behaviour of complex systems adheres.

Such strange attractors are found to underlie all manner of such systems from weather patterns to the trends in stock markets. And it is the mathematics of fractal geometry, which in turn describes their structure.

In attempting to model weather patterns, the meteorologist Edward Lorentz, discovered the strange attractor now named after him. Shaped like a butterfly – and epitomising the iconic 'butterfly effect' of chaos theory - the loops of its two 'wings' cross at ever changing points. And whilst the behaviour of the system can be predicted qualitatively, as is typical for a complex system, the precise values of its variables at a particular time cannot be.

With the knowledge of strange attractors, we will now return to Kauffmann's research and how the understanding of their characteristics may be applied to the interactive behaviour of genes.

Specialised cells

The attractors, which operate within a network comprised of three-fold nodal connections, when started from any randomly chosen pattern, settle into stable cycles incredibly quickly.

And Kauffmann discovered that the number of attractors inherent in such a system bears a simple mathematical relationship to the number of nodes in the overall network – approximately the square root of the number of nodes.

When applying these insights to the genetic makeup of an organism, Kauffmann has postulated that each of the specialised cell types within an organism equates to a particular cycle of genetic states.

To test this he has mapped the amount of DNA in a cell against the number of different cell types for different organisms, validating his hypothesis by discovering that they adhere to a power law – and so providing evidence for their scale-invariant fractal nature.

The couple of hundred specialised cell types in the human genome are thus attractors in a network of tens of thousands of genes interacting with one another on a trinity basis. In each type of cell, most of the genes are inactive, but a minority interact with each other in a repeating pattern, which continually reiterates through the cycle in accordance with the type of cell it is.

Genetic mutation and variation may then be a response to environmental signals mediated by the perceptive nature of the cellular membrane, as hypothesised by Lipton. The issuing of new instructions to the genome, would then change the nodal interactions between genes.

Such changes trigger forks, or bifurcations, in the evolution of systems. In the study of complex systems they are known to produce sudden alterations in the configuration of attractors and the sudden appearance of new forms of order.

Whilst much work still needs to be done, the profound insights of Lipton, Kauffmann and others are confirming that biological life too is intrinsically fractal and thus essentially holographic in nature.

Let us now take a wider look at the evolution of the planetary being we call home.

Dead Mars, living Earth

James Lovelock is a renaissance scientist who, whilst consulting for NASA, became involved in the design of experiments, which would enable a spacecraft landing on the surface of Mars to detect life.

Lovelock concluded that the best way to test for life would be to look for the evidence of entropy reduction – an increase in order – as living systems characteristically bring local order as long as they have an external energy source to feed on.

If there was no life present on Mars, Lovelock reasoned that its atmosphere would be in a state of equilibrium and dominated by stable compounds such as carbon dioxide. Whereas if life was present, he posited that, its life cycles would involve the creation of reactive gases such as methane and oxygen.

In September 1965, French astronomers were able to analyse the Martian atmosphere and discovered that it was made up almost entirely of carbon dioxide. They were thus able to show unambiguously that today, and at least on its surface, Mars does not support biological life.

It was hearing this news, which set Lovelock to considering the differences between the Martian atmosphere and that of the Earth.

The inspiration suddenly came to him, that for the reactive gases, which make up the Earth's atmosphere to remain as they have been for hundreds of millions of years, that 'something' must be acting as a regulator. And given that most of the gases come from living organisms, that life on the surface must be intrinsically involved.

This insight was the seed from which grew the idea of Gaia, the perception of the Earth as a self-regulating and integrated system.

Self-regulating cycles

During the last four billion years, the average heat output of the Sun is known to have increased by about a third.

But for life to have begun and then evolve, the surface of Gaia has needed to remain within a narrow range of temperature. And one early question asked of Lovelock's Gaia theory, was how this could be.

In the absence of life, as Lovelock had noted in regard of the Martian atmosphere, non-reactive gases such as carbon dioxide are the norm, and this was the state of the early atmosphere of Gaia. As a so-called greenhouse gas, carbon dioxide absorbed and trapped the heat from the Sun and thus warmed the surface of the young planet sufficiently to ensure liquification of water and the conditions supportive to the emergence of life.

Lovelock was also able to show that single-celled bacteria grow at their maximum rate at a temperature of 25 degrees Celsius, but less vigorously at either higher or lower temperatures. The dynamic interplay between the bacteria, which absorb carbon dioxide to build their carbon based bodies, and the atmosphere ensured the steady removal of the greenhouse gas from the atmosphere.

So as the Sun's heat output continued to increase, the self-regulating relationship between bacterial life forms and the level of greenhouse gases enabled the surface temperature to hold steady for over a billion years. And this environmental stability set the scene for the emergence of more complex forms of life, which began to release oxygen into the atmosphere.

But as the heat from the Sun then continued to increase still further, other processes began to play crucial roles in the unfolding drama of life on Earth and the maintenance of a stable and nurturing environment.

One such critical process was the creation of a cloud cover over the oceans of Gaia. Today this reduces the surface temperatures around the planet by an average of 20 degrees Celsius, due to the ability of oceanic clouds to reflect sunlight back into space.

Lovelock and atmospheric scientist Robert Charlson realised that an unexpected key to the creation of the oceanic cloud cover is the recycling of the element sulphur throughout the global web of life.

Microscopic marine algae throughout Gaia's oceans release sulphur in the form of dimethyl sulphide (DMS), which we can detect as the tangy smell of sea air. Whilst over land, dust motes provide the seeds from which clouds can form, over the oceans it is the minute specks of DMS which provide this service.

Carried inland by the oceanic clouds and discharged in the rain they carry, the sulphur nutrients then reach the soils of the planet. And subsequently washed into streams and rivers, the sulphur eventually makes its way back into the oceans and is again ingested and released through the algae.

The whole cycle is self-regulating. Fewer clouds mean that more sunlight reaches the surface of Gaia resulting in the growth of more algae and the ingestion of more sulphur from the waters of the oceans. In turn, more sulphur is released in the form of DMS back into the atmosphere, seeding the formation of more clouds, which then regulates the number of algae.

This harmonic cycle of DMS is just one of a vast number of interrelated and self-regulating processes, which over the aeons, have ensured that Gaia remains a wondrously nurturing home for life.

Cycles of Ice Ages

There is another way in which DMS plays a crucial role.

The most likely, although probably not the only, cause of the climatic cycles of Ice Ages and the periodic warming called inter-glacials, is due to astronomical factors associated with Gaia's orbit around the Sun – and to which we will return in the next chapter.

The onset of cooling, leads to drier conditions over land at high altitudes, which in turn allows wind-blown dust from the land, carrying iron compounds, to spread over the oceans at high latitudes.

Here, thanks to the clouds seeded by DMS, it is rained out and fertilises the seas. The increase in marine algae which results, breathes carbon dioxide from the air, reducing the greenhouse effect and encouraging more cooling, thereby allowing more dust to be blown off the land and so on. At the same time, with more DMS being produced, the cloud build up will continue, reflecting heat back into space and thus encouraging the cooling further.

Conversely, inter-glacial warming may then occur when the continuing wave of the astronomical cycle flows the other way to produce maximum heating in the northern latitudes of the planet. Melting some of the ice and damping down the dry land around the edges of the ice sheet reduces the level of wind-blown dust.

As a result, there is less iron raining down on the oceans and the feedback cycle goes into reverse, with life in the oceans going into decline and life on land flourishing as more areas become available for environmental exploitation.

This simple model predicts that there should be more DMS in the atmosphere during an Ice Age. Ice cores from Antarctica dating back 160,000 years show that this has indeed been the case – and also reveal that more dust did fall with snow during those times. It all fits.

During the onset of Ice Ages many life-forms were unable to adapt to the changing conditions and became extinct.

But such extinctions also form an intrinsic element in the cycles of life and death, essential aspects of the evolutionary story of Gaia. So let us now review the history of death on Earth, as the completion of life and the precursor of re-birth.

Extinctions

Palaeontologists around the world discovered that 65 million years ago, not only the dinosaurs, but 75 percent of all other life forms on Earth became extinct, in a sudden catastrophe.

In1980, physicist Luis Alvarez proposed that the cause, which triggered the mass extinction, was the impact of a huge asteroid or comet about six miles across. He came to this view after discovering that the boundary between the two geological eras known as the Cretaceous and Tertiary Ages and whose fossil record reveals the global extinction, was marked by the presence of significant amounts of iridium. An element rarely discovered on Earth, it is commonly found in meteorites and in the same proportion as that present at the extinction boundary.

Alvarez's hypothesis, which again was initially derided, gained dramatic support when, in 1992, a crater over one hundred miles across was discovered by geologists to underlie the Gulf of Yucatan off the coast of Mexico. Named Chicxulub, geologists were able to date its creation to exactly the age of the demise of the dinosaurs.

But the Yucatan cataclysm and its global impact is only one of five mass extinctions, which have punctuated the story of the evolution of life on Earth.

Two hundred and fifty million years ago, another catastrophe, and the most severe to date, destroyed at least eighty percent and possibly as much as ninety-five percent of all life on the planet.

This extinction event, which has been calculated by geologist Samuel Bowring and colleagues to have occurred over no more than ten thousand years, and possibly a great deal less, appears to have resulted from a precipitous fall in temperature. Causing the ice caps to enlarge considerably, vast areas of the continental shelves were exposed to the atmosphere. And it has been postulated, that the enormous biomass which then interacted with the atmosphere, absorbed huge amounts of oxygen, causing suffocation on a gigantic scale.

The reasons for the other three extinctions, which occurred about 440, 360 and 215 million years ago, are as yet unknown. It is likely that a combination of environmental factors both terrestrial and possibly astronomical is involved. But if, as for the Yucatan extinction, a meteoric impact was implicated, no one has as yet identified a crater or craters of the right ages, which could be the primary or contributory cause.

Of all species, which have been children of Gaia since her birth, ninety-nine percent are now extinct. But not all extinctions of species occur during the mass events described above. It is estimated that only about a third of extinctions happen during such sporadic catastrophes - the two-thirds majority form part of wider evolutionary cycles of life and death on an ongoing basis.

Rapid climate change is likely to be the general cause. Those species, which can adapt do so, but there may not be the time and alternative coping mechanisms - such as migration may not be possible. But there is no consensus as yet on which influences predominate and a long list of possible causes are still being debated. However, almost all scientists agree they are caused by some combination of shocks or dramatic changes that disrupt the environment on a regional or global scale.

In 1996, physicists Ricard Sole and Susanna Manrubia reviewed a massive dataset of species extinctions compiled by palaeontologist Jack Sepkowski. They found that the distribution of the size of extinctions as measured by the number of genera – or species groups - which died out; follows the scale-invariant rules of a power law.

In fact, their findings revealed that the power law relationship for extinctions is the same as for earthquakes - an extinction twice the size of another is four times as infrequent.

As we have seen, such power laws characterise phenomena that are inherently resonant and fractal and thus scale-invariant. This is indicative of complex systems in a critical state where an extinction of any size can thus happen at any time. Such systems are also non-linear in that a small trigger can have a large effect, but equally a large trigger can be dampened down.

But as each mass extinction has caused the demise of the prevailing life-forms on the planet, it has facilitated the emergence of others. The extinction of 215 million years ago enabled the rise of the dinosaurs. And the demise of the dinosaurs 65 million years ago, encouraged the evolution of a tiny shrew-like creature, which evolved into the rich diversity of mammals – and thus of human beings.

Fitness landscapes

Evolution accomplishes its ends through three-phase cycles of variation, selection and replication. A variation in an organism which allows it to better fit an environmental niche, will, through natural selection, enable it to survive longer and produce more offspring, thus replicating the variation and so on as the species evolves to better fit its environment.

Evolutionary scientists map this process onto so-called fitness landscapes, two-dimensional representations, which plots the physical characteristics – or phenotypes – of an organism in regard to its fitness in relation to its environment.

Species progressively climb from the 'valleys' of such landscapes, which represent a less than optimal fit with their surroundings, up to the 'hills' of the optimum compatibility with their environment.

However, the environment too changes. And so the ongoing co-evolution between the organism, its environment and with other species, which are also undergoing such processes results in fitness landscapes which are continually undulating like the surface of an ocean.

And the omnipresence of fractal patterns and attractors underlying the collective self-organised criticality of such co-evolution is the intrinsic nature of Gaia.

Water

As we have explored the evolution of Gaia, we have needed to consider at all times the presence and involvement of water. And it is to this deceptively simple but ubiquitous and indispensable component of the web of life that we now turn.

In 1994, Japanese scientist, Masaru Emoto began to experiment with droplets of water taken from various sources. Using the simple technique of freezing the droplets and photographing them under a dark view microscope, he was able to produce hundreds of pictures of their resultant structure.

What he found is revolutionary.

Water from pristine mountain springs and streams display the exquisite geometric designs with which we are familiar from pictures of snowflakes. Their six-fold hexagrammic shapes, every one unique, epitomise Nature's underlying order and harmony.

But when he collected, froze and photographed water from industrial areas, urban water pipes and water drums, he saw completely different images, which were distorted, dissonant or randomly formed.

Exposing pure water to the sound of music and then freezing it also resulted in a variety of different forms. Classical or folk music was embodied within the crystals of ice as exquisite harmonies, whereas the sound of heavy metal music was reflected in the crystals as disrupted and deformed shapes.

Emoto also discovered that words either spoken or written had ordering or disordering effects on the water crystals. Whereas the words 'love' and 'gratitude' created beautiful and harmonious patterns, words of disparagement or fear resulted in crystals, which were misshapen and apparently stressed.

Essentially, what appears to be occurring is that, like the cymatic shapes discovered by Ernst Chladni two centuries ago, which we discussed in Chapter 4, water will take on the resonant shape of the vibrations it is encountering whose standing waves are then frozen into the shapes recorded by Emoto.

Nature's methods

But Emoto is not the first scientist to investigate the amazing properties of water.

Viktor Schauberger grew up amidst the forests and mountain streams of the Austrian Alps during the last years of the nineteenth century. From childhood his astute powers of observation and insatiable curiosity led him to profound insights about the nature of water and discoveries of how to generate energy using Nature's own methods.

Studying the way in which trout are able to stay motionless in a fast moving current and able to screw their way up a vertical waterfall, he realised that they create and utilise the implosive energy of vortices.

Schauberger saw that the fish remain in the centre of the stream where the water is at its coldest and most dense and thus embodies the most potential energy. Their gills have powerful guide vanes on the surface, which directs the water flow into a powerful backwards vortex current and also creates a series of small vortices that amplify the upstream counter current. A zone of negative thrust is thus created along the entire length of the trout's body, which counteracts the current and enables it to stay in the same place.

He showed that natural living water is composed of many strata with subtle differences in temperature and electric charge, which influence the water's motion, its form of flow and its physical properties. He saw water as a pulsating living substance that energises all of life, both organic and inorganic. And when it is healthy it has a complex structure that enables it to communicate information, retain its memory, carry energy, nutrients and healing, to self-cleanse and discharge waste.

From his deep knowledge of water, Schauberger was able to extend the principles of its energy flow to a generic realisation that Nature consistently uses vortical spiralling motion which is implosive or centripetal, for creating and evolving - and conversely the explosive or centrifugal form of motion for dissolution and decomposition.

Water makes up approximately two-thirds of both the surface biosphere of Gaia and the human body. Its molecular composition of one oxygen and two hydrogen atoms reflects Kauffmann's findings for the tripartite connectivity, which optimises the ability to create life. And its tetrahedral geometry also embodying such tripartite structure facilitates the exchange of electric charges – and thus the energies of electro-magnetic fields crucial to all biological life.

As a bearer and transformer of energies and a harbinger of life, water is unsurpassed. But before we take our leave of the story of Gaia for the time being, we need to consider how energies are mediated by one further and crucial aspect of her web of life - electro-magnetic fields.

Electro-magnetic fields

Electro-magnetic fields pervade the universe, and all biological life is dependent upon them as are our modern technological societies. Yet we have little understanding of what electric charge, the fundamental quantum of the field actually is.

At an atomic level, the basic unit of such charge is embodied by the electron, which holds a negative charge and the proton, which holds an exactly corresponding positive charge.

An electric field is a property of electric charge at rest whereas a magnetic field is a property of such charge in motion. And acceleration or deceleration of electric charge results in electro-magnetic radiation, in the form of photons.

We are familiar with the huge spectrum of electro-magnetic radiation, which spans wavelengths ranging from high-energy short wavelength X-rays, through visible light, microwaves and radio waves, to extra-low frequency (ELF) waves with very long wavelengths.

All the physical realms of Gaia are intimately interconnected through an intricate matrix of such fields, which mediate her cycles and rhythms.

There is a now an enormous body of research, dating onwards from the pioneering work of biologist Frank Brown in the 1950s, which testifies to the innate sensitivity of animals to geomagnetic and other electro-magnetic effects of the natural environment. And it appears that such sensitivity is also prevalent in primary peoples worldwide.

Our current western lifestyles and worldview however, desensitise us to whatever natural energies may be prevalent in the environment as well as encouraging a disparagement of their existence.

Nonetheless, extensive research over the last fifty years has shown that the human body and brain act as a tuning device resonating powerfully with particular solar and lunar cycles and other environmental influences mediated through such fields. Many of these bypass our five-fold physical senses and resonate directly with the energy systems of the body. And this is why many people find it hard to sleep on the night of a full Moon, even though they are unaware of the influence of the Moon on their psyche.

Certain parts of the brain are extremely sensitive to electro-magnetic fields. And in the 1980s it was discovered that the cycles of change of the Earth's magnetic field affects the human pineal gland and by its links to the endocrine system of the body, affects sexuality, stress levels and emotional moods.

The influence of solar and lunar cycles and their interaction with the electro-magnetic fields of Gaia also regulates the body's biological clock and daily or circadian and longer-term rhythms.

However, perhaps the most profound and least understood of these interactions is through the agency of ELF or extra-low frequency waves which equate to the wavelengths of human brain waves

Schumann resonance

Such ELF waves are constantly created by internal geothermal movements within the Earth. And ever-present, seismic disturbances will affect their amplitude as will the type of geological strata through which they travel. The gravitational pull of the Moon, which raises the surface tides of the Earth, also causes tidal effects in the liquid magma beneath the crust, which in turn may generate such electro-magnetic effects and influence.

In addition, the space between the surface of Gaia and the conductive ionosphere - the uppermost layer of the atmosphere - acts as a resonant cavity for electro-magnetic waves in the ELF wave-band.

Such ELF radiation forms harmonic standing waves, which pervade the atmosphere and circle the Earth. The ionosphere is continually charged by the solar wind, the constant stream of high-energy particles emanating from the Sun. And excited by lightning discharges, the atmosphere then resonates in the ELF range, as discovered by W.O. Schumann in 1952.

The intriguing and crucial aspect of the Schumann resonance is that its fundamental frequency of 7.83 cycles per second (cps) lies in the mid range of the alpha rhythms of the human brain waves. And overtones of the Schumann resonance have also been measured at frequencies of 14, 20, 26, 33, 39 and 45 cycles per second, all of which lie within the range of human brainwaves.

As science is progressively appreciating the electro-magnetic sensitivity of the human biofield to its environment, the Schumann frequencies, which correlate with human cognition, represent our profound and yet little understood connection with Gaia.

Research into the overt and subtle interactions between Gaia and humanity are still at an early stage. Reductionist science has treated the environment as passive and its influences as peripheral. Only now is deep ecology and wholistic science beginning to perceive the intricate and exquisite harmonies, which underlie and pervade the cycles of life on the planet we call home.

We have aggressively and recklessly ignored the web of awareness, which comprises Gaia. And when people speak of saving the planet, perhaps they should realise that Gaia can look after herself – she has been doing so for over four billion years. However, unless we begin to hear the wise voices of those such as Emoto and Schauberger, it is we who will pass the point of being able to be saved.

Biofields

What is it that vivifies biological life - that enters at birth and withdraws at the death of the physical body?

We are energetic beings in a continuous state of vibration. Not only do our internal neurophysiological systems interconnect via energy exchange, but our perception and reality is dependent on such resonance.

Many traditions worldwide have perceived the manifestation of consciousness through many levels of energetic frequencies. Eastern healing teachings continue this holistic tradition, where dis-ease is treated as a blockage or an imbalance in the flow of a life-force energy known variously as *ch'i* (China), *ki* (Japan), *prana* (India), *pneuma* (Greece), *mana* (Pacific Islands), *waken* (North America) and *kurunba* (Australia).

Described generically by western researchers as biofields, such spiritual traditions, posit higher levels of energies and thus consciousness, as templates for the physical body.

The detection and measurement of such subtle energy fields and the understanding of how they interface into physical form, is probably the greatest quest of wholistic science.

The subtle energies of biofields are supra-physical. However, given the ubiquity of electro-magnetic fields, their ability to act both locally and nonlocally, the constancy of the speed of light as a fundamental attribute of spacetime, their facility to encode holographic information and to control and transduce energies, a deeper understanding of electro-magnetism appears to be the most likely key to the interface between consciousness, the nature of biofields and the physical world.

Gaia – the conscious Earth

Kinship with the subtle realms of Gaia is the heritage of us all. And our ancestors and the mystics of all traditions and times have learned from and honoured the beings of such realms. But for those who have disowned the existence of other planes than the physical, the limitation of that perception has impoverished their human experience of the abundance of Gaia.

Perennial wisdom perceives consciousness as all-pervasive. And in the Nature spirits of the devic and elemental realms of Gaia, the experiences of shamans and mystics offers us all a way to an understanding of levels of awareness with which we can communicate and from which we can learn a deeper wisdom.

As our individual and collective awareness expands, we are becoming more able to attune once more to the voices of the Nature spirits. And if we are prepared to hear them, we may begin to re-establish our ancient spiritual relationship with Gaia

The shamans of South America and Africa are now being asked by botanists and pharmacists to share their encyclopaedic knowledge of plants. And when queried by the scientists how they came to know so much, their replies have been consistent – the plants themselves have taught them.

Fig 7.1 A wave-like crop circle over 700 feet in length.
Reported on 5th June 2005 near Avebury, England.

And over the last two decades the enigmatic phenomenon of crop circles has offered us an opportunity to re-connect with Gaia, for despite the claims of so-called hoaxers, their creation remains a mystery.

For many people, their direct experiences within these temporary temples, which have lain close to many sacred sites of antiquity, have been transformational. And whoever the circle makers may be – and perhaps they are us – these mandalas formed of living crop, offer us insights into a deeper understanding into our own collective psyche and the mind of Gaia.

Our Solar System

For four and a half billion years, the grail of our planetary home – Gaia - has nurtured the exploration of consciousness as mediated through biological life.

The individual and collective expression of life-forms occupying a vast array of environmental niches and the continuing cycles of life and death and the emergence and evolution of new life-forms has maximised the opportunity to acquire and embody ever new and greater perceptions and awareness.

Philosopher Teilard de Chardin has called the collective mind of Gaia, the noosphere. And in later chapters we will return to consider the implications of this concept as we continue to explore not only what it means to be human but the potentiality of our expanding awareness.

But now we will broaden the vista still further and consider the harmonic resonances, which pervade the entire Solar System.

CHAPTER 8

THE SOULAR SYSTEM

Within the relationships between the five planets visible from Earth - Mercury, Venus, Mars, Jupiter and Saturn - and the two luminaries, the Sun and Moon, the ancient Greeks perceived the embodiment of cosmic harmony. And their intuitive insights into this interplay of planets, which they described as the music of the spheres, are now being validated by astronomers.

This fundamental inter-planetary resonance as it applies to the entirety of the Solar System is embodied in what is known as Bode's Law. Publicised in 1772, it confirms the perception of over two millennia earlier that the planets are spaced in harmonious ratios.

To arrive at Bode's Law, take the sequence of numbers 0, 3, 6, 12, 24, 48, 96, 192..., where, after 3, each number of the sequence is double - and thus an octave higher - than the preceding one. Then add 4 to each, to get 4, 7, 10, 16, 28, 52, 100, 196...

Bode's series then represents the relative distances of the planets from the central Sun, beginning with Mercury and extending out to Venus, Earth, Mars, Jupiter and Saturn.

The outer planet Uranus was not observed until 1781, but fits the Law at 196 in the sequence. And astronomers searching for a 'missing' planet at a distance from the Sun represented by 28 in the series subsequently discovered the asteroid belt at exactly this position.

In essence, the Solar System forms a gigantic harmonic musical scale!

But Neptune, discovered in 1846 and Pluto, in 1930, do not ostensibly fit Bode's Law – although both of them embody other harmonics in that Neptune takes twice the time to orbit the Sun as does Uranus, and Pluto takes three times as long.

Intriguingly though, the continuation of Bode's harmonic sequence predicts the presence of a planet twice as distant from the Sun as is Pluto.

Pluto was discovered by Clive Tombaugh after fellow astronomer Percival Lowell had proposed the presence of a 'planet X' from calculating its gravitational influence from known deviations in the orbits of Uranus and Neptune.

But whilst considered a planet, Pluto's actual size, being smaller than our own Moon, is insufficient to account for those orbital deviations that had led to its discovery.

The increasing power of telescopes has recently enabled further discoveries of similar sized objects far beyond the orbit of Pluto – but it may well be that Lowell's planet X remains to be discovered in the furthest reaches of the Solar System.

In 1995, geometer John Martineau discovered even deeper patterns of harmonic relationships pervading the Solar System. Working with the most accurate astronomical data available, he showed that the size of the planetary bodies in addition to the average size of their orbits are related to each other in a series of pentagrams and other fundamental geometrical figures, to an accuracy of more than ninety-nine percent.

For example, the orbit of Venus, as seen from the Earth, traces out a perfect five-pointed star in the sky. As we saw in Chapter 2, this geometric form embodies the cosmic relationship of phi. And amazingly, just as the numerical value of phi - 1.618 – is thus embodied in the spatial relationship between Venus and the Earth, the tracing of each pentagrammic pattern takes 1.618 years to complete, co-creating perfect harmony in both space and time.

Such resonances may be treated by scientists as 'coincidences'. But as we have seen repeatedly, these harmonic relationships are being progressively revealed as the innate nature of the universe and fractal manifestations of the holographic principle.

In the last chapter, we explored the perception of our planetary home as a conscious entity and saw in the intricate inter-relationships of Gaia, the pervasive evidence of underlying order and purpose.

We will now expand our perception still further and begin to consider the entirety of the Solar System as an inter-connected matrix of consciousness, in essence a group soul – our 'Soular' System.

A perfect balance

Certain things are so ingrained within our everyday experience that we lose sight of just how extraordinary they are.

Each day the passage of the Sun and the Moon through the sky elicits hardly a mention from most of us. As the Moon journeys around the Earth, its orbit is at a slight angle of just over five degrees to that of the Earth's orbit as the latter pursues its path around the Sun. But twice yearly, when the orbit of the Moon intersects that of the Earth, the three bodies are lined up in such a way that a solar or lunar eclipse may occur.

And when the Moon is exactly aligned between the Sun and Earth, that most glorious of natural phenomena, a total solar eclipse ensues.

As the disc of the Moon encroaches across the face of the Sun, the awesome moment of totality arrives when for a few brief seconds the entirety of the Sun is covered. And the matching of the two is indeed so perfect that sunlight shining through the canyons and craters of the Moon's surface creates an intermittent circle of light, which astronomers call the 'diamond bracelet'.

But in acknowledging this incredible balance, let us consider how remarkable it really is.

The Sun is an enormous 865,000 miles across and an average distance of 93 million miles from the Earth. In contrast, the Moon is a mere two thousand miles in diameter and just a quarter of a million miles away. And yet, by an apparent 'coincidence' as seen from Earth, they appear to be the same size!

And not only this, but the inclination of the Moon's orbit to that of the Earth's around the Sun is such that it enables the three bodies to line up in space to enable the miracle of eclipses to occur.

A cosmic dance

But the astronomical dance of the Sun, Moon and Earth also embodies a symphony of other astounding harmonies in space and time, which have been explored by mathematician and astrologer Robin Heath.

The twice-yearly seasons for eclipses frame a so-called eclipse year of 346.62 days. And their timing moves backwards around the calendar by 19.618 days each year, taking 18.618 years to complete a full cycle.

To the ancient astronomers, the node points where the Moon's orbit intersects that of the Earth thus enabling eclipses, were seen as the head and tail of a cosmic dragon and the entire18.618 year cycle, is therefore termed a Draconic year.

And as the eclipse year itself of 346.62 days, may be expressed as 18.618 x 18.618 days, so may the Draconic year be denoted as 18.618 x 18.618 x 19.618 days.

But this cosmic dance doesn't stop there.

The solar year of 365.242 days may be expressed as 18.618 x 19.618 days.

The tilt of the Moon's orbit around the Earth extends its rising and setting positions beyond that of the Sun with a full cycle, known as a lunstice, lasting 18.618 years.

And against the backdrop of stars, the relative positions of the Sun and Moon journey in a great spiral, known as the Metonic cycle, each lasting 19 years.

The further relevance of 19 is revealed when we consider the relationship between the Sun, Moon and Earth which gives rise to series of different types of partial and total eclipses. The harmonics of the system provide for these series of eclipses, to run in 'families' over centuries and even millennia.

These so-called Saros families trace spirals across the Earth from pole to pole over the long durations of their complete cycles, but the members of the same 'family' are separated by a period lasting 19 eclipse years and 18 solar years to 99.9 percent accuracy.

There are other harmonics in the trinity relationship of Sun-Moon-Earth, but all are characterised by the same numbers we have seen above. In earlier chapters, we saw how the fundamental ratio of phi, which numerically equates to 1.618, pervades Nature and is profoundly expressed throughout evolutionary processes.

We also saw in Chapter 2, how, in two-dimensional geometry, six circles fit perfectly around a central one - and in three-dimensions, how twelve spheres also form a perfect fit around a central one. If we continue the progression, we would expect to find the four-dimensions of spacetime to be characterised by eighteen around one and thus to encounter the numbers eighteen and nineteen – as we indeed do in the harmony embodied by the trinity of Earth, Sun and Moon.

And again, as we did in the relationship between the Earth and Venus, we see in the evolutionary spirals traced by their cosmic dance, the harmonies of phi perfectly manifested in space and time.

Perfect partners

Because the Earth is tilted on her axis, throughout the year the Sun rises and sets at different positions, like a huge pendulum moving along the horizon. And at the solstices in June and December, this daily change is reduced to zero at these extreme positions of the solar pendulum – where for three days the Sun's rising and setting positions appear to stand still.

The Moon is the perfect partner to the Sun and each month approximately reflects the range of rising and setting positions of the Sun's entire yearly journey. The two mirror each other throughout the year and at the solstices the mid-winter Full Moon's rising and setting positions reflect those of the Sun in mid-summer and vice versa.

The 27.3 day cycle which the Sun takes to spin on its axis, is also the exact time the Moon takes to complete an orbit around the Earth and return to the same position.

Against the stellar background, this lunar period is known as a sidereal month. These cycles too are intimately involved with human life – a woman's menstrual cycle harmonises with this timing, as does the 273-day gestation period between human conception and birth.

As the Moon orbits the Earth, the latter continues on her path around the Sun. and so the Moon takes a further two days to catch up, taking 29.5 days to complete the full cycle of phases, such as between Full Moons – known as a lunation cycle. And in a solar year, there are just over thirteen sidereal months and twelve lun ation cycles.

To the ancients, the perfect harmonies embodied in these astronomical cycles were not coincidences but revelatory of the ordered purpose of the Cosmos and in the earliest calendars they sought to harmonise life on Earth with this cosmic order.

In doing so they correlated the rhythms of the calendars into months or 'moonths', which reflected either the thirty day (rounded up from its 29.5 day exactitude) cycles of the Sun-Moon-Earth rhythm or the twenty-eight days (rounded up from 27.3 day) of the lunar cycle in relation to the stars.

Perennial wisdom also perceives such cycles as aspects of a wholistic Cosmos where the microcosm of the human experience inter-relates with and embodies the macrocosmic archetypal essences of the luminaries and planets of the Soular System.

And now to further understand how this perennial perception is being restated by wholistic science, we first need to return to the harmony of Number, which we explored in Chapter 2 and the archetypal and mythological basis of expanded awareness we first discussed in Chapter 5.

Archetypal harmonies

In Chapter 2, we began to perceive the fundamental wholeness of creation expressed as three-in-oneness and its archetypal presence throughout the Cosmos. And we have also considered how the elemental aspects of processes and experience are embodied and revealed through their fundamental four-fold nature

But to the ancient metaphysicians, it is not only through the embodiment of cosmic principles of three-ness and four-ness, but their additive and multiplicative aspects of seven (three plus four) and twelve (three times four) which are expressed in the psychological and physical aspects of human experience.

And we see this reflected in the archetypal presence and interplay between seven and twelve, which weave through myth and symbolism.

Perennial wisdom teachings exhort Numbers as intrinsically powerful aspects of the Cosmos and as being revelatory of underlying harmony. Thus the seven-ness and twelve-ness reflected in Nature, supports the embodiment of the symbolic and energetic attributes of their cosmic ideals and their interplay with and within the human psyche.

Seven-ness is expressed through the seven-fold family of visible luminaries in the heavens, the colours of the rainbow and the notes of the musical diatonic scale, all of which were perceived as macrocosmic resonances with the microcosmic seven-fold nature of human personality.

And in the ancient Vedic teachings from which the tradition of yoga arose, these influences are mediated into physical expression through seven energy vortices, or chakras, in the human body. Whilst chakras are perceived to resonate at subtle levels beyond physical measurement, they have been associated with the endocrine system of the body and thus with the generation of hormones and thereby the management of bodily functions and the regulation of emotional and mental states.

And in the extended notation of the chromatic musical scale and the ancient Chinese understanding of the energy meridians of the human body, the resonance of twelve around one is also seen as being manifested.

Twelve around One

In the cosmic dance of the trinity of the Sun, Moon and Earth, other archetypal resonances may be perceived. The twelve Full Moons or lunation cycles in a year, when at the culmination of each, the Earth is positioned and balanced between the Sun and Moon, is a powerful expression of our human inner and outer journey of exploration as we find our balance between light and dark.

And the three-dimensional geometry of twelve spheres around a central one, reveals the transcendental essence of the thirteenth whole, which again embodies the transformational completion of the journey.

That the ancients perceived this inherent initiatory empowerment is clear.

In ancient Egypt, the great deity of regeneration, Osiris, had twelve companions. In Greek theology, the deity Zeus led a pantheon of twelve gods and goddesses and in Greek myth the hero Hercules completed twelve labours to attain redemption. In the enduring mythos of King Arthur and the round table, reflecting the circle of the heavens – the solar hero Arthur was accompanied by twelve knights.

And Jesus chose twelve disciples to accompany his ministry of spiritual transformation.

The sacred science of astrology

Let us now see how these resonances may be archetypally embodied in the luminaries of the Soular System and interpreted by the ancient sacred science of astrology.

The first known attempts to bring a sense of order to the mapping of the heavens dates back over four millennia. And by around 500BC, Babylonian astronomer-astrologers had divided the sky into the band of twelve constellations, known today as the zodiac and which in their totality, complete cycles of personal and collective initiation.

The path of the Sun against the background of fixed stars is known as the ecliptic and its cycle traces a complete wave around the celestial dome over the course of a full year. And during that time, the Sun rises each morning against the backdrop of one of the twelve zodiac constellations.

The plane of the Soular System means that the Moon and planets also appear to journey around the circle of the sky in this zodiacal band, which extends thirty degrees above and below the Sun's yearly path.

The way in which the twelve signs of the zodiac have then been sub-divided in three aspects for over two millennia, provides a profound basis for further psychological interpretation.

The first is a three-fold division into qualities, representing the perennial wisdom teachings that all experiences embody waves which encompass the coming into being, consolidation and falling away. In astrological terms, the zodiac reflects the three-in-one quality of experience in its division into Cardinal signs (Aries, Cancer, Libra and Capricorn), which are associated with initiating activities, Fixed signs (Taurus, Leo, Scorpio and Aquarius) with their manifestation, and Mutable signs (Gemini, Virgo, Sagittarius and Pisces) with their integration.

The second is a four-fold division into the four elements. People who have Fire signs in their astrological makeup, (Aries, Leo and

Sagittarius) are seen as being enthusiastic and out-going. Earth signs (Taurus, Virgo and Capricorn) are associated with caution and practicality, Air signs (Gemini, Libra and Aquarius) with clarity of mind and communication, and Water signs (Cancer, Scorpio and Pisces) with sensitivity and empathy.

The third division is into the cosmic polarities of what the ancient Chinese term yin and yang, which essentially characterise passive and active attributes. Passive or Receptive signs are Taurus, Cancer, Virgo, Scorpio, Capricorn and Pisces - and Active signs are Aries, Gemini, Leo, Libra, Sagittarius and Aquarius.

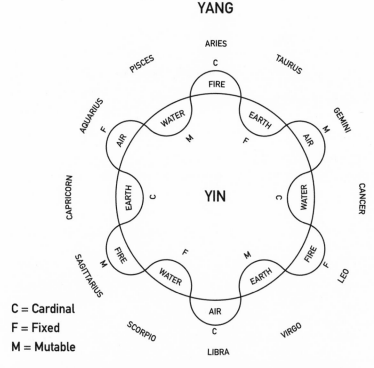

C = Cardinal
F = Fixed
M = Mutable

Fig 8.1 The initiatory cycle of the zodiac incorporates the continuous wave of the cosmic polarities of yin and yang, the trinity of cardinal, fixed and mutable qualities and the four-fold cycle of the physical elements.

The ever-changing interactions of influence encompassing the entire harmonic system comprise the most comprehensive personality based psychological tradition known. Eminent psychiatrist Carl Jung used astrology as a powerful psychological tool and Isaac Newton, when chided by the astronomer Edmond Halley for believing such apparent superstition, responded, '*It is evident that you have not looked into astrology. I have.*'

Cosmic correlations

The positions of the seven visible luminaries at the time of birth, within the various signs of the zodiac and their relationships to each other, form the holographic pattern of influence denoted by an individual's birth – or natal - astrological chart.

This interference pattern of correspondences between the archetypal patterns embodied in the Soular System and individual human consciousness, is seen by astrologers as essentially comprising the personality in conjunction with genetically inherited pre-dispositions. And given the unique time and place for everyone's birth, the specific pattern embodied by any individual is unique to them.

In 1950, psychologist Michel Gauqelin began what would become a study lasting three decades, during which time he produced a large body of data to support a relationship between planetary positions at the time of birth and subsequent professional eminence.

Gauqelin correlated the positions of the Moon, Venus, Mars, Jupiter and Saturn in relation to two traditionally significant astrological aspects: the Ascendant – the intersection of the Sun's position at the time of birth and the eastern horizon - and the Midheaven, the intersection of the Sun's position at the time of birth and its highest position in the sky.

Traditionally, the Ascendant is seen as indicating the foundation of someone's personality and how they will adapt to their environment. And the Midheaven position indicates what someone will identify with in their life. Both the Ascendant and Midheaven are thus guides to the profession to which someone is vocationally attracted.

Reviewing over eighteen thousand professionals in five European countries, Gauqelin found statistically significant correlations. For example, for sports personalities Mars was found in those positions far more often than would be expected by chance, as was Saturn in the natal charts of eminent scientists.

These associations agreed with those traditionally ascribed by astrology, but were only found for those professionals who had achieved eminence in their field of endeavour

An additional sample of over five hundred Belgian professionals independently reported similar results in the mid 1970s.

And psychiatrist Hans Eysenck, reviewing Gauqelin's findings, took them a step further predicting links between the personality descriptions of eminent professionals and in particular linking Saturn with introversion and Mars and Jupiter with extraversion.

The outer planets

In 1781, the discovery of Uranus, followed by Neptune in 1846 and Pluto in 1930 brought additional influences into the consideration of astrologers.

The orbital periods of the visible luminaries are all within a human lifetime, the slowest being Saturn which orbits the Sun in approximately 29 years. However, the outer planets take much longer: Uranus 84 years, Neptune 165 years and Pluto nearly 248 years. Their influences are thus seen as being primarily generational and collective.

To the ancient astrologers, the visible luminaries and planets completed the seven-fold perception of human personality. With the discoveries of Uranus, Neptune and Pluto and the inclusion of the Earth herself, the archetypal family of the Soular System grew to eleven members.

The discoveries of these outer planets have been encompassed within the astrological framework as embodying transpersonal and collective influences. Whilst still applicable to an individual personality, they are thus more commonly considered in aspects of astrological interpretation as involving deeper and more transfigurative influences in human awareness.

And a number of astrologers have drawn attention to the actual timing of the discoveries of the outer planets and their relationship to the collective raising of awareness.

For instance, the discovery of Uranus in 1781, at a time between the American and French revolutions and in the early stages of the Industrial Revolution, correlates with the astrological view of Uranian influence as individual and collective expressions of independence and the awakening to new possibilities.

Neptune and Pluto are also perceived by astrologers to embody archetypal characteristics, which resonate with the evolution of collective perception at the time of their discovery – Neptune with idealism and heightened awareness and Pluto with regeneration of the psyche.

And with recent discoveries of planetoids beyond Pluto and the possibility of Lowell's planet X lurking in the furthest depths of the

Soular System, to metaphysicians, such a discovery would complete a twelve-fold harmonic scale of archetypal correspondence around the human 'One', and thus, signify a transformation of human consciousness.

Cycles of destiny

The seasons we experience on Earth are caused by the tilt of Gaia's axis to her orbital plane. But the current angle of 23.4 degrees is not constant and varies over an approximate four degree range in a cycle which lasts 41,000 years.

In addition, the shape of Gaia's orbit around the Sun is not circular but an ellipse whose eccentricity varies over a second cycle lasting for 100,000 years.

And thirdly, the time of the year when she is closest to the Sun also changes over a cycle that lasts for 21,000 years.

This interweaving trinity of long-term astronomical cycles is named after Milutin Milankovitch who postulated the theory of its influence, which is thought to have at least a contributory role in the triggering of Ice Ages and is yet another example of how the evolutionary cycles of life on Earth are mediated.

But astrologers also perceive another influential cycle in the way in which Gaia wobbles about her axis of rotation, essentially like an enormous gyroscope and completing a full cycle nearly every 26,000 years.

This period, which is known as a Great Year, is the culmination of twelve zodiacal ages, each lasting just over two millennia. Each age is named after the zodiacal sign against which the Sun rises at the spring equinox and the process is called the precession of the equinoxes.

After the last two thousand years of the Age of Pisces, we are now entering the Age of Aquarius. Astrologers debate how the psychological wave of influence of each era manifests in the collective psyche. One view however, is that the wave of a specific zodiacal influence commences at the beginning of the era named after it, but only finds its full expression in the following era before falling away in the third era. As such, the complete psychological influence of each era, comprises the cardinal aspects of the current age, the fixed aspects of the prior age and the mutable aspects of the age before that.

And so, we should expect as we enter the Age of Aquarius, to experience the beginnings of its astrological influence denoted by personal empowerment and co-creative co-operation, the full expression of the previous Age of Pisces embodying the manifestation of compassion and the falling away of the influence of the Age of Aries and its solely individual self-expression.

The Soular System

As we have seen, astrology essentially perceives that the macrocosm of the Soular System is embodied within the microcosm of humanity. Such fractal correspondences then may be seen as resonating on both nonlocal levels, which transcend spacetime, and localised levels, which may be mediated through physical influences.

As such, rather than seeking an ultimate 'cause' of such influence, perhaps we should consider that they operate as manifold interactions of correspondences and resonances. Jung called such a-causal correspondences, 'synchronicity', and suggested that whatever is born or enacted at a particular point in time, resonates with the quality or essence of that moment.

Such correspondences may be effected by energetic resonance on both subtle and physical levels. And astronomer Percy Seymour has proposed the possibility of their physical mediation by electro-magnetic fields. He has suggested a model in which the planets resonate with the Sun's electro-magnetic field and, through the differential rotation of the gaseous layers of the solar surface, affect the continuous stream of high-energy particles known as the solar wind, and thereby the Earth's geomagnetic field.

Research in this field is in its infancy. However, it is becoming evermore clear that human sensitivity to electro-magnetic field effects, not only those generated within the biosphere of Gaia herself, but also by solar and lunar influences, is far greater than hitherto supposed by mainstream science

As we have seen, our own planet resonates with extra-low frequency (ELF) electro-magnetic radiation, on both sub-surface and atmospheric levels. If other planets do the same, it is conceivable that such influences are radiated across the intervening space. And given that planetary orbits are also in octaval harmony with each other, this could induce further resonance and, in certain planetary alignments, the energetic effects of coherence.

The effects of planetary alignments have been studied by astrologers since antiquity. And their influences are psychologically deemed to be those which would also apply to the interference of waveforms.

For instance, when two planets are said to be in conjunction and thus in the same position in the sky, their influence is additive. Conversely when they are 180 degrees apart, they are said to be in opposition and their influences oppose and counteract each other.

In the mid 1970s, astrologer John Addey published an extensive study of harmonic alignments and suggested that two of these, known as quintiles and septiles - where planetary positions are aligned in five-fold and seven-fold geometric relationships - are associated with creativity.

Research by scientists Nick Kollerstrom and Mike O'Neill has collated data of scientific Eureka! moments – named after the famous occasion when the Greek philosopher Archimedes is said to have jumped out of his bath, crying Eureka (I have found it), and ran naked into the street after a spontaneous insight into the displacement properties of water.

The findings of Kollerstrom and O'Neill support Addey's premise, that at such moments of creative insights there are astrologically much higher incidences of quintiles and septiles.

There may even be other harmonic laws associated with the speeds of the orbiting planets, which would literally represent the frequency of their periodic 'note' and - when planets align with each other - create chords of resonant influence.

Whilst the study of astrology is millennia old, the consideration of the entire Soular System as a self-organising entity is embryonic and our understanding continues to unfold. However, just as we are now appreciating the profoundly harmonic nature of our planetary home, as we begin to see with new eyes, we will perhaps appreciate the holographic principle at work in the extended spiritual family of our Solar – or Soular – System.

Cosmic chords

Our Sun is 'merely' an average star, one of a few hundred billion, which make up our Milky Way galaxy, which is itself typical of the few hundred billion galaxies which make up the visible universe.

The Milky Way itself is a so-called spiral galaxy comprised of a flat rotating disc in which spiral arms encrusted with stars, revolve around a central hub, made up of yet more stars and possibly a gigantic black hole at the very centre.

Our galaxy is about a hundred thousand light years across and around ten billion years old and the periodic cycles and feedback processes, which are being discovered as being embodied within it, are also vast in both space and time.

Astronomer Lee Smolin is researching the relationship between the clouds of gas and dust, which collapse to form new stars, the sizes of stars and the range of their subsequent lifecycles.

Smolin and others have shown that the vast blast waves from massive exploding stars or supernovae, in addition to seeding the interstellar medium with elements, interact to create energetic interference patterns.

Where the peaks of the waves of energy combine, nodes of interstellar gas and dust clouds are created like the beads of dew on a spider's web. And as over time these collapse under the force of gravitational attraction, new stars of varying size and brightness are birthed.

Computer simulations have shown that there is a resonant density of cloud for this self-sustaining process to continue and that the feedback of supernovae events moves the entire system towards this optimum condition.

Smolin and others are also discovering that the density of the interstellar medium throughout the galaxy is far from uniform and varies by up to a factor of a billion. Such significant inner variations reflect a system far from equilibrium and maintained in a critical state by the self-organising processes relating to the birth, life and death of stars.

And just as we have seen with the organisation of Gaia and our entire Soular System, such research is now suggesting that our galaxy also appears to be self- organising. Here too order is being created and sustained by the flow of energy through the system and the optimising processes of feedback are exquisitely balanced to sustain life.

On this level, the galaxy passes the test for life proposed by James Lovelock, and Smolin argues that galaxies too should be treated as living systems.

From this perspective, the boundary between what has been considered as living and what as non-living becomes blurred. If Gaia, our Soular System and our entire galaxy are deemed to be living then surely we are fully reconciled with the perception of perennial wisdom that the entire universe is an interconnected living whole, pervaded and ultimately directed by conscious intention.

A journey into wholeness

Over the last four chapters, we have taken an enormous out-breath, as we have continued to explore the innate harmony and order that underlies the physical universe on all scales of space and time.

We have also begun to consider the nonlocality of phenomena, which transcend spacetime and we have expanded our understanding of consciousness and human awareness.

In the next chapter, we will resume our exploration of personal and transpersonal awareness and take further steps in our journey of understanding what it means to be human and how we can heal on all levels of our being into the wholeness of who we really are.

PART III

HEALING THE WHOLE

As we continue our journey into the heart and mind of the Cosmos, and our awareness continues to expand, we begin to see that consciousness is universal. And we become ever more empowered to perceive and ultimately experience ourselves as the co-creators of our realities.

The word 'health' has the same ancient linguistic roots as the words 'whole' and 'holy'. All three embody the essence of wholeness, as does the word hologram.

In these next four chapters, we will discover how each of us may journey towards such health on physical, emotional, mental and spiritual levels.

And we will see how the holographic principle, which we have seen pervades the natural world is also embodied in ourselves and throughout our human relationships

As we do so, we will gain further insights into the ways in which we may each engage our heart, mind and intention to follow our own unique inner and outer journey home, to the wholeness of who we really are.

To see a world in a grain of sand
And a Heaven in a wild flower
Hold infinity in the palm of your hand
And Eternity in an hour

William Blake (1757 – 1827) English poet and visionary

CHAPTER 9

THE BIOLOGY OF BELIEF

One of the most sublime images in the world is high up on the ceiling of the Sistine chapel in Rome, Italy. Painted by Michaelangelo in the early sixteenth century it depicts God, holding out his arm to Adam.

Adam too extends his arm. And between their outstretched index fingers crackles a tiny bolt of lightning – the electro-magnetic carrier of consciousness - spirit made manifest in the physical world.

Embodiment of the soul

Western medicine is the only healing tradition, which trains its practitioners on cadavers – dead bodies whose life essence is no longer present. In contrast Eastern traditions of healing, such as those of India or China, teach and share their understanding through the study of living energies.

These Eastern traditions share another fundamental belief, common to all perennial wisdom – that we are spiritual beings undergoing a physical experience as a human being – and thus when diagnosing the cause and effecting the healing of a dis-ease, they do so on a holistic basis, which considers body, mind and spirit as a whole.

In perceiving spirit as the all-pervasive intelligence of creation, perennial wisdom teaches that consciousness is embodied in a soul, which is its manifestation at individual and collective levels of experience.

Souls express consciousness as a continuous spectrum of multidimensional energies, ranging from subtle or supra-physical levels, through octaves of mental and emotional levels to their embodiment on the physical plane.

The transpersonal aspects of the human soul are essentially its expanded awareness which incorporate higher realms of archetypal consciousness and its perception of the profound inter-connectedness of the Cosmos.

At the mental, emotional and physical levels, consciousness is expressed through the energy fields, which form the personality of the ego-self, the aspect of our individual soul that is undergoing the experience of all it means to be human.

The template of our physical form is thus perceived as initiating in higher levels of subtle energies - biofields - which harmonically extend into physical form. These higher vibrational energy bodies are the subtle counterparts to the physical and as perennial wisdom emphasises, they are not separate from it.

All such traditions of perennial wisdom, and indeed almost all non-Western approaches to medicine, conceive the consciousness that is embodied in such biofields as a life force, which vivifies a biological entity at birth and withdraws on the death of the physical body.

Health

Energetic imbalances show up in the subtle energy fields before becoming apparent as physical symptoms. As such, where psychological or emotional trauma is the causative trigger, if this is addressed and released sufficiently early, it does not degenerate into physical dis-ease.

Whereas the Western allopathic approach to healthcare waits until physical disease is perceptible and then seeks to heal its symptoms, the Eastern approach aims to prevent such illness from manifesting in the first place by the holistic care of body-mind-spirit and promoting an understanding of the causative factors underlying physical distress.

Clearly, individuals are subject to bodily injuries sustained for example in accidents. But here too traditions diverge in that the Western approach would tend to primarily, and very often solely, address the physical trauma, whereas the Eastern would also attend to its psychological and emotional implications.

In recent years, an integrated approach has gradually been emerging in the West, combining its technological innovations with a more holistic approach and the gradual recognition of the efficacy of a number of Eastern techniques of energy healing, such as acupuncture.

As such techniques however, cannot be seriously adopted without an acceptance of their underlying philosophy, the understanding of the energy fields pervading the body is progressively becoming an area of pioneering research.

And the importance of the very low energy electro-magnetic fields intimately associated with the body's physical component of energy flows, is now being recognised and measured.

Energy meridians

The twenty-four volume *Nei Ching*, is considered to be the oldest known text relating to the Chinese understanding of meridians of energy flowing through the human body, carrying the biofield energies they term *ch'i*.

Energy meridians are considered to carry both the subtle and electro-magnetic components of these energies throughout the physical body, just like the arterial system carries blood. And distributed around the body are approximately a thousand points, which are the nodes for such energies and where they may be accessed via the skin.

The Chinese tradition of acupuncture utilises extremely fine needles inserted painlessly into the skin at these points to free energy blockages and stimulate energy flow in the meridian system, often facilitated by gently tapping or rotating the needles.

Medical doctor Reinhold Voll has shown that within a few millimetres of the acupuncture points there is a significant decrease in the electrical resistance of the skin compared with non-acupuncture points. He has also demonstrated that there are measurable differences in the resistance levels at these points between healthy and non-healthy bodies.

In a 1992 study involving three hundred volunteers, medical doctors Jean-Claude Darras and Pierre De Vernejoul injected radioactive tracers into acupuncture points and were able to trace their paths through the body. Such tracers were found to follow the traditional meridian paths of Chinese medicine whereas the tracers injected at non-acupuncture points merely dispersed.

The rate of diffusion through the energy meridian system was also found to be in line with the ancient perception that the energy flow through a healthy body correlates with its circadian, or daily, biorhythms.

And in 2005, a study by a combined medical team from the Universities of Southampton and London have confirmed the value of acupuncture for pain relief, a benefit that Chinese doctors have known and used for millennia.

Let us now see how these energy fields may act as causative agents in the development and maintenance of biological organisms in general and the human body in particular.

Biofields

We have seen in Chapter 7 how the research of biologists Bruce Lipton and Stuart Kauffmann is suggesting that underlying fractal patterns may energise both the overall structure of biological organisms and the initiation of cell specialisation.

And it is becoming clear that the holographic template of the overall structure of an organism, its energetic pattern – or biofield - is as real a part of its body as are its cells, heart or limbs.

Cell biologist Bruce Lipton has proposed that it is the membranes of individual cells, which perceive the environment and actively mediate information and thus awareness. And in the development of multi-cellular organisms, whole-body membranes surrounding the organism would then seem to act as the information processors for the biofield template of their overall structure.

In the earliest stages of a human embryo, every gene in every chromosome is active and available to every cell. As the organism develops, the cells form three rudimentary tissue layers, which are essentially membranes. The inner layer; or endoderm develops into the glands and viscera of the body. The middle layer, or mesoderm grows into the bones, muscles and circulatory system. And the outer; ectoderm becomes the skin, sense organs and nervous system.

By the time the three membranes of the human embryo are developed, some of the genes within the chromosomes are already being deactivated. And as the cells progressively differentiate and specialise into mature tissue, only one specific set of genes stays switched on in each case, for example as blood, muscle or liver cells.

And as we shall now see, research is suggesting that the biofield, the causative energetic template for the organism, is mediated in physical form by coherent electro-magnetic fields.

Back in 1960, biochemist Albert Szent-Györgi pointed out that the molecular structure of many other parts of the cell are ordered enough to support the semi-conduction of electricity.

And physicist Cyril Smith and researcher Simon Best have likened the ordered array of cells in a biological system to a mathematical Shah function. This is a specific Fourier transform – the mathematical language of the holographic principle – that is self-referential and able to generate a holographic image of itself when illuminated with coherent light.

Neurophysiologist Ralph Gerard has also found that nerves throughout the human body are uniformly polarised; positive at the input fibre (or dendrite) and negative at the output fibre (or axon), guiding electrical impulses to move in one direction only and thus giving electro-magnetic coherence to the nervous system.

And the involvement of electrical fields in stimulating cell differentiation processes – the means by which cells change to and from being functionally specialised - has been investigated by medical doctor Robert O. Becker.

The electro-magnetic body

Becker has pioneered the use of electro-magnetic fields to stimulate cell re-growth, initially investigating limb regeneration in salamanders and other amphibians that are well known to have powerful natural regenerative abilities.

In such creatures, he found that electrical fields operating at the site of a wound, trigger cell de-differentiation in adjacent blood cells and subsequent re-differentiation to enable the regeneration of a missing limb.

The electric current appears to interact with the cell membrane, supporting Lipton's view of its intelligent function. And as repair continues, the electrical field, whose strength is initially boosted after the injury, returns to its normal level as the healing process is completed.

The ability to naturally regenerate declines with increasing evolutionary complexity. And this appears to be associated with proportionally more nerve tissue being concentrated in the brain, reducing the amount of nerve fibre available in other parts of the body to below the critical level needed to stimulate regeneration.

However, there appears to remain within mammalian physiology a residual capability to regenerate naturally. Even though controversial as a treatment, it seems that fingertips of children up to the age of about eleven years old, if cleanly sheared off beyond the outer crease of the outermost joint, will regenerate themselves if left to do so without intervention.

Becker has also discovered that it is the specific electrical activity in the epidermis, the outer layer of the membrane of the skin, which initiates re-growth.

Following an injury, re-growing nerve fibres make unique connections with the epidermal layer creating what are called neuro-epidural junctions (NEJ). Such NEJs act like plugs fitted into sockets to complete the exact electrical circuit to then carry the necessary biofield information to trigger the de-differentiation of surrounding cells and their subsequent re-differentiation into healthy tissue.

The direction (polarity) plus the amplitude and force of the electric current in such injuries, as indeed for all such currents throughout the body, then serve as a vector system giving distinct values for every area of the body.

This is equivalent to the way in which complex systems are mathematically mapped in phase space, which as we have seen in Chapter 7, reveals the underlying patterns of fractal systems and holographic processes at work.

The research of Becker and others is demonstrating how such low energy electro-magnetic fields play a crucial role in structuring the form and maintaining the health of all biological organisms including ourselves. But it may also be offering us even more profound clues as to how the subtle energies of biofields may interface with and manifest in the physical world.

The biology of belief

In Chapters 5 and 6, we discussed how the scientific evidence for the ability of our minds to perceive and exert nonlocal influence has progressively been amassed over the last three decades.

But if mind and consciousness can apply such influence on others, what about the ability of our mind to influence our own circumstances and physical well-being?

Generally, the ego-self is culturally conditioned. Thus it not only acts in accordance with its prevailing worldview and beliefs, but it literally is unable to see what it cannot imagine. In essence, there is no resonance on that basis and so the ego-self has no way of attuning itself to the reality of a new and effectively unimaginable phenomenon.

But where the ego-self can imagine a phenomenon and believes in its reality, it is able to directly experience and essentially co-create that reality.

For millennia, the meditative techniques of a number of traditions have taught initiates how to overcome pain and embody greater well-being. Today more and more people are benefiting from these teachings by employing these simple but effective means to reduce stress and manage chronic pain.

We have discussed Bruce Lipton's model of the cell membrane as an organic information processor, dynamically linked to the environment. And how the behaviour and internal conditions of the cell reflect the recognition of perceived environmental stimuli – both physical *and* energetic.

But as Lipton points out, such perception may be distorted and thus represents a 'belief' about reality. And so, energetic environmental signals such as thought processes and emotions, whether 'real' or otherwise, influence the behaviour of the cell.

Lipton has thus identified the process whereby the attunement of our mind and our emotional state, both conscious and subliminal, are able to influence our physical body – guiding it to health or dis-ease.

But now as we consider these influences still further, we need to appreciate how research over the last thirty years has progressively demonstrated that intelligence and thus 'mind' is not constrained to its physical mediation through the brain.

The intelligent heart

In the 1970s physiologists John and Beatrice Lacey pioneered the understanding that the heart is able to perceive, and has inherent intelligence. They found that not only are signals sent from the brain in the cranium to the heart, which the heart considers but does not necessarily follow, but that the heart can also send signals to the brain, which the latter does obey.

And the subsequent discovery that the heart has its own nervous system, comprising at least forty thousand nerve cells, or neurons - as many as are found in various sub-cortical centres of the brain - has led to the recognition that a two-way bio-communication system operates between the heart and the brain.

Within a human embryo, the heart forms and starts to beat before the brain begins to develop. The earliest evolutionary part of the brain, relating to its emotional centres (known as the amygdala and hippocampus) then grows and only thereafter is the 'thinking' part of the brain generated.

The primacy of the heart and its innate intelligence significantly affects how we perceive and interact with the world, as was reviewed by Daniel Coleman in 1996.

Coleman noted that measurements of human IQ, which determines the quotient of intellectual and cognitive abilities, do not change significantly from childhood onwards regardless of educational opportunities and attainment. And he also found that success in life appears to depend less on IQ and more on our ability to manage and develop our emotional intelligence quotient, or EQ.

EQ relates to self-awareness and our perception of the inter-relationships between our thoughts, emotions and actions and their consequences on others. And unlike our IQ, our EQ can continue to be educated and indeed re-educated throughout life.

Since 1991, stress researcher Doc Childre and his colleagues at the HeartMath Institute in California have undertaken and collated research to demonstrate how negative emotions such as insecurity, anger and fear, throw the body's nervous system out of balance and engender heart rhythms that are jagged and disordered.

Conversely, they have found that positive emotions of love, compassion and gratitude, create coherent energy signals, which increase order, reduce stress and bring balance throughout the nervous system and are reflected in harmonious rhythms of the heart.

There is now substantial evidence that by enhancing emotional intelligence and invoking the intuitive wisdom of the heart sends energetic signals to every cell of the body, re-educates areas of imbalance and dis-ease and facilitates health and well-being.

Energy medicine

These new insights are reconciling with the perennial wisdom of spiritual awareness and correlate with the evidence of nonlocal influence described in the last two chapters. By retrainig our consciousness, we *can* reshape our lives; and enhance and regain well-being.

All techniques of energy medicine utilise the same underlying principles as we have seen throughout *The Wave* that consciousness is all-pervasive and expresses itself as energy.

It is not the energy that heals, but the information, and perception it carries. Thoughts and emotions are patterns of energy configuration and it is the re-arrangement of these patterns, which either inhibit or restore health.

In addition to the re-appraisal in the West of ancient Eastern techniques of energy medicine, such as acupuncture, many new techniques are emerging, which are based on the same, or similar principles.

Whilst these in general require qualified practitioners who are knowledgeable of the details of a specific technique and its effects, the principles of energy medicine empower each of us as individuals, for there are simple and effective techniques that we can use ourselves.

We have already mentioned the benefits of regular meditation practice. And holistic modalities such as yoga benefit mind, body and soul. The ancients also recognised the healing power of sound and music. And the fundamental harmonics expressed through the toning of many Eastern mantras – the simplest of which is the OM, the expression of primordial cosmic creation – is an everyday means of aligning our energies with the flow of all life

A number of new techniques are also being developed, which are intended to release the energetic patterns associated with past emotional or psychological trauma.

Whilst such techniques are also now appearing to be effective in the short term, given their recent development, there is little research as yet to attest to their long-term efficacy. And also their use in general appears to be best suited for the resolution of specific issues or phobias.

It is likely that if health issues are embodied in deeper and possibly archetypal energetic patterns that the symptoms will return, unless their underlying attitudinal and behavioural patterns are amended, or the mental and emotional causative reasons for the imbalances are fully resolved.

And to do this requires us to develop self-awareness and undergo an inner journey of discovery and a deeper understanding of who we really are.

Chakras and the inner journey to wholeness

The Vedic wisdom of India, perceives that the subtle energies of the human biofield interfaces with the physical body through the spinning vortices of subtle energies, known as chakras, which are located just in front of the spine and extend from the tailbone up to the crown of the head.

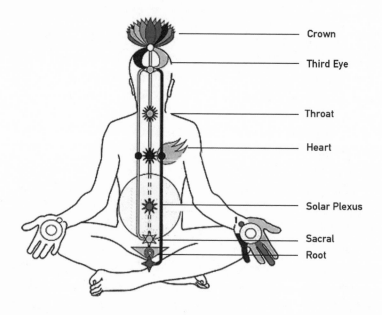

Fig 9.1 The seven chakras of the biofield of the human personality.

Unlike the energy meridians of the body, which have both subtle and physical energy components, the latter of which are mediated by electro-magnetic fields and are measurable, it appears that chakric energies are constrained to subtle levels.

And on these subtle levels, the chakras are considered to connect with a triad of energy meridians, or *nadis*, known individually as the *ida, pingala* and *shushumna*, acting as conduits for the life-force and biofield.

The locations of the chakras have been correlated with the major glands of the endocrine system, which secrete hormones and thus regulate an enormous range of physical and emotional responses. And each chakra energetically resonates with an essential aspect of the experiences of the personality of our ego-self.

Chakras are deemed to determine our use of energy. And the freedom with which energies at subtle and physical levels flow is directly correlated to our health and well-being. Any blockages or restrictions to either the reception or expression of subtle energies and the free flow of physical energies will result in imbalance and dis-ease at psychological, emotional or physical levels.

By understanding the chakric system, how it works and how it should operate optimally, we can perceive our own energetic blockages. And by becoming aware of each of their influences we can extend our attention beyond the manifestation of the dis-ease, and towards the actual energetic causality, which lies behind its ppearance, which is where real healing and sustained change can occur.

To gain an understanding of the energetic and psychological attributes ascribed to the seven chakras we will now briefly consider each in turn and their associated aspects of our human personality and experience.

The root chakra

The root chakra is energetically located at the base of the tailbone and represents the 'root' of our physical being and the deepest connection of our physical body with the Earth.

The energies of the root chakra are the most primal and instinctive of all seven chakras and are primarily associated with survival. The clearest and thus most healthy expression of its energy is when we live and work in an environment that most effectively supports our individual personality and needs.

Our primary clue to a condition of imbalance of the root chakra is a feeling of insecurity. And if we have insufficient resources to sustain our basic requirements, the needs of this chakra will be so consuming that we find it very difficult to focus on anything else until they are met.

One of the challenges of meeting these needs is in recognising that they are different for everyone. And a further challenge is understanding that our true needs may be different from that which we want – which is conditioned not only by our own perceptions but those of family, friends and our wider society.

The sacral chakra

The second, or sacral chakra, is energetically located in the pelvic area. And its primary drive is the search for pleasure and relationship of all kinds.

Its energetic attribute is to connect with the world of sensation and awaken feelings of emotional engagement. And its perspective is constantly to experience the polarities of attraction and repulsion and ultimately seek their balance.

Imbalances of this chakra lead to insensitivity, and ever-stronger doses of pleasure are then required to penetrate the emotional numbness that ensues. Alternatively, a common experience is to seek to avoid the perceived pain of relationships or their loss, by emotionally shutting down the energies of this chakra.

When we emotionally or mentally hold onto the traumas of previous experiences or live in fear of losing our pleasures, energetic blockages in the sacral chakra will result, and ultimately, their only release is when we are able to let go of the issue and resume balance.

The solar plexus chakra

The third chakra is located at the solar plexus, which many traditions have considered to be the energetic centre of the entire body and the seat of the will. From this centre is derived the principles and ethics for which we are willing to take a stand and the purpose to which we apply our efforts.

The solar plexus chakra energises and facilitates our ability to initiate activity and both project and defend ourselves within our environment.

Development of self-control and discernment are attributes of a healthy solar plexus chakra, as are courage and creativity in the deciding and optimum use of choices.

Imbalances in the energies of this chakra arise from an over, or under-use of willpower and intention. Over-use is seen in a pervasive competitive attitude where everything is a test or a battle and characteristically, an ongoing feeling of 'justifiable anger'.

Under-use of its energies is often revealed in an inability to express ourself, and feelings of helplessness and frustration at living life according to 'shoulds' and 'shouldn'ts' rather than following our own inner guidance and truth.

Becoming aware that it is the underlying energy that causes events, rather than events causing energy, facilitates our returning to the source of attitudes and behaviour, rather than continuing to be embroiled in the imbalances or dysfunctional patterns of their effects.

These first three chakras primarily resonate to the energies of our ego-self which perceives itself as separate and individual – and if out of balance, they will encroach on our experience of life as mediated through the upper chakras, which we will now go on to discuss.

The heart chakra

The opening and clear expression of the fourth chakra – the heart - represents our essential re-membering of the wholeness of creation and at its most fundamental, the difference and choice between love and fear.

The aim of the heart chakra is ostensibly simple – it is to experience love on personal and transpersonal levels and it is through the heart chakra that we begin to expand our sense of being and become aware of higher and greater realities.

With an opened heart, our human experience is able to consciously embody the awareness of spirit – to experience the vitality of the lower ego-based chakras and begin to connect with the higher awareness mediated by the upper chakras.

When emotional trauma causes us to close down our heart chakra, from cynicism, callousness or mistrust, this apparent refuge, our perceived 'security' from the world, actually becomes an imprisonment of our own making.

But as we awaken or re-awaken our hearts, imbalance in our lower chakras, unless resolved, may interfere with the natural expression of love. The words 'I love you' are then really saying 'I want you' or 'I need you'.

And typically the other expression of imbalance experienced with the awakening heart is inappropriate giving, when we willingly give to others but are unwilling or awkward in receiving the gifts they offer to us.

But with balance in the lower chakras, our awakened heart then enables us to become ever more aware of our soul purpose in this life and inspires us with the enthusiasm to embody and fulfil its destiny.

The throat chakra

The fifth chakra is centred at the throat and opens as we discover our authentic voice and express it through whatever creative forms are appropriate to us. Whilst the throat is associated physiologically with speech, our true self-expression is not limited to the voice but may take any creative form

The opening of this chakra represents the beginning of our personal empowerment. And the free expression of its energies opens us to transpersonal and collective perception and service – not servitude – to higher values and inspiration. It expresses our connection with greater realities, which we begin to experience with the opening of our heart chakra and supports us in developing an independent worldview beyond cultural and other conditioning.

Imbalances in the energies of the throat chakra, are typified by someone who has awakened to the appropriateness of independent thought, but who has no discernment or discipline with its expression.

Sometimes this is experienced in an inability to assert our ideas and we may then incur frustration and feelings of being an outsider.

And if ego is attached to the self-expression, the process of expanding our awareness also becomes stultified. We become defensive and attached to our new beliefs, rather than recognising our perception as being inevitably partial and being open to its continuing unfolding.

The 'third eye' chakra

The sixth or third eye chakra is energetically located in the centre of the brow above the bridge of the nose.

Traditionally, access to its energies has been deemed to accompany our inner urge to encounter the magic and deeper purpose of life, and experience a transcendental reality beyond the mundane.

When open, the intuitive awareness of higher realms of existence becomes increasingly available for us to consciously experience. And whilst initially, such encounters may be ascribed to 'imagination', the insights and understanding which emerge lead to such transcendent revelations.

The energetic balance of the third eye is to discern whether the experiences it facilitates leads to inspiration and empowerment or depletion and dis-empowerment.

And such balance is again predicated on the need to first achieve balance in the lower chakras. Otherwise accessing the energies of the sixth chakra will intensify such lower chakra issues. Residual feelings of unworthiness or insecurity will be heightened. And conversely, feelings of inappropriately heightened self-worth will encounter opportunities to become trapped in such ego-attachment.

But when the lower chakras are balanced, opening of the 'third eye' empowers the alignment of our human experience with our higher purpose and destiny. In doing so a sense of 'going with the flow' of life beyond the ego-self, effortlessly and abundantly supports our needs.

In this heightened awareness, we begin to appreciate what the mystics of all traditions have expressed, and we begin to experience the inner peace of living synchronistically and inspirationally – being and trusting that we will always be at the right place at the right time – without effort or stress.

The crown chakra

The seventh and final chakra of our personality based energy field, is located at, and takes its name from, the crown of our head.

The energies of this chakra support our conscious awakening to our higher soul purpose and a perception of the unity transcending the apparent polarities of the physical world.

To sustain awareness at this level requires the integration of all the other chakras. As such, this is a state of grace and the allowance of our higher awareness to flow through and be embodied by our human experience. It is a state of ego-surrender, which should not be confused with sacrifice. With this expanded awareness, there is direct communion with *All That Is* – and no need for intermediaries. And in such conscious harmony with the Cosmos, we become a participating co-creator in the dance of life.

The alter major chakra

Both the sixth and seventh chakras energetically resonate with the essence of the mind of our ego-self. When open, the sixth, or third eye chakra, reveals a more profound 'inner' view of our realities. And the seventh, or crown, chakra accesses an expanded and clearer vision of the 'outer' realities of both our human experience and of the Cosmos.

At the base of the skull, where it meets the top of the backbone, mystics have identified a further energy centre, known as the *alter major* chakra, which energetically connects with both the sixth and seventh chakras. When this is opened, it reconciles our expanded 'inner' and 'outer' awareness and reveals them to be reflections of each other.

When the energies of the *alter major* chakra are available to us, we are ready to undergo a dramatic shift in our perception into a profound experience of ourselves and the Cosmos which transcends our personality based perspective.

The universal heart

In Chapters 3 and 4, we discussed the energetic essence of Number and the ancient scales of music that embody the innate harmony of the physical world. Throughout *The Wave* we have also seen how the resonant relationship of the octave – where the frequency of a fundamental note, is doubled to derive a higher note - is fundamental to this pervasive harmony.

Throughout Nature, the octave is embodied within the wide array of power laws we have discussed, where a doubling in the frequency of a phenomenon is accompanied by a simple relationship to the scale of its expression.

As we saw in Chapter 4, the diatonic musical scale of seven notes is incomplete without the eighth note, which completes the octave. Only when the rising scale of doh, re, mi, fa, so, la, ti – is accompanied by the higher doh – is it fulfilled, sounding satisfactory to our ears and feeling so to our being as a whole.

And so it should, because in a profound sense, the seven chakras of our personality-based energy field are in themselves incomplete.

Only when we resonate to a higher octave of awareness do we begin to fully comprehend the wholeness of who we really are.

Over the past few years, more and more people are becoming aware of higher energy centres and beginning to directly access such transpersonal chakras. And the experience of such expanded awareness is enabling a profound resonance with the consciousness of Gaia and that of the entire 'Soular' System to become available to us both individually and collectively.

The eighth chakra, being termed the 'universal heart', is the portal to these higher connections. Most people, who are beginning to feel its energies, perceive it as an energy centre positioned midway between the 'personal' heart and throat chakras. On a collective level, it is through our emerging resonance with this eighth chakra that we are experiencing as our increasingly collective compassion.

Energetically, it brings together and balances the trinity of energies formed by our 'personal' heart, mind (alter major) and solar plexus chakras - the essence of our personality and ego-self expressed through our heart, mind and will - and raises them to a higher octave of vibration.

The trinity essence of the universal heart chakra, thus combines and creates a portal to transcend the ego-self and embody the self-realisation of higher consciousness. Unconditional love is the essence of this connection and its opening is a joyous portal of awareness and re-membering of the higher consciousness which guides our human experience.

The inner journey continues

Perennial wisdom has always perceived that each step of the inner journey to self-awareness and empowerment embodies a three-stage process of initiation.

The first is the initiate's instigation of the circumstances, which offer the opportunity for such a step to be taken.

The purpose of spiritual initiation is to gain a more profound awareness and understanding of the Cosmos and the initiate's place within it. And such inner-tuition or gnosis forms the second stage of the process.

The third and completing stage, is the integration of the experience, physically, emotionally, mentally and perhaps most importantly, within the psyche of the initiate.

Individually and collectively, we are evolving, not only physically, but also on the more profound levels of emotional, intellectual and spiritual awareness.

And we are experiencing the evolution of our spiritual perception, by our yearning to reconcile with a greater and authentic reality and purpose beyond our ego-selves, and its embodiment within our human expression.

Such yearning is not to subjugate ourselves to others but rather to empower ourselves as individuated sparks of the Divine and to become co-creative participants in what we know, in the unconditional love of the universal heart, to be our destiny.

Relationships with others

We see mirrored in others, the challenges and issues with which we continue to struggle. And in our relationships with our families, friends and communities and our collective relationships on a global basis, we see reflected the steps of our journey into wholeness

So let us now look at these wider relationships, at how we may see them in a new light and aspire to reconciliation and a future, which embraces the wholeness of our collective destiny.

CHAPTER 10

ONE HEART

There are more than six billion people living on Earth today. And every one of us is descended from a small group of anatomically modern humans who once roamed the plains of East Africa between 150,000 and 200,000 years ago.

Tracing back key aspects of our genetic lineage, such as the mitochondrial DNA passed down the female line and the Y chromosome passed through the male, strongly suggests that this original group may have only totalled a few thousand people.

Since then, what we identify in our modern global population as ethnic characteristics, including skin colour, has evolved from the differentiation of only a few nucleotides, the building blocks of the DNA molecule, amongst the billions comprising our DNA.

Our apparent ethnic diversity is truly only skin deep and the richness of our behavioural characteristics is overwhelmingly derived from a combination of our cultural heritage, our individual personalities and the circumstances of our life's journey.

Underlying and emphasising the totality of the collective coherence of our human family, geneticists have discovered that there is twice as much variation in the mitochondrial DNA of a family group of chimpanzees living on a single hillside in Africa than across the entirety of the human race now living.

The complexity of our inter-breeding over millennia has also meant that whatever our appearance, each and every one of us, to a greater or lesser degree, embodies a diverse ethnic heritage which writer Steve Olson has described as a patchwork quilt stitched together from the DNA of our ancestors.

If we can learn to celebrate, rather than fear such diversity and recognise the underlying unity that births its creative abundance, we can surely begin to heal the rifts which have divided us for so long.

Human affairs

In the last chapter, we briefly explored ways in which perennial wisdom has guided human awareness towards self-realisation and the ways in which each of us undergoes an inner journey that is both unique for everyone and yet universal to human experience.

Whilst recognising its individual expression, such universality offers us ways in which to reconcile our differences and establish sustainable harmony within human affairs.

Two thousand years ago, Jesus expressed the golden rule as, *'do unto others as you would be done by'*. Its simple message asks us to treat every single individual within the human family, as we would ask for them to treat us.

Without ignoring or condoning harmful behaviour or proposing a generic relativism that sees every action as equally acceptable, it guides us towards inclusion and away from exclusion, towards authentic behaviour and away from artifice and towards justice and away from exploitation.

But in the complexity and apparent chaos of human affairs, how can we discern the possibility of order, not imposed by hierarchical controls but brought about through individual and collective empowerment?

To begin with, can it be possible that the same order and resonance, which underlies the complexity of natural systems throughout the universe, also apply to human affairs? And if so, are such insights, combined with the guidance of perennial wisdom, able to offer us a way forward?

To try to answer these questions, let us begin with the lessons of history.

History and the critical state.

Whilst historians study history for a variety of reasons, ultimately their concern and our own interest in the past is to understand the journey which has led us individually and collectively to this point in time. We want to appreciate what we have done that has engendered benefits, and perhaps even more importantly, to understand our perceived mistakes and seek to identify ways of avoiding them in the future.

During the last few chapters, we have explored many different complex systems that exhibit the characteristics of the critical state – open to outside influences, far from equilibrium and close to the edge of instability.

The apparent chaotic behaviour of such systems belies their underlying simplicity and order, which obeys the resonant principles of power laws and which reveals their scale-invariant and thus fractal and holographic nature.

We have considered how these naturally occurring power laws are helping to explain phenomena such as weather patterns and the occurrence of earthquakes. But can their principles be applied to the interactions of human societies?

It appears that they can.

War

Let us first consider the natural example of earthquakes and how they come about. We now know that the crust of the Earth's surface is made up of about twelve so-called tectonic plates, which gradually move in relation to each other and in so doing create stress in their constituent rocks.

The innate friction within and between the layers of rock, which bear the stress, prevents its immediate release. But sooner or later, as the stress increases beyond a threshold level, the rocks suddenly give way and an earthquake ensues.

As we have seen, the non-linearity, which is characteristic of such systems, means that a small additional stress can result in a minor or major earthquake and only when such events are statistically analysed are they seen to obey simple rules.

In the case of earthquakes, this is known as the Gutenberg-Richter power law and states that as the power of an earthquake doubles, its occurrence becomes four times less frequent.

Back in the 1920s, and over half a century before the development of computers and scientific advances that enabled the mathematical framework of complexity theory to be developed, physicist Lewis Richardson sought to understand whether reasons for the catastrophic breakdown in human relations, which result in warfare, could be analysed.

Richardson considered over eighty conflicts that took place between 1820 and 1929. And to judge their scale he considered the number of deaths reported in each war and plotted them against the number of conflicts.

What Richardson found was a power law – and one in which the relationship between the scale of a conflict and its frequency followed exactly the same relationship as Gutenberg and Richter found much later, also applies to earthquakes.

Further analysis by Jack Levy in the 1980s refined Richardson's approach by relating the death toll of a particular conflict to the global population at the time of its occurrence.

Levy reviewed the fatalities associated with wars ranging from that of the League of Venice in 1495 right up to the Vietnam War of the 1970s. He too found that they followed a power law – albeit given his refinement of Richardson's methodology, one where a doubling of casualties equates to wars that are 2.62 times less frequent.

Like the natural phenomena described by such laws, the scale of the cataclysms of warfare are unable to be specifically predicted. And an apparently small insurgency can become a major conflagration.

Because of its power law characteristics, whilst general causes or trends may help to account for warfare in general, the specific reasons for a particular war are also unable to be fully determined. However, what is apparent and undeniable is that imbalances within societies, if un-addressed and un-adjusted, build up fault lines of stress - which may, without any warning give way.

And peace

Our communities comprise fabrics woven from political, social, cultural and economic threads of inter-connection and influence.

The influences that pervade such inherent connectivity, are manifold and take place on many levels of awareness. Whilst we are consciously aware of some of these, many are subliminal and indeed include influences emanating from higher levels of consciousness, which we may only become aware of as our perception expands.

Such influences are non-linear too. As we know from our own experience, an apparently insignificant cause can have a major effect. And equally, an apparently significant impact can appear to have an important effect in the short term but over the longer term it can be seen to have been transient and insubstantial.

Awareness of stresses and the flexibility to engender the ongoing adjustments needed to prevent their build-up is a pre-requisite to limiting – but almost certainly never eradicating – their effects.

In the case of conflicts and their ultimate expression in warfare, the influence for peace and the third way of active reconciliation is the balance between conflict 'resolution' by unilateral imposition, and its perpetration.

As in personal resolution, the ability to forgive does not condone or indeed forget the initial act. What it does in reality is to release and free the one able to forgive from the imprisonment of corrosive pain and anger.

But now let us consider other influences, which affect us every day of our lives - those that relate to economics.

Economics and the critical state

Throughout history, rulers, governments and more recently corporations, have sought political and social influence and control through the management of economics. But despite the different means and motivations of their various interventions, it appears that here too, there are underlying and simple principles that belie the complexity of their expression.

Before Benoit Mandelbrot began to investigate fractal geometry and the underlying order of chaotic systems, in the 1960s he focused his attention on seeking to understand the fluctuations of financial markets and the way in which the prices of commodities such as cotton, varied on the New York Stock Exchange.

What he discovered was that the rise and fall of stock prices follows a familiar power law and thus that economics too is subject to the same principles that were later found to underlie other complex systems.

In the 1980s, and aided by increasing computer power, the methods that had been developed to investigate such systems, were applied to economics by Brian Arthur and others.

The classical theories of economics deal with systems that are assumed to be close to equilibrium. And in their classical analyses, such systems obey linear rules. In other words a small intervention results in a correspondingly small outcome. For example, the sales of a marginally better product creates a marginally increased return or profit.

But Arthur recognised, as Mandelbrot had done previously, that economic systems - like warfare and earthquakes - are non-linear and thus inputs are not directly matched to corresponding outputs.

By treating economics as dynamic open systems that involve feedback and through which energy - in the form of money – flows, their innate nature may be revealed. And whilst incredibly complex on the surface, their underlying holographic principles are again simple and the same as those inherent to a vast array of natural phenomena.

Influences

From the study of what is being termed the physics of society, it is emerging that the behaviour of both naturally occurring complex systems and those relating to human societies seem to be subject to the same underlying principles.

As we have seen, all such systems involve continual interaction and influence between their various elements.

Human intervention and influence, such as governmental sanctions on the export or import of major commodities, or the influence of a large-scale war, if sufficiently great, can affect a socio-economic system in a significant way;. But as we have seen with other non-linear complexity, such influences have specific outcomes that cannot be predicted. And the non-linear effects of small adjustments are highly unlikely to be able to be managed or determined.

We influence each other in ways that are great and small and our human family of over six billion people is intimately and closely connected. And it is the 'sound' of such influences, which ripple throughout the system and whose energy resonates with others to create the dynamic interference patterns of our entire cultural, political and economic inter-relationships that make up our collective experience.

And so in the horrors of war, the interplay of economics and the ebb and flow of cultural trends, we see the same fractal geometry and the workings of the holographic principle as throughout the natural world.

But how do such influences permeate our perceptions and lives?

To understand this, we need to recognise that it is a small world.

Six degrees of freedom

In 1967, psychologist Stanley Milgram decided to test the reality of this anecdotal truism by writing a series of letters to a number of people in Kansas and Nebraska.

In the letters, he explained that he was attempting to make contact with a friend of his in Boston. And he asked the recipients of the letters, to pass them on to anyone they felt might help the letter reach his Boston friend.

The nub of the test however, was that Milgram only gave the name and profession of his friend, but no details of his address in Boston.

He then sat back to see what happened.

Incredibly, all the letters eventually reached his friend in Boston. And in tracing the paths of every one, he found that they had each passed through about five intervening contacts and had thus taken about six steps to reach their correct destination.

The successful completion of Milgram's test gave rise to the familiar notion of 'six steps of separation'. And intriguingly, perennial wisdom perceives in the number six, the ordered integration of structure and function, and the embodiment of the maximum efficiency in the use of energy.

Small worlds

In 1998, mathematicians Duncan Watts and Steve Strogatz decided to study networks and the principles that underlie Milgram's findings.

They began by mathematically modelling the linkages within graphs – grids of dots connected by straight lines - with the dots of their model representing people and the linking lines, their connections to each other.

They combined the features of a regular graph where the grid forms an ordered pattern looking like figure 10.1a and a random graph

where the links are randomly distributed and which looks like figure
10.1b. And by taking the regular graph and simply replacing at
random a few of its ordered links by ones of random length, they
arrived at a graph looking like figure 10.1c.

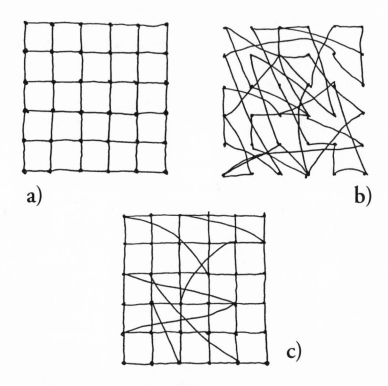

*Figs 10.1 The ordered but inflexible communication of graph a),
the random but unfocused connections of graph b), and the
small world of graph c).*

This hybrid form of graph depicted by figure 10.1c, combines the
clustering which is characteristic of social groups and which is
indicative of a regular graph and the freedom of movement enabled
by the short-cuts of the random graph.

In other words, they had discovered the principles of a small world. And to determine whether their small-world graphs applied in the 'real' world, they turned to playacting.

The details of cast lists for American films go back over half a century and provided Watts and Strogatz with an ideal network of connections to study. In starting with a particular actor, they were then able to identify his connections – via appearing on the same cast list as other actors and through his cast colleagues on their various films, connections with other actors and ultimately back to the actor they started with.

The actor Kevin Bacon's appearances in a large number of films without being the lead actor, made him 'special', and caused them to choose him. And their analysis showed that within three or four steps, Bacon was connected with every other film actor in the entire filmography of the network.

Further analysis has confirmed that indeed, whilst a fine actor, Mr Bacon is indeed not special in his acting connections and that the film world is indeed small.

But the investigation of small worlds has other more important insights to offer than filmography. It shows how a few random connections within a network are able to substantially extend its influence and the speed by which such influence is spread.

And such influence can of course be benign or malign.

The spread of infectious diseases is an example of how a malign influence can extend through such a network. But a deeper understanding of how such networks operate also enables the development of more effective strategies to combat and minimise such malign effects.

In February 2003, the first case of SARs was reported in Hong Kong, but within only a few days, cases were being reported throughout Asia, Canada and Germany. In seeking to understand its spread the doctors of the World Health Authority recognised that carriers – the shortcuts in the small world network - were travelling by air and thus were both rapidly and potentially disastrously extending the network influence of the outbreak.

And by understanding the underlying nature of its spread, effective steps could be quickly taken.

Global communications and the extent of international travel are making our small world ever smaller. And as we shall now also see, some worlds are inherently smaller than others.

The Internet and the World Wide Web

The global communications and information networks of the Internet and the World Wide Web are a combined self-sustaining complex system, although no one planned it this way.

The initial structure of the Net was based on ideas put forward by communications engineer Paul Baran. In the early era of centralised computer processing, Baran radically suggested a highly decentralised, or distributed, network where each computer 'node' is connected to several others.

Whilst incorporating a high level of redundancy, such a network is robust, flexible and less vulnerable to attack.

Baran's communications ideas were called upon in 1967 by computer scientist Wesley Clark when designing a pioneering database system for US military-sponsored universities to share information.

Over two decades later, computer scientist Tim Berners-Lee provided the third and final key to set in place the foundations for the global network – a gift he gave freely to the world. By devising the computer language of hypertext to uniquely identify information he thus enabled documents to be hyper-linked to any and all others throughout the system.

But from these rudimentary beginnings, the entire system has grown organically without a master plan. Essentially the Net and the Web have evolved into what many analysts describe as an ecosystem, where it is no longer possible to draw a comprehensive map of its connectivity pattern – the structure is already too vast, complex and deeply embedded for it to be traced.

Nonetheless, it appears to have self-developed the highly redundant and distributed topology initially proposed by Baran.

In 1999, Réka Albert, Hawoong Jeong and Albert-László Barábasi, sent a robot into the Web in an attempt to map its pathways. Given its already huge scale, they limited its investigation to their university database which itself comprised over three hundred thousand documents and about one and a half million connective links.

And what they found was that once again, when they analysed the number of incoming and outgoing links, that they followed the scale-invariant rules of a power law.

Anyone who sets up a document on the web is free to decide how many outgoing links to specify and of course is unable to control how many incoming links their web page attracts. Yet from this free multiplicity of choices is derived a law of fundamental and harmonic order.

The Net and the Web have co-organised themselves into a small world network, but one throughout which the relationships of data and communications are resonantly fractal and thus scale-invariant and holographic.

The specific pattern of their power law adherence shows that the probability of finding a node point in the system with a large number of connective pathways to other node points is far higher than for the distribution that applies to the scale-dependent small world graphs of Watts and Strogatz.

The scale-free nature of the Net and the Web allows them to continue to grow and evolve whilst still enabling the access pathways to information to be maintained. And as a result, they are leading the way in the development of new cultural and institutional structures that are decentralised and non-hierarchical.

The global community

The exponential increase in such communications is essentially creating the holographic field of a global community. Carl Jung's collective unconscious is rapidly becoming a collective consciousness mediated through the electro-magnetic interplay that is facilitating the emergence of the noosphere – the global mind of Gaia.

After hundreds of thousands of years of family-based independence, over the last ten millennia the human race has progressively evolved our inter-relationships to dependency and now co-dependency.

As the inflexibility of our established institutions are proving no longer able to support our burgeoning inter-dependency, it is flexibility, the empowerment of individuals and their coming together as co-creative participants that will need to be our watch-words to a sustainable collective future.

We have rights as human beings – as indeed does all life – but we also have commensurate responsibilities.

And as the prescience of minister Martin Luther King cautioned us - we either swim together as brothers or we drown alone.

Our issues on a personal scale are mirrored and exacerbated at the larger fractal levels of our families, societies and on a global scale. When we heal the one, we heal the whole.

As such our co-operation with each other is a fundamental requirement. And the necessity of our developing better ways to collectively co-operate and adjust for societal tensions is urgent.

Tit for tat

As individuals living in a society, we can regard co-operation as being law abiding and offending as breaking the law for one's own gain at someone else's expense. The fact is that, whilst co-operation may be beneficial, as everyone has ruefully noted at one point or another, selfish and anti-social behaviour can reap material rewards that are as great or even greater.

So with this in mind, how can societies evolve ways in which co-operation prevails?

In the 1970s political scientist Robert Axelrod devised an experiment to investigate how people came to co-operate when there was the opportunity to offend and where, if taken, individual advantage could be gained.

Axelrod did so by inviting professional games theorists to submit strategies for the co-operation or otherwise between two agents, which gave the best cumulative outcome as measured by the benefits of mutual trust and harmonious relationships.

The key to Axelrod's game was however, that the two agents were unable to communicate with each other and thus explain their positions or negotiate – a situation not uncommon in human affairs.

The fourteen entries to Axelrod's game proposed a variety of strategies, but the tournament was eventually won by the simplest approach - that submitted by Anatol Rapaport and which he termed Tit For Tat or TFT.

The only rules of Rapaport's strategy were that the game began by the two participants co-operating and thereafter a participant did whatever their opponent had done in the previous round.

By mirroring their opponent, TFT ensures adaptation to whatever the situation calls for – if an opponent is co-operative, the second agent will co-operate. But if one agent offends, the other will react accordingly. So, in situations where one agent does not know the other, the flexibility of TFT enables both to reap the benefits of co-operation where possible but neither can be exploited.

Another significant aspect of TFT is that its strategy is one that commences with co-operation, and Axelrod found that all such strategies ultimately do better than those that begin by offending.

Following the games tournament, Axelrod identified four characteristics of a successful strategy. Don't be the first to offend. Always reciprocate. Don't be too clever – in effect respond rather than second-guess. And don't be envious, in other words do the best you can for yourself (and those you represent) without trying to out-do the other agent.

Choice

Axelrod's tournament demonstrated the benefits of co-operation, and we may indeed be predisposed to co-operation. Biologist

Edward O. Wilson has argued that as civilisation evolved, such modes of human behaviour will have been converted from such instinctive impulses – observed in other animals - to social norms, legal imperatives and the impulse of moral principles. Essentially we return full circle to what we consider as being 'natural' justice.

But a fundamental aspect of Rapaport's TFT strategy is its assumed lack of communication between the two agents involved. Its simple rules do not allow for any other than the prescriptive tit-for-tat response to an offence. But if that offence is not deliberate, but a mistake, not only does TFT respond with a further offence but the strategy becomes locked into and is unable to escape from such a cycle.

Human fallibility means that TFT is unable to offer a means of harmonious resolution, and its strategy needs to be modified. And when it offers the choice to allow for some offences to either go unpunished or for an agent to decline to retaliate to an offence, which follows an offence of their own – the strategy takes on a more benevolent sustainability.

So, what happens when agents learn from their past mistakes and evolve a deeper understanding of each other?

In 1992, games theorists Martin Nowak and Karl Sigmund decided to find out.

Reconciliation

Nowak and Sigmund simulated a diverse variety of strategies involving co-operation and offence. In all of which the choice of whether to co-operate or offend was taken in response to what the opponent did in the previous round.

Through hundreds of thousands of iterations, they discovered an ebbing and flowing as co-operation and offence won through. But eventually after two earlier outbreaks of co-operation, which then succumbed to a reassertion of offending, there emerged the evolution of a third and sustainable co-operative environment.

These researchers have shown that tit for tat responses are unable to ever get out of a pattern of offending, as has been the prevailing tragedy throughout the Middle East and Northern Ireland.

Only by being willing to forgive a degree of fallibility by both sides or by being willing to be contrite, will the pattern be broken and the opportunity for peace emerge.

Reconciliation requires honesty, a willingness to forgive and an attitude of respect and inclusion. In South Africa, following the end of apartheid, brokered by courageous and visionary leaders, the courts of truth and reconciliation aimed to do just that. Without denying or condoning the widespread abuses which had prevailed under the apartheid regime, they sought to openly acknowledge those years, bring to justice the perpetrators and release individuals and society from their collective guilt and anger.

But South Africa had two major advantages. In F.W. de Klerk, they had a courageous leader willing to embrace radical change. And in Nelson Mandela, a visionary and wise future leader who was himself able to authentically forgive nearly three decades of incarceration.

For communities to move forward in this way, leaders of vision who are willing to truly embody the aspirations of their people within themselves are the primary catalysts for change.

And more and more, it will be the empowerment of people throughout societies, who themselves are able to embody that aspiration and vision, that will bring about lasting peace.

The Universal Heart

Hierarchical institutions are inherently inflexible. And like organisms they become extinct where they are unable to adapt to new circumstances.

As we have seen, the reach of our individual and collective influences at all scales of our global society is changing exponentially - and flexibility, co-creativity and relative balance are key to our collective future.

Global trade and communications, if not already, are carrying us to an imminent state of global inter-dependency. No longer is it feasible to have an attitude of 'not in my back yard'.

And as we have seen throughout *The Wave*, our collective social networks have all the hallmarks of scale-invariant ecosystems. And we are beginning to see that their fractal geometries, which reveal innate coherence and resonance on all scales throughout Nature, apply to us too.

Novelist Ian McEwan noted that as the unbearable horror of the 11th of September 2001 unfolded, the last messages from the people who perished in the New York conflagration were of love.

And as the almost unimaginable human suffering of the catastrophe of the Asian tsunami of 26th December 2004 continued, our initial reactions of shock and horror were almost immediately overwhelmed by our feelings of compassion and a desire to offer help, in whatever way we could.

On that bright September morning in New York, people of many nationalities died. And during those terrible few days throughout south-east Asia, hundreds of thousands of men, women and children perished and twelve nations were devastated.

We commonly aver that we speak our deepest truths from the heart. And as we reconcile our hearts, minds and wills in the universal heart of humanity, in love and not fear, we can come together to resolve ancient rifts and re-establish the sustaining balance of natural justice.

The energetic awareness of the eighth chakra – the universal heart of humanity - marries the compassion of our hearts, with the clarity of our minds and the co-creative courage of our will, and embraces and transcends our sense of self into the loving service of and fellowship with all life.

Eight cosmic principles

There is an octave, an eight-fold group of cosmic principles, which, in their various expressions, throughout history and across all cultures, form the basis of perennial wisdom. In the wholeness of their embodiment, they resonate to the fundamental harmony by which consciousness expresses itself and which we have explored throughout *The Wave*.

Together, they may be perceived as guiding our experience of co-creation and act as way-showers for our journey home into wholeness.

The principle of balance describes the principle that throughout all dimensions and realms of the Cosmos, the energies of consciousness ultimately seek to come into balance. But only at the highest level of perception, that of Source, is unity consciousness fully revealed. At all other levels of consciousness, the aspiration towards the wholeness of such balance guides the experiences and evolution of awareness.

The principle of polarity, or relativity is probably best represented in the ancient Chinese expression of yin and yang. Polarities pervade the Cosmos and within each polarity, as in the yin-yang symbol, is the seed of its partner.

For much of our recent history, we have perceived such cosmic polarities as being separate and expressed as their extremes of light and shadow. But by describing their interplay as expressing their inherent relationship - or relativity - rather than 'polarity' or 'duality', we can perceive the innate dance between them. And it is through their relationship – and its ultimate balance - that consciousness is experienced.

Whilst incarnating on the physical plane as a man or woman, we embody *both* male (yang) and female (yin) aspects on emotional, mental and higher levels of vibration. And the balance of their relationship within us forms an innate and crucial aspect of our journey into wholeness.

But in seeking the wholeness of who we really are, we also need to acknowledge and embrace, not only these cosmic essences of 'male' and 'female', but that of the cosmic 'child' within us. And it is this third and reconciling aspect of the wholeness of the trinity that births our creativity – a new way of being, which joyously and openly explores the Cosmos and its experiences

Our choices are ultimately between those of love and fear.

When through the illusion of separation, our feelings and choices are based on fear – our entire being essentially shuts down.

But as we have seen in Chapter 9, when we feel love – not as needy dependency, but as an unconditional joyous reality – our entire being resonates with the wholeness of the Cosmos.

The principle of correspondence expresses the resonant interconnection through all things and experiences of the principles and primary energetic forces of the Cosmos.

Such correspondences are inherent to the expression of the holographic principle. And as we have seen, they are found in all aspects and at all scales throughout the physical world. The wisdom of this perception, is embodied in the ancient Egyptian and hermetic teachings of '*as above, so below*' and the fractal and holographic nature of the Cosmos

We are energetic beings. And so, as we have seen, the energies of how and what we think and feel resonate on both inner and outer levels. And such resonance finds its correspondence in the situation of our health and the circumstances of our life.

As our awareness expands, we become more coherent in our energy patterns. In doing so, we become more authentic and embody greater integrity. And both the resonance and the coherence of the higher vibrations of our intention and attention corresponds with the underlying harmony of the Cosmos

The principle of reflection describes this outer mirroring of our inner circumstances. The opportunity to develop self-awareness and move towards inner balance is reflected in the outer circumstances of our experience, as individuals, families and on the levels of societies and globally. When we heal the one, we heal the whole.

The principle of change underlies the gaining of awareness through experience of individuated consciousness and the evolution to higher vibrational frequencies. This is accomplished through the continuous co-creation of change - challenge or opportunity depending on our perspective – that is intrinsic to our experience and the development of self-awareness.

The principle of cause and effect is the wider metaphysical context of the physical law of every action producing an equal and opposite reaction. Linked to the principle of balance, within the experiences of consciousness, such action – reaction processes are ultimately equalised.

Both the principles of change and of cause and effect are contained in the ancient Vedic concept of *karma*, whose essence represents the flow of the energies expressing consciousness and, as understood by perennial wisdom, is not a reflection of perceived morality or the judgement by others or by a higher consciousness of our actions.

Nonetheless, as our awareness expands, we become profoundly perceptive of the wholeness of the Cosmos and naturally align our choices to its ultimate unity. And in our doing so, the energies of the implications of our choices become balanced and *karma* is resolved and released.

The principle of conservation reflects the continuous flow of energy that applies throughout the Cosmos. Again, this is the metaphysical expression, which equates to the law of physics, that applies throughout the physical world, in that whilst the form that energies take may change, they are ultimately conserved.

And in order to enable the flow of energies to be balanced in our own experience, the principle of conservation requires us to both give and receive, and to allow the ebb and flow of the waves of life to pass harmoniously through us.

Finally, the eighth cosmic principle which completes the octave of the expression of consciousness, ***the principle of allowance*** is linked to the principle of cause and effect. It maintains that once an intention is set and manifested, allowance of its consequences forms part of the learning and integration of the experience and the development of our greater awareness.

Return to Gaia

And now we will explore how the unfolding of our wholistic understanding of the Cosmos is showing us the urgent need and the ways to re-establish our relationship with Gaia.

CHAPTER 11

ONE WORLD

Since the 1970s, the increasingly urgent rallying call of environmental groups has been the need to 'Save the Earth'.

Given our careless and aggressive polluting of Gaia and the rape of her resources, such sentiments are eminently appropriate and laudable.

But we should be under no illusions. Gaia can take good care of herself. Global climate change and our rampant exhaustion of the natural resources we rely upon to support the lifestyles of over six billion people, will not destroy the Earth – they will destroy the human race.

Restoring our harmony with the environment and re-connecting with the physical and metaphysical realms of Gaia is ultimately about preserving humanity. We are the ones who need to re-learn that our planetary home is the only home we have – at least for the foreseeable future.

And as the philosopher Saint Exupery also reminds us, we do not inherit the Earth from our parents, we borrow it from our children.

To paraphrase Einstein, it is also a truism that a problem cannot be solved using the same thoughts or approach, which caused it in the first place. To re-establish our relationship with Gaia, rather than continuing a futile and self-destructive attempt to control her, we need to co-operate with her cycles and rhythms rather than seek to overcome or ignore them. And we need to hear once again, the voice of her wisdom.

Harmonious technologies

The fossilised materials, primarily coal, petroleum and natural gas, which have fuelled the industrial processes of the nineteenth and twentieth centuries are malign in their environmental impacts, non-renewable and are being exponentially depleted.

The industrialisation of China, India and other emerging nations are also adding dramatic levels of further stress to the demand for energy, and the view of most experts is that the global availability of oil has already peaked and has begun its inevitable decline.

It has been estimated that OPEC, the oil-producing cartel of the Middle East, will need to produce close to capacity during the winter of 2005 in the main to meet China's growing energy needs. And new oil recovery programmes, even discounting their adverse environmental impacts, are highly unlikely to be able to meet the projected rising demand.

Any resumption in the use of nuclear fission would also surely be a retrograde and deeply disturbing prospect. Whilst potentially easing the challenges of developing alternative energy strategies, unless new technologies of decontamination are discovered, it would result in an inheritance of poison, not only for our children and their children but for many more generations beyond.

In a world whose human population continues to increase, the search for renewable, environmentally responsible and sustainable alternative energy sources and technologies is now urgent.

But given the likely timescales to transition to new technologies and the installation of their requisite infrastructures, we need not only to continue and intensify the search, but also to significantly reduce our overall use of energy.

We cannot afford to allow the colossal waste inherent in current technologies to continue and on all levels of our societies we must overcome our ignorance and carelessness in our everyday energy usage.

Waste not, want not

It is estimated that between the point at which it is generated, to its place of end-use, over two-thirds of the total electricity produced throughout the world is wasted - lost as heat from the electricity grids of wires and cables which transport the energy from place to place.

Whilst government and utilities companies will all need to undertake significant investment to mitigate this issue, what can each of us do individually?

Perhaps surprisingly, there are two simple actions we can put into immediate effect, and which have significant impacts on our use of electricity.

We can save up to three-quarters of the electricity we currently use to run such electrical appliances as televisions and computers if, rather than keeping on their stand-by mode, we simply switch them off.

And by turning down the thermostat of our centrally heated homes or workplaces by only one degree centigrade we can save on average an estimated ten percent of our overall heating costs - or for those of us with air conditioning, reducing the cooling of our homes one degree would have the same benefit.

But not only do we waste energy resources directly, we do so indirectly in the vast amounts of materials we throw away. Significantly reducing the volume of such waste and recycling materials wherever possible are now urgent measures we all need to take.

In addition to segregating our waste materials and lobbying for and using recycling facilities wherever possible, we as consumers have individually and collectively more empowerment than perhaps we realise.

We can for example lobby manufacturers and retailers to minimise product packaging, phase out the use of plastics, wherever possible and introduce biodegradable packaging in their place.

We can encourage manufacturers to make products for which spares are more easily and cost-effectively available. And we can be more discerning in buying products, which have longer lives and replaceable parts, rather than those which are disposable or which become obsolescent in the short-term.

To date, the adverse environmental and indirect energy impacts of products have rarely been required to be borne by the manufacture. Because such impacts have been seen as being 'external' to the manufacturing process, their costs have not been included in the price of the product, and so such imbalances and adverse practices have been perpetrated.

But some governments are beginning to legislate for the full costs of buildings, cars and consumer durables to be accounted for, including the impacts of pollution throughout their entire lifecycles and the cost of their ultimate disposal. And so, as property developers and manufacturers become obliged to consider the entirety of the impacts of their products, these will be progressively reflected in their prices – enabling consumers to choose options based on real costs.

We face huge challenges in making a transition from where we currently are to where we need to be, and we will only be able to do so if we act collectively and responsibly. In overcoming them, we will either all be winners, or our selfishness and lack of care and foresight will make us all losers.

Sunlight

The sunlight, which reaches the Earth over a twenty-four hour period, has more energy than all the conventional oil that has ever been or will ever be extracted from the planet. And so the development of technologies, which directly or indirectly harness solar power, is at the forefront of the search for alternatives to fossil fuels.

Solar panels of various kinds, photovoltaic cells that convert solar energy into electricity and other systems that store the thermal energy of sunlight are becoming more effective and cheaper, as the take-up of these technologies is economically encouraged.

Another approach, where energy is again ultimately derived from sunlight, is the utilisation of organic materials, from which we have benefited since our distant ancestors began to build fires from wood.

Such biofuels are essentially non-fossilised equivalents of coal and oil. Whilst they do release the greenhouse gas of carbon dioxide, their continuing replenishment with growing plants breathing in carbon dioxide from the atmosphere enable their net emissions to be balanced.

The natural resources comprising the biomass from which such fuels are derived, not only include fast growing woods and grasses but otherwise waste products, such as parts of the leaves and stalks of maize and wheat that remain after the grains are harvested (called stover), and the pulp left after sugarcane stalks are crushed to extract their juice (called bagasse).

Effective biofuels are also derived from many other animal and plant waste products such as silage and animal manures, and by being both produced and utilised at local levels, obviate the energy cost of long-distance transport.

And in addition to the ever-present benefits of sunlight, two other natural forces are being harnessed to produce energy that is abundant and environmentally safe.

Wind and water

Wind turbines are becoming a widespread feature of those landscapes that have predictable and consistent weather patterns and that produce sufficient wind power to make their use economic. But the appearance of such turbines is perhaps rightly being seen as blighting areas of natural beauty and their extended use may well be curtailed if other technologies are available.

And the power of moving water – from inland hydroelectric projects transforming the energy inherent in the flow of rivers, to the use of tidal barrages and technologies that benefit from the rhythms of coastal currents, continues to be utilised.

Technologies, which use the energies innate in water, namely hydrogen and oxygen are also being developed. Theoretically, the energy stored in the hydrogen atom – the most common atom in the universe, is sufficient to provide an unlimited and non-polluting resource when released. Whilst the technical difficulties however in effectively and safely harnessing and storing such energy are formidable, the potential rewards are so great that every effort must be made to support its attainment.

And as the insights of Viktor Schauberger into the implosive power of water are being rediscovered, we may hope that these too are able to be utilised in ways, which realise his dream of our working with and alongside Nature.

Deep heat

The combination of the pressure from overlying rocks and heat released from their natural radioactivity, means that the deeper we drill into the Earth, the higher is the temperature of the rocks themselves and of any water accumulated there.

The use of this natural heat, or geothermal energy, is clean, reliable and available everywhere. And a number of approaches to its extraction are already in use. Drilling wells to various depths either into aquifers – regions of underground water – or into hot dry rocks, offers a variety of techniques for providing high-pressure hot water or steam able to be used either directly for heating, or via heat pumps and heat exchangers for heating or cooling or to drive turbines and thus generate electricity.

The zero point field

The perhaps ultimate attainment of alternative energies would be to harness the unlimited energies innate in the zero-point field of quantum fluctuations, which pervades the entire universe. As yet, whilst there is a great deal of speculation and a number of suggested means by which extraction of such energy may be attained, it is as yet a dream – but one which may yet come true.

Fractal power

In the last chapter, we saw how the development of the Net and Web, have created essentially an electro-magnetic ecosystem, whose robustness and ability to self-organise is due to its distributed and fractal nature.

It may well be that, unlike the current reliance on fossil fuels, in the medium term, no single energy source will become predominant. Instead, unless and until we are able to safely and effectively harness for instance the almost unlimited energies embodied in hydrogen or even more amazingly, the zero point field, it is likely that we will need to generate energies from a variety of sources and through a range of techniques.

But many of the technologies now being developed, have the capability to directly or indirectly generate electricity, which where appropriate will have the ability to interconnect with regional grid networks.

The current infrastructure, updated and rendered more energy efficient Should then continue to be able to be utilised. Where any local generation of electricity exceeds local consumption, the excess can be fed into the grid and offset against the energy being taken from it. The technology to measure such two-way energy flow is already developed and such reverse meters are already installed in a number of countries.

During the next twenty years, it is almost certain that our ways of generating and using energy will change as radically, if not more so, as other aspects of our lives have during the last generation. And the search for sustainable and safe energy, whose generation and usage is in harmony with Gaia, will go on.

The food chain

Perhaps one of the most significant areas in which we have distanced ourselves from the natural rhythms and wisdom of Gaia is in the ways in which we now grow and process the food we eat.

In the last fifty years, the introduction of industrial production methods in farming and the radical moves on a global scale away from the poly-cultural diversity of crop growth to monocultures have been a revolution probably as far reaching as the first introduction of agricultural methods ten millennia ago.

But the methods of agri-business that have been developed over this time have involved massive use of artificial pesticides, which have resulted in the continuing depletion of soils and the destruction of eco-system balances.

As consumers, we are now literally spoilt for choice in foods, which look aesthetically appetising but which are generally full of artificial additives and residual toxins. And not only are such toxic additives endemic within the growing process itself, but to ensure food retains its appearance throughout its transport, storage and on the shelves of the supermarket, it undergoes yet more modification and artificial treatments.

The amount of 'convenience' food, snacks, fast food, processed 'ready meals' in our average diets and the extensive use of the microwave oven – which destroys nutritional values - was also unknown only a generation ago. And it is not surprising that the levels of allergies, food intolerances and obesity are now at epidemic levels in the US and UK. Besides this, symptoms of hyperactivity, aggression and an inability to concentrate among both children and adults are also progressively being linked to processed food.

The range of food we can buy is greater than it has even been – and yet it is making us ill! Incredibly during the years of the Second World War, when food was rationed, British people were healthier overall than they are in 2005. And after a more than fifteen-year health programme in the US to counter obesity, people are fatter than ever before.

But not only are we eating much food that is bad for us, a recent 2005 survey in the UK has also shown that overall, more than a quarter of food is thrown away unused – a statistic which is likely to be at least matched by the US.

Not only do we individually waste an enormous amount of perfectly edible food, but restaurants and food retailers do too. Such levels of waste are not only unacceptable in a world where people are still starving, but also have huge associated costs.

The two greatest factors in wastage related to food, are, the rejection of food that is only marginally past its sell-by date, even though it is nutritionally perfectly edible. And the discarding of fresh food, such as vegetables and fruit, which does not pass the stringent aesthetic appearance requirements of the retailers.

If retailers are to change their attitudes, we as consumers, need to change ours. Let us re-focus on the *real* issues of health and safety in our environment rather than the spurious ones we currently emphasise, such as the current regime of sell-by dates. And let us modify our attitudes to the appearance of food, and rather increase our focus on its nutritional aspects.

As we have recognised that fossil fuels have polluted our environment and are unsustainable, there is a growing realisation that the processed food, the inner 'fuel' developed for our 'convenience', is polluting our bodies and is equally unsustainable.

Just as we urgently need to radically re-think our outer energy resources, we need to do so for our inner energy resources too.

Respect

About ten millennia ago, in what is known as the Fertile Crescent, which geographically, is now where Europe and Asia meet, the beginnings of pastoralism and agriculture appear in the archaeological record.

The Fertile Crescent has native to it, four species of big mammals; cow, pig, sheep and goat. It appears that in these early times after the last Ice Age and throughout the world, many animal species had been 'auditioned' for domestication, but very few were chosen, then or subsequently, as the role is difficult to fulfil.

All four domesticated species are herbivores or omnivores with a docile disposition and a low tendency to panic. All four have a well-developed social structure in groupings with a dominant hierarchy, where humans can take over the 'leadership' role. Both within species and in combination, they tend to have over-lapping, relatively non-exclusive territories. All produce an array of secondary products and finally all are relatively prolific in breeding.

The mutual benefit to both humans and animals of their domestication has been termed co-evolutionary. But with the relatively recent adoption of factory methods to the raising of domesticated stock, has begun the sustained abuse of animals, who have been our evolutionary partners for ten thousand years.

Such methods are inimical to the animals they treat so callously. And the widespread use of growth hormones, and antibiotics to suppress the disease rampant in the appalling conditions endemic to most factory farming not only affects the animals, but inevitably the people who then consume their meats, eggs and dairy products.

Surely we cannot allow such abuse of our fellow creatures to continue.

All we have explored in *The Wave* has shown the inter-connection of the web of life. When an animal is reared in misery and killed inhumanely the energies of its pain are retained within its cellular structure. Is this the kind of food we want for ourselves and our families?

We have co-evolved with domesticated animals over millennia and by treating them honourably and humanely, we can re-establish a relationship that benefits us all.

Farming methods

From the very beginnings of agriculture, farmers have sought to improve the yields and qualities of their crops and biologically 'married' different plants to develop hybrid strains to attain those aims.

But until the genetic revolution of the 1990s, there had never been any intermingling of DNA between plant and animal species. Genetically modified (GM) crops however do just that and create hybrids, which would never naturally occur in Nature.

The potentially catastrophic implications of such truly unnatural technology are unknown and their effects both on the environment and on human beings, have not been tested to any significant degree.

And the claims by the biotechnology companies who have developed such GM products, for their increased productivity of such crops and their need for lower levels of pesticides are not only yet to be proven in the medium term, but their adverse effects on ecosystems are already obvious.

Until much more rigorous testing has taken place and we are fully convinced of their benefits and honestly aware of their adverse effects, we must be responsible and cautious and ban the expansion of such crops and clearly label their existing inclusion in products.

Inherently, GM crops are the technological outcome of a reductionist approach and are innately disharmonious with Gaia. And ongoing research is demonstrating that over the long term, organic farming methods, the re-introduction of poly-culture and permaculture, which work alongside Nature, are as productive as so-called factory methods and dramatically more sustainable.

As consumers, we collectively have enormous power. The supermarkets will not put on their shelves what we do not buy. And our lobbying can have significant success when it relates to the need for example to clearly label the inclusion of food additives or genetically modified ingredients or ban them outright.

We currently see a vast choice of relatively cheap food in our shops, but when the true costs of agri-business in terms of its high-energy usage, unfair and restrictive trade practices, environmental damage and adverse effects on human health are considered, such apparent abundance is shown to be illusory.

We do have viable alternatives and can reverse the current explosive and destructive cycle to a positive implosive one. Physiologically, our bodies have been used to certain patterns of foods, free from the currently enormous level of additives, for millennia. Moreover, we have historically grown food relatively locally and generally eaten it in season.

Re-focussing our intention and energies in finding beneficial solutions to our needs rather than our wants, may enable us to regain true and sustainable abundance, in balance and not in conflict with Gaia.

Clearing up after ourselves

Nearly four billion years ago the first life forms inhabiting Gaia were minute single celled microbes. Able to survive and indeed thrive in the extreme environment of the young planet, they still continue to be responsible for many of the processes that sustain Gaia and the entirety of biological life on Earth.

Science is now realising that such microbes may be used in what is called bio-mediation, to clear up toxic waste and groundwater contamination. Research is underway to determine whether microbes are able to capture carbon dioxide and produce hydrogen in sufficient quantities to be made economically viable.

And the recent discoveries by Masaru Emoto as we discussed in Chapter 7, of the ways in which the physical attributes of water are affected by and resonate to different frequencies of intention, may be able to be developed into powerful means of cleaning and vivifying water.

We need to hear the voice of Gaia and listen to her wisdom - to study and understand the deeper processes of her cycles and apply them in the development of resonant technologies, which seek to optimise rather than maximise returns and where we co-create win-win solutions to the urgent challenges we face together.

The sacred Earth

Perceiving our planet as a sacred being – the embodiment of Gaia – is fundamental to our directly experiencing her harmony and hearing the profound wisdom of her voice.

Our ancestors, and contemporary primary peoples demonstrate a profound empathy with the natural world and its rhythms. They 'feel' their way, incorporating within that process, empathy with the mountains, the caves, the rivers, the rocks and the trees of their environment, and the animals with whom they co-habit landscapes.

All are part of a living interconnected world of energy formed into matter, but fluid, flexible and changeable. Hunter and prey in this Cosmology are brothers-in-arms with a contract of honour and affection between them – and this empathy extends to all aspects of life. For example, constructing a dwelling or creating a monument requires a similar contract between the human builder and the materials used – and ritual and ceremony to co-create and maintain the harmonious relationship needed to ensure the best outcome for the project.

To harmonise and align with both Heaven and Earth, in the creation of sacred buildings, the ancient geomancers incorporated idealised geometries, alignments to the Heavens and the cardinal points of the Earth and incorporated physically and symbolically the balance of elemental forces.

The ancient geomancers of China, India and Britain were not only masters of their physical environment but also of its metaphysical realms and their subtle energies. And in order to benefit from the abundance of Gaia, they studied her rhythms and sought to live in harmony with them.

Subtle energies

Our current scientific understanding of the subtle energies which perennial wisdom perceives as pervading the Cosmos and from which the physical universe is derived, is rather like our understanding of electro-magnetism in the mid nineteenth century. Then the connection between electricity and magnetism was not understood, nor the nature of either. Yet now electro-magnetism forms the basis of the technologies that support our global economy.

A letter sent in 1919, to Albert Einstein by physicist Theodor Kaluza may be the key to our deeper understanding of such energies.

Kaluza had recognised that the mathematical description of Einstein's theory of relativity could be extended to a supra-physical universe with an additional large-scale spatial dimension. And the equations, which emerged from this higher-dimensional description of general relativity, were exactly those which the physicist James Clerk Maxwell had discovered in the nineteenth century that describe the electro-magnetic field.

Of the eighteen equations, which Maxwell originally devised to describe electro-magnetism, only four have been used to develop all the technologies that currently utilise electro-magnetic energy. Maxwell's genius and Kaluza's insights may yet demonstrate that the subtle energies, which interact with and inform the physical world, are higher dimensional attributes of the electro-magnetic field.

Geomancy

The ancient wisdom of the Chinese masters is embodied in the teachings of feng shui that encompass the resonant beliefs of Taoist philosophy. This holds that the Cosmos is an inter-connected matrix of correspondences in which actions on Earth can affect the Heavens and vice versa.

Perceiving the subtle energies of *ch'i* as pervading and vivifying the universe Feng shui seeks to create buildings that are in harmony with and are microcosms of the macrocosmic order.

Even earlier than the Chinese tradition, the sacred science of the Vedic culture of India is similarly enshrined in the teachings of *vaastu*. Here, the premise of a living Earth is extended to incorporate buildings as part of the living landscape.

For both traditions, the location, positioning, structural form and materials used are considered to be auspicious or not - in harmony with and nurtured by the living eco-system of physical and subtle energies – or not.

The aim of both traditions within the wider context of a human life lived wholly in harmony with the Cosmos, is to co-create buildings which resonate with their environment and their intended purpose and which nurture such balance and purpose in the people who live and work in them.

The two traditions however, tend to emphasize different aspects with regard to solving issues relating to the built environment. Feng shui tends to pragmatically seek solutions to problems of energetic imbalances, whilst often appearing to be less concerned with their underlying cause.

In contrast, vaastu tends to focus on the telluric and geomantic aspects of a particular situation, primarily offering idealised rather than practical suggestions. For example, if the proposed site for a new house is deemed unpropitious, a feng shui consultant might offer alleviating solutions, without necessarily seeking to resolve the innate cause of the problem. The advice of a vaastu consultant might well be to change site!

For both, the environments and cultures, which brought forward their understanding millennia ago, were radically different from what we experience today. They originated in times when the availability of land and feasible alternatives were far more prevalent than they are now.

Nowadays, most of us live in older houses rather than new, specially commissioned homes. And we live and work on land, which energetically embodies the historical imprints of previous human occupation and events.

Most of our homes and other buildings were built without taking account of such geomantic wisdom, and the focus of most geomancers today is primarily remedial, seeking to alleviate those issues, which are inherent in the site or building and the restoration of harmony.

As such, it is not only helpful but also necessary for us to understand and differentiate between what is perennial in the ancient wisdom and what is environmentally and culturally specific.

Empowerment

In common with the experiential wisdom of the Earth's primary peoples, all geomantic traditions stress the inter-connectedness of the Cosmos, which as we have seen throughout *The Wave* is being verified and enhanced by the discoveries of wholistic science.

They also perceive the primacy of consciousness and the influence of higher vibrational energies creating and pervading the universe.

Most of these ancient Cosmologies, however, saw our human experience as being at the behest of greater forces over which we have little influence. Depending on whether a culture viewed the Cosmos as uncertain and chaotic or discerned an underlying order, the interaction with such forces were attempts either to derive a temporary respite or to sustain innate harmony.

The shamanistic cultures of the Americas, Asia and Africa have tended towards the former view, whereas geomantic cultures such as those of China, India and Egypt tended towards the latter.

The shamanistic traditions have emphasized direct experience and intuitive wisdom, seeking to walk lightly on the Earth and in harmony with nature. And the shamans of such traditions hear and are intuitively guided by the subtle voices of the spirits of Nature.

The ancient geomantic cultures, in contrast, followed a more intellectual path, and perceived the cosmic cycles of space and time and the inherent harmony of creation as embodied in sacred geometry, music and number.

The universal principles of their combined wisdom balance heart and mind – intuitive attunement and mental acuity.

However, whilst such perennial wisdom reveals deep insights into the realities of the Cosmos, today's wholistic science is enabling still more profound comprehension, taking our spiral of perception to new heights.

One crucial development from the teachings of the shamans and geomancers of old, is that of personal empowerment. Within the priesthoods and metaphysical traditions of the ancient world, adherence to prescribed teachings was stressed. And to attain the understanding of the techniques of sacred science and accomplish the inner search for enlightenment, the involvement of a *guru* or teacher, was required.

The experience of the last three centuries has, especially in the West, supported social and intellectual individuality. And the discoveries of the new wisdom facilitate personal empowerment. Where they differ is between the lonely separation of a materialistic worldview and that of the new wisdom, where the aim is to balance and harmonise individual ego with the collective and cosmic whole.

Our exploration of the holographic principles of resonance which pervade the Cosmos and which underlie such shamanistic and geomantic traditions, will enable us to bring greater awareness in perceiving and understanding the causes of energetic imbalances and our own growing intuitive insights will progressively facilitate their resolution.

Dowsing

The ancient art of dowsing, where nonlocal awareness is utilised to discover things that are beyond the five physical senses, has, over the last few years enjoyed a resurgence. Whilst dowsing for water or water divining is the best known and most common use of dowsing skills, practitioners can attune themselves to dowse for virtually anything.

Utility companies in a number of countries including Britain, employ dowsers as a matter of unpublicised course for the finding, not only of water, but for example, to rediscover buried gas pipes and electricity cables whose paths have been forgotten. And mining companies also employ dowsers to find and trace mineral deposits and estimate their extent.

The process of dowsing involves the energetic attunement by the dowser to whatever he or she is seeking to find - similar to tuning a wireless or television to the wavelength of a particular radio or television station.

Such attunement is essentially the same as the nonlocal awareness achieved by remote viewers. And for most dowsers, such awareness appears to be subliminal and registered by a bodily reaction – as is often the case for psi responses as we have seen in Chapter 6.

So, whilst the usual tools of the dowsing art are either hand-held bent rods of wood or metal, or pendulums, the tool itself is merely a means to register the attuned response and any 'tool' – or indeed nothing – can be used, if it works for the individual.

We all can dowse. Attuning to our inner and outer environment develops our intuitive awareness and enables us to attain greater harmony in our lives. And dowsing, like meditation, by requiring us to be centred and still, enables us to attune to and hear not only our own quiet voice of inner wisdom, but also the voice of Gaia and the wisdom of the Cosmos.

Crisis

In previous chapters, we have discussed the significance of electro-magnetic fields and our emerging perception of their crucial significance for biological life and the mediation of consciousness.

Just over a century ago our understanding of such fields was rudimentary, and yet we have become almost wholly reliant on technologies that utilise their principles. And our environment is now suffused with the artificially produced energetic waveforms of such fields to an extent unthinkable even a few decades ago.

Scientific reports are increasingly revealing evidence that close and continuing proximity to high level E-M fields, such as those of overhead power lines and mobile phones have adverse health effects – issues which geomancers have appreciated for some time.

The high numbers of electrical appliances in offices and homes almost certainly account for levels of ill health, especially when their effects are combined in people who are already energetically stressed by other factors.

It appears that the accumulation of such stress may be the critical factor in reducing our natural immune system to levels that are below the threshold for our body to re-attune itself to these new energetic circumstances.

We are in crisis. But as the Chinese double glyph for the word depicts, a crisis comprises both danger and opportunity.

Globally, our ways of relating to each other and to Gaia are unsustainable. But at the same time, there are positive signs that the perceived separation engendered by a materialistic worldview has reached its extreme expression.

Our collective psyche, so long unconscious is waking up to a collective awareness and compassion. And as we begin to truly perceive our global danger, a clearer vision of the way forward is emerging.

The tide is turning. And as we embrace a wholistic vision of the Cosmos, we will individually and together overcome the danger and embrace the opportunity of these momentous times.

Co-evolution

Gaia too is evolving.

The Earth's magnetic field has been reducing in strength and shifting for some time, presaging a flip in the polarity of the poles. Whilst this has happened a number of times in the past, – the last over 750 thousand years ago – it is now well overdue, and may be imminent or millennia away.

But whilst no one knows what the physical and energetic implications of such a flip in electro-magnetic polarity will be, there is no evidence that when the last pole reversal occurred, our distant hominid ancestors suffered in any way.

And we are all becoming conscious of climate changes. Our current levels of pollution arising from the prevalence of reductionist technologies are at least contributory and are likely to be their primary cause. Whilst the exact causes and their interplay are still hotly debated, their implications are incontrovertible and will almost certainly increase in coming years. And we will need to work together to do everything possible to alleviate their effects.

Throughout the long history of Gaia, there have been continuing Earth changes, some gradual and some cataclysmic, and climate change and a forthcoming pole reversal are inherent aspects of her cycles of evolution.

During the cataclysm of the Boxing Day tsunami of 2004, when nearly three hundred thousand people died, very few animals perished. It appears that their innate sensitivity enabled them to become aware of the encroaching disaster and flee inland. The last remaining tribes of Stone Age peoples of the Andaman and Nicobar islands of the Indian Ocean were also able to detect the coming wave - before it appeared on the horizon - and escaped to the highest point of their tiny islands. And as we re-connect with Gaia, our inherent harmony with her, which is our heritage as human beings, can be re-established.

Whatever the evolutionary and revolutionary future of Gaia, she is our home. We and she are co-evolutionary partners and we need to re-establish our relationship and harmony with her. And only then will we be able to fully appreciate and embody our own destiny by consciously embodying the wholeness of our spirituality within our human experience.

We are not alone

Our Sun is an average star, 'merely' one of a few hundred billion stars, which comprise the Milky Way galaxy. And we saw in Chapter 8 how astronomers are beginning to consider that the galaxy too is a self-sustaining system, which not only supports the emergence and evolution of biological life, but which itself may be considered to be living.

There are projects currently underway to detect the presence of Earth type planets orbiting other stars. To date over a hundred non-solar planets have been discovered using a technique that detects tiny wobbles caused by the gravitational influence of these planets on the motion of their parent stars.

All such non-solar planets as yet found are about the size of Jupiter, as any smaller planets are beyond our current ability to detect. But most astronomers are confident that if Jupiter sized planets exist so will smaller, Earth sized planets. And it is only a matter of time before even more powerful telescopes will herald their presence.

By 2009, NASA hopes to launch a satellite called SIM – the Space Interferometry Mission - which will utilise the technique of inter-locking several small telescopes, which then combine to produce the observing power of a single larger telescope.

Its stupendous accuracy should enable the detection of Earth sized planets orbiting the nearest 200 stars to the Sun. And both NASA and the European Space Agency ESA, are working on the next generation of satellites which hopefully by 2030, will be able to measure the spectra of the infra-red radiation emitted by such planets to gauge the presence of biological life

Each of the two projects involves six satellites, which will fly in a hexagonal formation. And to maintain their perfect alignment, the distances which separate them are controlled by lasers.

It is fitting that they will conform to the exact geometry which perennial wisdom perceives as embodying conscious harmony and order. And as they seek to discover life beyond Gaia, within their web of lasers we see again a microcosm of the holographic principle that shapes the universe.

A new wave of understanding

In the next chapter, we will harmonise the emerging understanding, which we have explored throughout *The Wave* to propose a paradigm of consciousness and a model of the Cosmos, which empowers each of us to re-member who we really are and to real-ise our kinship with all life.

CHAPTER 12

A CONSCIOUS COSMOLOGY

Over the last three hundred years, as we have scientifically explored the universe, we have intellectually persuaded ourselves that the material world is all there is.

And the scientific mantra has been that whatever cannot be measured, and thus scientifically proven, does not exist.

However, less than a century ago, we were unable to detect or measure much of the electro-magnetic spectrum, including the microwaves and radio waves that now form the basis of our global technologies.

As is so often the case in science, those discoveries came about through indirect rather than direct measurement - then as now, able to impute the realities we cannot confirm with our physical senses.

Physicists are also now recognising that supra-physical dimensions are required to explain the realities of the physical world. And whilst such dimensions appear transparent to our current technologies, they are already imagining the means by which we may be able to discern their presence.

The fundamental premise of perennial wisdom and of *The Wave* is that consciousness is primary to its expression throughout the Cosmos. That it is all-pervasive, manifests itself as energy and that all energy is waveform in nature.

And it is through the nature of waves, in all their various forms and their interactions, resonance and coherence, which enables the harmonious integration by which consciousness co-creates the physical world

Consciousness and 'spirit' are thus not separate from 'matter'. God is not 'out there', but is the wholeness underlying all manifest expression. And we are spiritual beings – individuated expressions of consciousness - undergoing a physical experience.

Wholistic science is beginning to show that not only is this the case, but the holographic means by which the heart and mind of creation is real-ised.

The holographic revolution

A Cosmology which is based on the primacy of consciousness and which has as its underlying principle, the understanding that consciousness purposefully creates the universe, is not incompatible with the findings of science.

But any new paradigm, which emerges from our deeper understanding must accommodate the anomalies and inconsistencies which, as we have discussed in *The Wave,* are unable to be explained by the prevailing worldview - of a universe which is wholly materialistic, which has randomly emerged and in which consciousness is merely the outcome of physical evolution.

The prevalence of the current worldview is the logical culmination of the first scientific revolution, led by Isaac Newton. Ushering in a mechanistic paradigm, which sought to understand the whole by separating out its constituent parts, its reductionist approach has however, been described by healer Deepak Chopra as akin to taking apart a radio and then wondering where the music has gone.

A century ago, a second scientific revolution unfolded when physicists became aware of the deeper realities of the quantum world and the relativity of space and time. The world was re-envisaged, and the materialistic universe perceived by Newtonian science was transcended by a vast matrix of inter-connecting fields of energy.

In the last decade, an even more profound understanding has emerged and the fundamental wave/particles of those energy fields have been replaced by the concept of ultra-minute waveforms called strings. Reverberating harmonically in eleven dimensions, they produce the various fundamental 'notes', which we discern as the energies and matter of the physical world.

The materialistic world of Newton was transformed a century ago, and yet its approach is still upheld by many scientists. And of those who have made the leap of understanding to perceive the quantum world, many are as yet completely unfamiliar with the cosmological discoveries of the last decade.

The wave of this new revolution however may offer us not only further answers as to *how* the universe is as it is, but provide a key to our understanding of consciousness, the wider multidimensional Cosmos and a perception of *why* the world is as it is.

A further consequence of M theory, the theoretical framework from which strings are derived, is the concept that the physical universe of spacetime may be bounded by so-called branes.

And the discovery in the 1960s of the phenomenon of the holographic principle whereby the splitting and re-convergence of light beams projects a three-dimensional image from a two-dimensional boundary, is now finding in M theory, the waveform nature of strings and the spacetime boundary of branes, a natural and unifying complement.

The holographic universe

A new paradigm, which incorporates consciousness as being primary - and thus as creating the manifest universe - must encompass the laws of physics as we know them and expand their applicability. And it appears that our emerging understanding of the holographic universe may do this.

In the latest comprehension of cosmologists, the universe is a four-dimensional (the three familiar dimensions of space and one dimension of time) spacetime holographic projection of processes, which take place on the two-dimensional spatial surface of a vast brane.

Parallel research into the entropy, or states of organisation, inherent within the three-dimensional interior of black holes has shown that their maximum value is proportional to the two-dimensional surface area of the black hole.

As this level of entropy can be equated with the maximum amount of information able to be stored and processed, such research offers a profound insight into how the holographic projection from the universal brane, may enable the greatest level of information – perception – consciousness, to be experienced in the physical world.

The mathematical language of the holographic principle was discovered by Jean Fourier, and enables any pattern to be transformed into simple waveforms and be subsequently recreated in its original form. And inherent within this harmonic nature of holograms is that the entirety of an object or system is recreated in every part of the geometrical relationship of its three-dimensional image.

Such harmonic relationships form the structural frameworks of physical materialities, depicted in the classical geometries of the Greek philosophers and the fractal geometries of those modern researchers studying complex and dynamic systems.

The deeper we peer into the fabric of the physical world, at all scales of its manifestation, from the minute to the mighty, the simpler and more resonant the principles on which it is founded appear to be. And the more they reconcile with perennial wisdom.

M theory requires higher dimensions, and solutions to Einstein's equations of relativity also imply a higher dimensionality to electromagnetism. Is this the light by which consciousness holographically projects the manifest universe?

The holographic brane

As we have seen, it appears that the maximum consciousness expressed throughout the universe, may be proportional to the vast branes, which are its holographic boundary. And it also seems that the maximum information able to be processed by a biological cell, may be proportional to the surface area of its surrounding membrane.

In Chapter 7, we discussed how the membrane of the biological cell, the first organelle – or rudimentary organ - that appeared in evolution and the only organelle common to all 'living' organisms, may represent the cell's 'brain'.

The cellular membrane is thus a processor of consciousness and forms the dynamic interface between the cell and its inner and outer environment. The fractal evolution of multi-cellular organisms enables increasing perception to be embodied and thus optimises the ability to adapt, survive and thrive and provide ever more abundant opportunities for conscious co-creation to unfold.

Biological organisms are thus essentially microcosmic holograms. And the subtle energies of their biofields, the causative templates for their physical forms, are mediated by coherent electro-magnetic fields – the *modus operandi* of the holographic principle.

Let there be light

There are a number of characteristics of electro-magnetism – or light – that strongly suggest that a deeper understanding of its nature may offer us the key in perceiving how consciousness interacts with its physical manifestation of energy/matter.

Let us enumerate these:

The waveform properties of electro-magnetic fields are key to the holographic principle, which within spacetime is based on the interference patterns created by coherent light.

As depicted in figure 12.1, electro-magnetism itself is three-dimensional and essentially shapes the dimensionality of the physical world

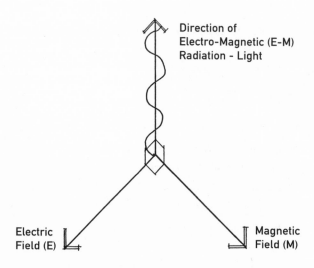

Fig 12.1 The three-dimensional matrix of the electro-magnetic field.

Within spacetime, energy and matter are intrinsically correlated by the speed of light 'c', as in Einstein's equation, $E=mc\approx$.

Both Kaluza and Maxwell identified a supra-physical dimensionality, which embodies higher overtones of the electro-magnetic field and which provide solutions to Einstein's equations of relativity.

All consciousness in the physical body is transferred and mediated by electro-magnetic processes.

The physical counterparts of the subtle energy meridians of Vedic and Chinese medicine are measurable as electro-magnetic conduits both within the human body and the body of Gaia.

Electro-magnetic waves have all the properties ascribed by perennial wisdom to conscious manifestation – intention, focus, attunement, resonance and coherence.

And finally, both space and time themselves may be seen as fundamental attributes of light. As an object travels towards the limiting speed of light, time itself slows down and space contracts.

Coherence and underlying order

For a holographic projection to create a three-dimensional hologram, the light source needs to be coherent. And for the holographic principle to create the physical world, the coherent intention of higher consciousness is required.

Such coherence should surely reveal itself in the initial set up conditions of the universe, which are crucial to the evolution and self-organisation of Nature.

And as we saw in Chapter 3, the universe is indeed set up in an extraordinarily special way. Six cosmic numbers whose values are profoundly embedded throughout the manifest world were incredibly finely tuned from the very beginning. And were any of these to have values only marginally different from those measured – we, and the entire universe, would not now exist.

We have explored throughout *The Wave* how harmonious order is being revealed to underlie the apparent complexity of the natural world, and is progressively being discovered to apply equally to the holographic nature of human experience.

And as we begin to see with new eyes, we may perceive the co-creative signature of consciousness pervading the Cosmos and the cosmic principles of perennial wisdom at work.

Nonlocality

There is no explanation within the tenets of a materialistic paradigm for the nonlocal psi effects of human consciousness and the expanded awareness that is evident in holotropic states. And there is no mechanism yet offered by that paradigm for the development of nonlocal mind and such higher-level awareness to arise from a purely physical evolutionary process.

But by considering the primacy of consciousness as the source and purposeful creator of the universe, and ourselves as individuated consciousness – spiritual beings undergoing a physical experience - such awareness is both logical and inherent.

And yet, for us to fully experience what it means to be human, it appears that the purpose of our ego-self – our human personality - is to maintain an illusion of separation and to co-creatively embody such awareness at mental, emotional and physical levels of consciousness.

In the transient and ever-changing waveforms of our experiences, we co-create and perceive the implications of cause and effect. And throughout, we dance the interplay of the fundamental relationships of yin and yang.

Within the confines of spacetime, the illusory but apparent flow of time and the limiting nature of the speed of light enables the relativity of such experiences to be undertaken and perceived by the ego-self. But beyond the holographic boundary of the physical world, the immediacy of nonlocal or cosmic perception enables us transpersonally and collectively to assimilate the totality of consciousness.

A conscious Cosmology

Any 'new' paradigm needs to be wholistic, able to describe and explain the whole as well as its constituent 'parts'. And to both encompass and expand our awareness.

Rather than the cosmology of materialistic science, such an emergent Cosmology is indeed comprehensive and is able to reconcile the entirety of our experiences and perception of the multidimensionality of the Cosmos.

Wholistic science is beginning to perceive the holographic principle as the means by which the exquisite order and harmony of the physical world is derived.

And although we do not yet have the answers, as we seek further insights into the mind of the Cosmos, perhaps we are beginning to ask the right questions.

As we perceive the purpose whose holographic intent creates the harmony and order of the universe, we must now not only ask how it is as it is, but we can no longer avoid asking the deeper question of why.

And when we do so, we not only gain insights into the mind of the Cosmos, but into its heart. As we begin to hear its voice, we are starting to listen to our own higher awareness and to commence the journey beyond our ego-self to the spiritual wholeness of who we really are.

PART IV

CO-CREATION

We have in the twelve chapters of *The Wave*, like the initiates of all cultures and times, completed a twelve-fold inner and outer journey into the heart and mind of the Cosmos.

And like those initiates, we have arrived at a final threshold.

Like them, the question we now need to ask of ourselves, is what will we do with our hard won understanding.

In this final step, we will explore how the empowerment of our individual and collective intention offers us the opportunity to lift the illusory veils which separate us, enabling us to co-create a future where we can greet each other and all other beings as brothers and sisters, fellow travellers in our ongoing journey of discovery.

Our deepest fear is not that we are inadequate.
Our deepest fear is that we are powerful beyond measure.
It is our light, not our darkness, that most frightens us.
We ask ourselves; 'who am I to be brilliant, gorgeous, talented, fabulous?'
Actually, who are you not to be?
You are a child of God.
Your playing small doesn't serve the world.
There is nothing enlightened about shrinking,
so that other people won't feel insecure around you.
We are all meant to shine, as children we do.
We are born to make manifest the glory of God that is within us.

It is not just in some of us, it is in everyone,
and as we let our own light shine, we unconsciously
give other people permission to do the same.
As we are liberated from our own fear, our presence
automatically liberates others.

Marianne Williamson (1952 -) American spiritual teacher. Marianne's
words were read by Nelson Mandela at his inauguration as President of
South Africa.

CHAPTER 13

CO-CREATE

When a surfer rides an ocean wave, he or she does so by balancing on a surfboard, which is smoothed and polished to minimise friction and thus enable the surfer to flow freely as the wave rises, crests and falls away.

The surfer doesn't seek to control the wave but to be in harmony with it. Focussed and present, he or she is alert and balanced – flexible and responsive to the nuances of every moment.

We are all surfers, individually and collectively riding a tidal wave of change.

Whilst we can attempt to cling to the past or grasp at the future, we only have the power to make our choices in the 'now' of each present moment. In the eternal 'now', we have the   power to choose to be in harmony with the Cosmos and to make our choices on the basis of love – or we can choose to only perceive the sometimes chaotic foam on the surface of the wave and make our choices from the continuing illusion of separation and on the basis of fear.

We can perceive and choose to consciously align with the underlying harmony and purpose, which continually co-creates the physical world and align ourselves with its transcendent source.

And each and every one of us can contribute by choosing to focus our energies on the positive re-envisaging of the world – or remain mired in the negativity which the illusion of separation engenders.

Intend

Our familiar experience of the hologram is that it is produced by laser light that is thus coherent and focussed.

As our awareness expands and we actively value the wisdom of our hearts and the inner voice of our intuition, our consciousness becomes ever more coherent.

And by attuning our intention to the highest purpose, we become empowered to consciously co-create our realities.

What we can imagine, we can become.

Reconcile

Einstein once said that *'science without religion is lame, religion without science is blind'*

Perennial wisdom perceives unified consciousness as the ultimate source of the manifest Cosmos, the transcendent One from which is birthed the essential dance of yin and yang – the means by which consciousness explores the richness and diversity of its own creation. And in the universal experience of tripartite forms and processes – the mediation, resolution and completion of three within One – that wholeness is reconciled.

But the illusion of such expressed separation has become one that we have mistaken as being the only reality. We have dis-membered our psyche as we have collectively explored its diversity.

It is time to re-member the wholeness of who we really are and to make our choices from that deeper and ultimate reality.

It is time to make our choices from love rather than fear, to include rather than exclude and to co-operate rather than compete.

Co-create

We are spiritual beings undergoing a physical experience. And each of us is powerful beyond measure.

It is time for us to real-ise this. Empowered by our highest awareness and held in the presence of the universal heart, we can stand straight and lovingly offer the world our unique gifts.

Together, the resonance of our co-creation is greater than the sum of its parts. And each and every one of us can play our unique role in midwiving Heaven on Earth now.

Heal the whole

The spiritual teacher Sogyal Rimpoche has spoken of how, two and a half millennia ago, the Buddha compared the physical universe to a vast net woven of a countless variety of brilliant jewels, each with a countless number of facets. Each jewel reflects in itself every other jewel in the net and is in fact one with every other jewel. Everything is inextricably interrelated and we come to realise that we are responsible for everything that we do, say or think, responsible in fact for ourselves, everyone and everything else and the entire universe.

We are the jewels of creation and we are the creator.

The final step of any initiation becomes the first step of the next stage of the journey of discovery. It is time for us to take a giant leap.

SUGGESTED FURTHER READING

- Alick Bartholemew, 2003. Hidden Nature: The Startling Insights of Viktor Schauberger. Floris Books.
- Philip Ball, 2005. Critical Mass. Arrow Books.
- Robert O. Becker and Gary Selden, 1985. The Body Electric. Quill William Morrow.
- Mark Buchanan, 2001. Ubiquity. Phoenix.
- Don Campbell, 1997. The Mozart Effect. Avon Books.
- James D'Angelo, 2001. Healing with the Voice. Thorsons.
- Masaru Emoto, 2004. The Hidden Messages in Water. Beyond Words Publishing.
- Brian Greene, 1999. The Elegant Universe. Jonathan Cape.
- Brian Greene, 2004. The Fabric of the Cosmos. Penguin
- John Gribbin, 2005. Deep Simplicity. Penguin.
- Stanislav Grof, 1998. The Cosmic Game. Newleaf.
- Robin Heath, 1999. Sun, Moon and Earth. Wooden Books.
- Hans Jenny, 2001. Cymatics. Macromedia Publishing.
- Bruce Lipton, 2005. The Biology of Belief. Mountain of Love Publishing.
- Lynne McTaggart, 2001. The Field. HarperCollins.
- John Martineau, 2001. A Little Book of Coincidences. Wooden Books.
- Dean Radin, 1997. The Conscious Universe. HarperEdge.
- Elizabeth Roberts and Elias Amidon (eds), 1991. Earth Prayers. HarperSanFrancisco.
- Thomas Saunders, 2002. The Boiled Frog Syndrome. Your Health and the Built Environment. Wiley-Academy.
- Michael Schneider, 1995. A Beginner's Guide to Constructing the Universe. HarperPerennial.
- Cyril W. Smith and Simon Best, 1989. Electromagnetic Man. J. M. Dent & Sons.
- Michael Talbot, 1996. The Holographic Universe. HarperCollins.
- Eckhart Tolle, 1999. The Power of Now. Hodder and Stoughton.

O

is a symbol of the world,
of oneness and unity. O Books
explores the many paths of wholeness
and spiritual understanding which
different traditions have developed down
the ages. It aims to bring this knowledge
in accessible form, to a general readership,
providing practical spirituality to today's seekers.
For the full list of over 200 titles covering:

- CHILDREN'S PRAYER, NOVELTY AND GIFT BOOKS
- CHILDREN'S CHRISTIAN AND SPIRITUALITY
- CHRISTMAS AND EASTER
- RELIGION/PHILOSOPHY
- SCHOOL TITLES
- ANGELS/CHANNELLING
- HEALING/MEDITATION
- SELF-HELP/RELATIONSHIPS
- ASTROLOGY/NUMEROLOGY
- SPIRITUAL ENQUIRY
- CHRISTIANITY, EVANGELICAL
  AND LIBERAL/RADICAL
- CURRENT AFFAIRS
- HISTORY/BIOGRAPHY
- INSPIRATIONAL/DEVOTIONAL
- WORLD RELIGIONS/INTERFAITH
- BIOGRAPHY AND FICTION
- BIBLE AND REFERENCE
- SCIENCE/PSYCHOLOGY

Please visit our website,
www.O-books.net

SOME RECENT O BOOKS

BRINGING GOD BACK TO EARTH
John Hunt

Religion is an essential part of our humanity. We all follow some form of religion, in the original meaning of the word. But organised religion establishes definitions, boundaries and hierarchies which the founders would be amazed by. If we could recover the original teachings and live by them, we could change ourselves and the world for the better. We could bring God back to earth.

"The best modern religious book I have read. A masterwork." Robert Van de Weyer, author of *A World Religions Bible*

"Answers all the questions you ever wanted to ask about God and some you never even thought of." Richard Holloway, former Primus Episcopus and author of *Doubts and Loves*

John Hunt runs a publishing company of which O Books is an imprint.

1-903816-81-5
£9.99 $14.95

ZEN ECONOMICS
Robert Van de Weyer

Just as Zen sages taught that attitudes and behaviour can suddenly alter, Van de Weyer combines economic analysis with social and philosophical insight to reveal how the entire world is on the verge of an economic and social transformation. The thrift practised by the Japanese, which has caused their economy to stagnate, will soon spread to all affluent countries, because it is the rational response to the economic, social and spiritual challenges that affluent people are now facing.

But thrift on a global scale, far from causing stagnation, will enable many of the world's most intractable problems to be solved. Van de Weyer offers practical financial and personal advice on how to participate in and cope with this global change. This book carries several messages of hope, which are linked by the theme of saving and investing. It's single most important message is that in the western world most of us have reached a point of prosperity where the investment with the highest rate of return is investing in the self.

Robert Van de Weyer lectured in Economics for twenty years at Cambridge University, England. He has written and edited over fifty books on a variety of themes, including economics, religion and history.

1-903816-78-5
£9.99 $12.95

TORN CLOUDS
Judy Hall

Drawing on thirty years experience as a regression therapist and her own memories and experiences in Egypt, ancient and modern, *Torn Clouds* is a remarkable first novel by an internationally-acclaimed MBS author, one of Britain's leading experts on reincarnation. It features time-traveller Megan McKennar, whose past life memories thrust themselves into the present day as she traces a love affair that transcends time. Haunted by her dreams, she is driven by forces she cannot understand to take a trip to Egypt in a quest to understand the cause of her unhappy current life circumstances. Once there, swooning into a previous existence in Pharaonic Egypt, she lives again as Meck'an'ar, priestess of the Goddess Sekhmet, the fearful lion headed deity who was simultaneously the Goddess of Terror, Magic and Healing.

Caught up in the dark historical secrets of Egypt, Megan is forced to fight for her soul. She succeeds in breaking the curse that had been cast upon her in two incarnations.

Judy Hall is a modern seer who manages the difficult task of evoking the present world, plus the realm of Ancient Egypt, and making them seem real. There is an energy behind the prose, and a power in her imagery which hints that this is more than just a story of character and plot, but an outpouring from another age, a genuine glimpse into beyond-time Mysteries which affect us all today. Alan Richardson, author of *Inner Guide to Egypt.*

Judy Hall has been a karmic counsellor for thirty years. Her books have been translated into over fourteen languages.
1 903816 80 7
£9.99/$14.95

HEALING HANDS
David Vennells

Hand reflexology is one of the most well-known and respected complementary therapies, practised in many hospitals, surgeries, hospices, health and healing centres, and is enjoying a growing popularity. *Healing Hands* explains the simple techniques of Hand Reflexology so clearly, with the aid of illustrations, that "within a few days the reader could be competently treating themselves or others." It is aimed at those interested in learning the practical techniques (how to give yourself and others a full treatment), and also includes the fascinating history of reflexology, how it works with the hands and the various things we can do to support the healing process. As the reader learns the techniques step by step, they can gradually increase their knowledge of anatomy and physiology, together with developing a more accurate awareness of the hand reflexes and how to treat them accurately and successfully.

David Vennells is a Buddhist teacher of Reiki and the author of *Reiki Mastery* (O Books).
1 903816 81 5
£9.99/$16.95

THE WISE FOOL'S GUIDE TO LEADERSHIP
Peter Hawkins

Nasrudin is the archetypal wise fool, who lived in the Middle East over 600 years ago, though his stories have travelled the world and been updated in very generation. *Peter Hawkins* has given a modern spin to 84 of these stories by turning Nasrudin into a management consultant. Simple truths are told in a straightforward and highly entertaining way. They shock us into seeing situations and ideas with which we have become familiar from a different perspective. Each story slips into our house by its engaging good humour, but once inside it can start to rearrange the furniture and knock new windows through the walls of our mind-a process that can be releasing and refreshing, but at times disconcerting!
The book also provides an introduction to Nasrudin and his stories, and a chapter on "Telling Tales; the positive use of stories in organisations."

I commend this book to you-wiser even than The Hitch Hiker's Guide to the Galaxy, *far, far funnier than* In Search of Excellence, *so much thinner than* The Harvard Business Review Encyclopedia of Corporate Strategy, *and astoundingly cheaper than Catch 22!*
Professor Mike Pedler

Dr Peter Hawkins is co-founder and Chairman of Bath Consultancy Group, which operates internationally in helping all types of organisations manage change.

1 903816 96 3
£7.99/$11.95

JOURNEY HOME
Tonika Rinar

Tonika Rinar believes that everybody is capable of time travel. We can access history as it really happened, without later exaggeration or bias. We can also heal ourselves by coming to terms with our experiences in past lives.

Tonika escorts the reader into other worlds and dimensions, explaining her own remarkable experiences with an easy-to-read approach. At one level the book can simply be taken as a series of fascinating experiences with the paranormal, embracing past life regression, ghosts, angels and spirit guides. But it also encourages the reader along their own journey of self-discovery and understanding. A journey in which you can discover your own connection with the Universe and the many different dimensions contained within Creation.

Journey Home offers a multitude of insights, and along the way looks at some of the fundamental questions asked by all cultures around the world. Where do we come from? Why are we here? What is the point of our life? What happens when we die?

Tonika Rinar is an extraordinary psychic and visionary, international speaker and workshop leader, with 17 years clinical experience in working with people suffering injury and illness. She has been interviewed extensively on radio and TV.

1 905047 00 2
£11.99 $16.95